David Morgan was awarded the DSC for his services in the Falklands War. He left the forces in 1991 and now flies commercial jets for Virgin Atlantic Airways. A dedicated acrobatic pilot, he regularly flies at air shows.

D0257346

HOSTILE SKIES

MY FALKLANDS AIR WAR

DAVID MORGAN

PHOENIX

A PHOENIX PAPERBACK

First published in Great Britain in 2006
by Weidenfeld & Nicolson
This paperback edition published in 2007
by Phoenix,
an imprint of Orion Books Ltd,
Orion House, 5 Upper St Martin's Lane,
London WC2H 9EA
An Hachette Livre UK company

10 9 8 7 6 5 4 3 2

Copyright © David Morgan 2006

A CIP catalogue record for this book
is available from the British Library.

ISBN 978-0-7538-2199-2

Printed and bound in Great Britain by
Mackays of Chatham plc, Chatham, Kent

The Orion Publishing Group's policy is to use papers that
are natural, renewable and recyclable products and made
from wood grown in sustainable forests. The logging
and manufacturing processes are expected to conform to
the environmental regulations of the country of origin.

www.orionbooks.co.uk

This book is for my wife Caro and my children Elizabeth and Charles, for their love and support through my dark days. Without their encouragement, it would not have been written.

Also for Sally for saving my sanity.

And for Antje for saving my life.

Contents

List of Photographs

Acknowledgements

I WOULD LIKE to express my thanks to the following people who have been of great assistance to me in writing this account. Rodney Burden; Michael Draper; Douglas Rough; Colin Smith and David Wilton, joint authors of *Falklands – The Air War* published by the British Aviation Research Group (1986). Their brilliant research enabled me to place my part in the conflict in the correct historical perspective.

Thanks also to Air Chief Marshal Sir Peter Squire GCB DFC AFC DSc FRAeS RAF (Retd) for allowing me access to his Falklands diary and to Comodoro Hector Sanchez FAA, Commander Clive Carrington-Wood RN, Squadron Leader Ian Mortimer RAF (Retd) and Michael Vestey for their personal reminiscences. Also to Commander David Hobbs MBE RN and Jeremy Shore from the Fleet Air Arm Museum at Yeovilton for access to their contemporary records of the conflict.

I would also like to thank Brian Hanrahan and the BBC for permission to quote from Brian's Falklands dispatches and EMPICS for permission to reproduce Martin Cleaver's photograph of me next to my battle-damaged aircraft on 1 May 1982.

John Pudney's poems are included with the permission of David

Higham Associates and were published in *For Johnny* by Shepheard-Walwyn (1976).

My thanks finally to Richard Bach, aviator and author extraordinaire, for permission to use excerpts from his wonderful book *Illusions, The Adventures of a Reluctant Messiah* published in 1978 by Pan Books. This slim volume, together with John Pudney's poetry, was my haven from the tempests of war.

Prologue

THE SKY WAS a deep purple-pink, the sun well below the horizon and the distant coast a dark, foreboding smudge. I was sweating and cursing, trying desperately to pull my gunsight up onto the aircraft ahead, firing bursts from my 30-millimetre cannon but not hitting him. Time seemed distorted, the cockpit was dark and the instruments obscured and out of place. The aircraft was not performing as it should; it was heavy, unresponsive. Something was very wrong but I couldn't fathom what it was. Part of me tried to analyse the problem while the rest attempted to follow the target as he turned and jinked hard ahead of me. The G forces were crushing me into the seat and making it difficult for me to lift my head. My vision was blurring as I grunted and strained to keep the blood flowing to my brain.

Without warning a hole was punched in the port side of the cockpit, just by my left elbow. Pain shot up my arm and side. I couldn't move my left hand and when I opened my mouth to cry out, all I could manage was a strangled groan. I had screwed up; there was someone behind me, the oldest mistake in the book. I was going to die. I let go of the stick and fumbled for the seat handle. I had to eject. I had to get out of the aircraft if I was going to survive.

Blackness.

Suddenly I was on the ground trying to run, but I could not move my feet; they were trapped in a layer of thick clinging mud up to my knees. I struggled hard but could only move forward desperately slowly. My side was not hurting so much now and I had regained some of the use of my left arm. I checked the wound in my left side and found that my abdomen had been sliced open – organs glistened dully between my fingers. This was bad, very bad. I had to get out of the mire. Mud had already entered the wound and thoughts of gangrene flickered across my mind. I tried to force my legs forward one at a time, but each movement became harder than the last. I mustered every ounce of willpower but it didn't seem to have any effect. I attempted to cry out again but could only manage another agonised groan. I was terrified, disorientated. I couldn't understand what was going on but I knew that I was being pursued by something unspeakably evil.

'Are you OK?' came a small, distant voice. I felt a touch on my shoulder and opened my eyes.

Blackness.

'Are you all right, love?'

Thin slivers of diffuse starlight shining between the curtains, a dull green glow from the alarm. I am sweating, my pulse racing.

I become aware of Caro's concerned face looking over my shoulder and realise that it has been another nightmare. It has been over twenty years now. In the early-morning darkness I take the decision that it really is time to tell my story and lay these ghosts once and for all.

CHAPTER 1

INVASION

THE MORNING OF 2 April 1982 started with urban normality. It had been three months since the family and I had returned from our second tour of duty in Germany. We had been lucky enough to find a married quarter on the outskirts of the village of Ilchester in Somerset, within easy walking distance of the local school, and my two children were settling in well. Elizabeth was a bright seven-year-old who had been born during our first Germany tour and Charles was a mischievous five-year-old with a wicked sense of humour.

For the previous two months I had been converting to the Sea Harrier, or SHAR as it was universally known. I had flown some forty hours with 899 Naval Air Squadron (NAS) at Yeovilton and had just about got to grips with the basics of air-to-air radar work. It had been a nasty shock to discover that the navy expected me to operate in the dark as well as during daylight hours. In Germany, with our ground attack role being very much daylight only, we flew at night only on very rare occasions. In fact, in the six years prior to starting the SHAR course, I had flown a grand total of sixteen hours at night. Two months into the course, I had already notched up a further fifteen hours.

The Sea Harrier weapons system differed considerably from that of the Harrier GR3. The Sea Harrier had been conceived as an interceptor to deal with the Russian long-range bomber threat. Its radar was a very basic system which suffered terribly from ground returns, or clutter, over land but worked fairly well at medium to high levels over the sea. At low level it was useless over land and required a large amount of skilful handling over water to pick up and track a target. The idea was to use the radar as a long-range eyeball to get you into a visual fight where you could use your panache, skill and daring to down the target with missiles or guns. I was already finding that working the radar, computing the intercept geometry and not crashing into the sea from five hundred feet at night was stretching my abilities. One of the instructors on 899 at that time had already bounced off the sea twice, once in a Sea Vixen and once in a Phantom. It was not a recommended manoeuvre!

I was, however, apart from the night flying, finding the course very enjoyable and was looking forward to my three-year secondment to the Fleet Air Arm. I had amazed my wife Carol at the end of January by giving her a list of every single day I would be away from home for the next eleven months. This sort of stability had been out of the question in Germany and we had started to plan ahead for the first time since the birth of our children.

While the kettle was boiling for the morning cup of tea, I idly turned on the radio to catch up with the news. What I heard knocked me back on my heels: an Argentine invasion force had landed on the Falkland Islands. It took several seconds for this to sink in; I could not believe that it could really have happened. It seemed surreal that such an unprovoked attack could happen in the modern world.

I had only a vague knowledge of the Falkland Islands. I envisioned a small group of low-lying sandy islands, with a few basic houses and a large Union Flag defended by a handful of Royal Marines. My geographical knowledge was a little sketchy but I did realise that they were a hell of a long way away from the UK and there was going to be a huge political row. It did not occur to me then that I was about to be called upon to go to war.

War had been a constant concern in Germany. During my first tour there I had been heavily involved in intelligence work and had become convinced that an attack by the Warsaw Pact upon NATO forces was only a matter of time. Many of us kept spare cans of petrol in our cellars in order that our families might have a chance of making the Channel ports before Germany was overrun. Several times a year there were a few tense hours when the sirens would sound, summoning us all onto base, and no one was sure whether it was an exercise or for real. I had instructed my family to head west if they didn't hear that it was a drill within a couple of hours.

The Germany Harrier Force was trained to be able to deploy within hours of an alert and my first job in the theatre had been to plan the off-base sites that the aircraft would use in the event of hostilities. These sites were highly classified and varied a great deal in nature, some hiding the aircraft in farm buildings, others utilising strips of urban road and supermarkets. They all had one thing in common though – they were within a few minutes flying time of the opposing forces. We had no illusions about how long we could keep flying in such a hostile environment and reckoned on 30 per cent attrition every day. In other words, after three days we would probably cease to be an effective force. It would have been a bloody battle with little hope of survival.

That morning, as I drove through the main gates at Yeovilton on my way to the squadron, there didn't seem to be much unusual activity. The ensign was being raised to the customary shrill of the boatswain's call and the station had its normal air of purposeful chaos. This changed when I reached the crewroom, however. The rest of the pilots had been called in hours earlier and the place was buzzing like a hive.

IT WAS SOON made clear that the decision had been made to dispatch a task force to retake the islands. We learned that the army had told Prime Minister Margaret Thatcher that they would need at least 10,000 troops and that the RAF had said that they couldn't provide anything in the way of support at that range. We were then told that the first sea lord had promised that we would sail on Monday.

I felt a little left out of the initial flap, as I was still officially a 'student', and was told to begin with that I would be staying behind at Yeovilton to finish the conversion course, another four or five months' flying. This did not disappoint me greatly and I would have been very happy to wave the rest of the guys off from the safety of the wardroom bar.

That day passed in a whirl of activity. Personnel were recalled from leave, some being stopped on motorways by police patrol cars, and aircraft were prepared for deployment. Transport was organised and people were nominated to embark. By the afternoon it was realised that every single aircraft would be required to join the task force, which meant nothing left at Yeovilton for me to complete my training in. It was therefore decided that I would sail with HMS *Hermes* but would not be flying. I was to be the operations officer for the squadron; my main purpose in life would be running the flying programme with a secondary responsibility for writing the line book. This was the unofficial squadron history, consisting of interesting photographs and embarrassing quotes. Not really my idea of war! If I was going to expose my body to danger, I wanted a bit more control over my own destiny than that.

Before leaving for home, I paid a visit to stores to pick up some last-minute essentials. On my list was a shoulder holster for my service pistol but when I attempted to get this issued I was greeted with a classic storeman's answer: 'Oh no. I'm sorry, sir, they are war stocks and I can't let them go.' A fairly swift and to the point discussion followed and I walked out with my brand new holster.

This incident reminded me of the day at RAF Brawdy some four years earlier when I discovered that my Hunter leg restraint garters had become a little worn. These webbing straps fitted around the legs below the knee and were connected to the Martin-Baker ejection seat by thick cords which pulled the lower limbs tight against the seat pan on ejection. Without them you could end up with your legs flailing around your head at over 400 knots, which is not very comfortable, especially when you hit the ground.

My trip to flying-clothing stores was not entirely successful however. It is a fact that some storemen regard their equipment as their own personal property and can be very reluctant to part with it. On this occasion my request was greeted with a sucking of teeth and 'I'm sorry, sir, but . . .' 'Don't tell me,' I said. 'You have only got two in stock and you can't issue those in case anyone wants them.' A pained look crossed his face and he replied, 'Oh no, sir, you are welcome to what I have but I am afraid I only have one left on the shelf.' I gave him an obvious look of incredulity, whereupon he informed me that they came in packs of three! Oh, the mysterious wonders of the supply branch.

On my return home that evening I sat down and explained to Elizabeth and Charles that I was going off to war. They were very confused as they associated war with being in Germany and thought I shouldn't have to fight now that we were back in England. I had explained to them the need for us to have troops in Germany and we had visited East Berlin to examine communism at first hand. There they had found that the Coke tasted foul and there were no chips to be had anywhere; certainly reason enough to fight the Russian hordes. Now I could sense their concern as they watched the television newsreels of Royal Marines being marched into captivity along the waterfront at Stanley and the library shots of Argentine aircraft flashing across the screen. There were lots of hugs that night before they drifted off to sleep, Liz clutching her newly acquired kitten and Charles his very tatty blue bunny.

After the children had gone to bed, I packed my bags. It was difficult knowing what to take and what to leave behind. The last thing I wanted was to burden myself with too much rubbish but some things were essential. I packed my cameras and all my spare film. I also put in a couple of exercise books because I believed that this might – just might – be an important part of my life and I wanted to keep a diary. Little could I guess then quite how critical the next few months would actually turn out to be.

I also packed three books that had a very special meaning for me. The first was a well-thumbed copy of Richard Bach's classic, *Jonathan Livingston Seagull*. For those of you who have not read it, it is the quintessential book for all aviators who make their own rules and live by them. The second was his sequel, *Illusions: The Adventures of a Reluctant Messiah*. The philosophy in this small book came as close to changing my life as anything I have ever read. Finally, I took a slim volume of John Pudney's poetry entitled *For Johnny*. My father had come across a copy of this towards the end of his time as a naval fighter pilot in the Second World War. I first read it when, at the age of twenty-one, I lost one of my course mates in a flying accident.

Chris was a great teddy bear of a guy who was not a natural pilot but made up for this with hard work and a wonderful sense of fun. We had many a hilarious night barrelling through the Yorkshire countryside in my old Austin A55 with some girls and far too much beer. Then one day he tried to haul his Jet Provost off the short runway at RAF Leeming without having enough airspeed and mushed into the trees just short of the A1. I saw it happen from dispersal and can remember screaming to him to eject, not that there was any chance of him hearing me. He ejected about fifty feet above the ground and I caught a quick glimpse of the drogue chute on his seat deploying before it disappeared behind the trees. We found him next to his seat at the base of a hawthorn hedge, quite dead, with his partially deployed canopy undulating uselessly in the breeze.

My father sent me one of John Pudney's poems, which mirrored and explained the feelings of loss and sorrow which you have to learn to overcome if you are a service pilot, otherwise it would just be too wretched to carry on. Since then, that book has been my constant companion, to be brought out when melancholy strikes or when another funeral oration is required.

So it was with a meagre holdall of belongings and a heavy heart that

I said goodbye to my family the following morning and set off for Yeovilton and embarkation. However, in complete contradiction of the previous day, I was told that I would be flying onto the ship the following morning and would be accepted as a fully fledged pilot for the duration of the operation. I was absolutely delighted that I would now not be confined to the bowels of the ship while everyone else was carving the daylight above but I was still not overly keen on leaving my family. It also meant another night at home, which although greatly appreciated did cause a little confusion as we had already said our tearful goodbyes in anticipation of my departure.

On the Sunday morning the farewells were for real and I left with Charles' words ringing in my ears: 'Don't worry, Daddy, they have only got tatty old aeroplanes and you have got brand new ones!' Out of the mouths of babes and sucklings . . .

The squadron had been divided up between the two front line squadrons, 800 and 801, based on the carriers *Hermes* and *Invincible* respectively. Coming with me to *Hermes* were Lieutenant Commanders Neill Thomas, Gordie Batt and Tony Ogilvy, Sub Lieutenant Andy George and a fellow 'crab' (RAF officer), Flight Lieutenant Bertie Penfold. Neill was the 'boss' of 899, an experienced Phantom pilot and a gentleman of the old school, whereas Gordie was a most unlikely-looking fighter pilot. He was short and rather round in shape, with a face that looked as if it had been used as a punch bag. He had started as a helicopter pilot but had recently completed a tour flying A6 Intruders with the US Navy. He had a very sharp wit and could defuse the tensest of situations with a well-placed irreverence. Tony Ogilvy was in the middle of a refresher course and due to relieve Sharkey Ward as boss of 801 NAS on *Invincible*. Beneath Oges' piratical exterior beat a heart of pure gold and his expertise as an ex-Buccaneer air warfare instructor was to be of great value.

Bertie I had known in Germany. He was a first-class Harrier instructor and approaching the end of his sixteen-year commission with the RAF. His plan was to buy a smallholding in the Yeovilton area and fly Hunters for the Fleet Requirements and Air Direction Unit on the south side of the airfield. Andy George was a brand new pilot. He had only just emerged from advanced training and had been teamed up with me on the conversion course. Together we had covered about one third of the syllabus and he was still at the 'enthusiastic puppy-dog' stage. Andy was obviously a very capable pilot and possessed the boundless energy of the young but as Gordie warned him, 'Youth and enthusiasm will always be overcome by experience and low cunning.' He was like a dog with two tails at the prospect of going to war and couldn't quite believe that he was actually going to be given the chance.

By the time I arrived at the squadron on Sunday morning, eight aircraft had already embarked on *Hermes*. I was given a quick brief on deck operations and pointed at XZ 450, the Sea Eagle missile trials aircraft that had been hurriedly retrieved from British Aerospace at Dunsfold. It had no radar warning receiver and had been fitted with the Sea Eagle launch panel. In all other respects it was a standard aircraft. I carried out a very careful walk-round inspection, still rather hoping that there might be some sort of snag, which might delay me for a few more hours. Meanwhile, one of the ground crew manhandled my RAF blue holdall into the back hatch behind the airbrake. This was the only luggage space available in the Harrier and could only be accessed by lying on your back under the aircraft. Not too much of a chore on a warm spring morning but a right royal pain in a cold, muddy field.

As I got airborne at ten o'clock that morning I dropped my starboard wing and said a silent goodbye to my family as I flew just to the south of the married quarters. I was aware of a number of people waving madly in my direction and the roads at the end of the runway were crammed with sightseers. The locals were certainly out in force to see us off.

From Yeovilton I flew south-east towards Poole Harbour and then east along the Solent until I saw the old naval air station at Lee. It seemed a lifetime ago that I had arrived off the train there as a callow youth to be assessed for a naval scholarship. In one of those black hangars I had transported barrels and fellow applicants over crocodile-infested swamps (or was it bottomless pits?) with the aid of two coils of rope and a couple of pieces of timber. I remember receiving a massive bollocking for shinning up a rope and using a hangar roof support as a belaying point for a rope swing. Apparently it was supposed to be open sky. Still, I was accepted so someone must have recognised initiative when they saw it. Along the coast from Lee was Seafield Park, a minor country house on the beach appropriated by the navy during the war, which still housed the School of Naval Aviation Medicine. Here, on a balmy evening in 1967, I had been playing croquet with three other newly promoted midshipmen when a hedgehog had come snuffling onto the pitch. After some initial suggestions that the RSPCA would not have approved of, the little beast was allowed to continue on its peripatetic way without hindrance.

Beyond Lee lay Portsmouth, laid out like a map. *Hermes* stood out very well in the hazy sunshine, tied up alongside the Northwest Wall. The old lady of the fleet still had her mainmast shrouded in scaffolding as the dockyard 'maties' worked like hell to get her fit to sail. She had been in the middle of a maintenance period, with half her mast removed, when the call had come on the previous Friday.

I called Flyco (Flying Control) and was told to hold off at endurance speed as the deck was not yet ready for me. I therefore set up a lazy orbit to the south of Hayling Island at 5000 feet and reduced speed to an economical 240 knots. Before leaving Yeovilton I had been briefed to make absolutely sure I would be able to land on board before jettisoning fuel down to landing weight. Apparently, carriers had the habit of telling you to dump fuel and then changing their minds and expecting you to hold off for another half an hour. So when the call came, 'Yeovil five zero, dump down to landing weight and Charlie immediately,' I politely requested confirmation that the deck was clear. This confirmation came in what I considered a rather unnecessarily curt message. Oops, I thought. Just made myself unpopular – not a very auspicious start. Without more ado, I dumped down to 1500 pounds of gas and was just about to start my approach when a further call came: 'Five zero, change of plan. Hold off and endure.' Sod's law had operated.

I explained as politely as I could that I was unable to hold off for more than a couple of minutes and was given reluctant permission to land. I decelerated through the entrance to the harbour, speed nicely under control, nozzles moving down to the hover stop, the power of the mighty Pegasus engine increasing gradually to replace the reducing aerodynamic lift. All was going pretty well, I thought. I didn't want to screw up my first ever deck landing in front of the whole of the Royal Navy.

As my airspeed decreased below 90 knots, the point at which the Harrier becomes unstable in yaw, I saw the reason for Flyco's concern: the largest floating crane I had ever seen was being towed sedately around the stern, completely blocking my approach path. I had to make a rapid decision. I still had just enough fuel to divert to Lee-on-Solent but this would disrupt the ship's already fraught programme. The other option was to 'cuff it'. I had operated in some very tight clearings in the German countryside over the last few years, so a bit of wacky VSTOL* shouldn't be too difficult. I slapped the nozzles into the braking stop, wove my way around the crane, did a snappy spot turn alongside the superstructure and put the aircraft down firmly on 4 Spot, a rather unconventional approach but a respectable landing. I had the feeling it would be a little more exciting once we got under way.

As I shut the aircraft down and turned off all the electrics, the access ladder was clipped into the foot holes on the right-hand side of the aircraft and a grinning face appeared over the edge of the cockpit.

'W'ay aye, ya bugger! I told you we'd go to war together sometime!'

It was Fred Frederiksen, one of the pilots who had joined the navy with me in November 1966. I had not seen Fred for more than ten years; his rugged face looked a little more lived-in than before but his lyrical Geordie accent was unmistakable. After we left Dartmouth, he had gone on to fixed-wing training and ended up flying Sea Vixens. After this, he converted to Phantoms before becoming an instructor and later a test pilot. As a pilot his skills were unsurpassed and as a man it would

*Vertical/short take-off and landing

be difficult to find a more genuine, gentle or likeable friend. I was absolutely delighted that he was sailing with us.

The flight deck was humming with activity with the ship's crane swinging vehicles, stores and ammunition up into Fly 1, in front of the island. From here, everything was being rapidly moved to the forward lift and taken down into the hangar below. Both gangways leading to the dockside were teeming with people carrying stores on board. From high up on the flight deck they looked for all the world like the armies of leafcutter ants I had seen during my service in Belize, each one carrying a seemingly impossible load.

Fred chaperoned me down the deck to a watertight door at the base of the island. Such doors and hatches would become the bane of our lives. Normally they were held closed by two clips but at action stations, when watertight integrity had to be guaranteed, all eight clips were driven home hard. This meant that simply moving from the wardroom to the briefing room became a hand-bruising, finger-crushing pain in the arse.

Inside the island was the line office. Here the line chief kept all the paperwork required to record changes of aircraft serviceability. Even in wartime it was important to maintain records of work carried out and hours flown so that essential maintenance would not be overlooked. I dutifully signed my aircraft over to the maintainers and was taken up two decks to Flyco to meet commander (air). Robin Shercliff, or Wings as he was traditionally known, was a delightful person; he was tall and spare, with a slight stoop and a bright twinkle in his eye. I had known him briefly when I was undergoing basic flying training at Linton-on-Ouse in 1967 and he was one of nature's gentlemen. I was to see another side of him over the next few months. He was completely unflappable and I never heard him raise his voice to anyone, even when we were under attack or when an aircraft ended up in the catwalk. He was just the kind of man needed in this pivotal position and he would be largely responsible for the massive support we received from the ship during the coming conflict.

Next stop was my cabin, 5U4; the number is engraved on my memory even now. To get there entailed walking half the length of the ship, through numerous watertight doors, down several ladders, past the wardroom and finally down a very narrow, vertical ladder onto 5 Deck. I was sharing with Andy George, and since I was considerably senior to him, I grabbed the top bunk. It was a comfortable enough cabin, albeit a little cramped for two. Behind the sliding door was a space about ten feet by seven; on the left wall was a full-length wardrobe and a writing desk and opposite was a set of three deep drawers and a sink. Although the sink was plumbed with hot and cold running water, its waste pipe, as I soon discovered, merely ran into a two-gallon 'spit kit' in the cupboard below. This meant that if you used the sink, you had to cart the waste water quite a long way aft to get rid of it in the 'heads'. We soon agreed that this was not worth the effort. It amazes me to this day that this arrangement must have been in place ever since *Hermes* was launched over twenty years earlier and is unlikely to have changed now that she is INS *Viraat* with the Indian Navy.

The bunks were really very comfortable, being quite long and more than wide enough for the average person. They also had large mahogany leeboards to stop you being thrown out in a heavy sea. The later carriers, of the *Invincible* class, had settees that converted into extremely narrow bunks. Not only were these uncomfortable, they were so narrow that seat belts were required to keep you from ending up on the floor. They also had a mechanism which tended to unlock in a heavy sea, and numerous people woke up to find themselves incarcerated behind the back of a settee with no means of escape. This was known universally as being 'clam shelled'. Not a problem with the tried and trusted design of *Hermes*' sleeping arrangements.

I spent that afternoon finding my way around the ship. It was a confusing warren of passageways and hatches containing a bewildering array of pipework, damage control equipment and signs. There were no signs to guide you and apparently no maps either; it was just a case of learning where the essential places were. All spaces had a code which allowed them to be located on a three-dimensional plan of the ship. The three elements of the code started with the deck number, with the flight deck being No.1 Deck. Below this was 2 Deck and above, in the island, came 01 Deck. The second element referred to transverse divisions working aft from A at the bows, and the final element located the space within those divisions, odds to starboard and evens to port. Thus my cabin, 5U4, was on 5 Deck, right aft and on the port side, conveniently close to the wardroom in 4T.

There were fore and aft passageways running most of the length of the ship on 2 Deck and a further set on 4 Deck. These were the main highways from which most of the ship could be accessed. Most of 3 Deck was taken up by a hangar space which stretched from G Section back to Q Section. This was served by two enormous lifts, one aft and one forward on the port side. Each lift was capable of carrying a fully armed Sea Harrier from the hangar to the flight deck in a matter of thirty seconds.

I quickly discovered that there were a number of spaces it was essential for an aviator to be able to locate. The No. 2 Briefing Room in 2M with its adjacent aircrew refreshment buffet (referred to universally as the ACRB or Greasy Spoon) was to be the centre of our operations. The wardroom, with its dining room and bar, was the social centre of the ship, and up in the island were the bridge, operations room and Flyco.

Hermes had been designed as a fixed-wing carrier capable of carrying two squadrons of jet aircraft. To this end she had spacious accommodation for both personnel and equipment, unlike the newer *Invincible* class, which had been designed purely to take helicopters. This gave her a cavernous hangar with large workshops, a vast expanse of armoured flight deck, and more importantly a very spacious wardroom with a very large bar. On *Hermes* the compartment in which the bar was located was large enough to hold the entire ship's officer complement in comfort and still have a game of mess rugby. It also had the advantage of having large brass scuttles along the port side through which I found I could watch the Gosport ferry plying backwards and forwards across the harbour entrance. The bar itself was a mahogany counter about twenty feet in length with a fine set of mirrored panels behind the row of optics. Truly a bar fit for the cream of naval aviation.

During that afternoon Neill Thomas and Oges landed on with two more Sea Harriers from Yeovilton. These were brand new aircraft taken out of storage at RAF St Athan in South Glamorgan. Work on deck stopped only for a few minutes to allow their recovery before recommencing with a will.

By this time the hangar was stacked with stores and ammunition of all types. Small arms and grenades lay next to missiles and toilet paper. Incongruously, there were also large cases of Argentine corned beef, the equivalent of the D-Day invasion fleet being fed bratwurst. Gradually these stores were being distributed around the ship and stacked in every spare corner. The 3 Deck passageway heading aft to the quarterdeck became the potato store until, after several weeks, the paper sacks began to disintegrate and the whiff of the semi-rotten tubers became too much to bear.

On Sunday evening a group of us headed into Portsmouth for a Chinese meal and a few beers. The town was buzzing with the news of the fleet's imminent departure and I had the peculiar feeling that I was watching history being made. On the short walk back to the dockyard main gate I was lucky enough to find an empty phone box and made a short call home to say goodbye. As we made our way past Nelson's flagship I noticed that a number of bow planks had been removed for repair, exposing the four large hawse pipes for the anchor cables which led horizontally back into the hull of the ship. Some wag remarked that things must be desperate if they were refitting *Victory* with Exocet missiles.

Sleep did not come easily that night as I lay on my bunk wondering what the future had in store for me. I had not had any time to put my life in order. We were in the process of buying a house and I had managed to arrange an enduring power of attorney so that Carol could access all my accounts and sign documents on my behalf. I had also told her about an affair I had been having with a beautiful young German girl.

I had met Antje at a small flying club in the Westerwald area of Germany in July 1979, when she was twenty-one years old. I was stunned by her twinkling hazel eyes and her zest for life. The following year we met again and spent most of the weekend in each other's company, including a late-night sauna and nude swim in the club pool, where she made no attempt to hide her physical attributes. We discovered that we had a huge amount in common despite the ten-year difference in our ages. She was also a fan of Richard Bach's writings and those of Antoine de Saint-Exupéry, the pioneering French pilot. After a while we found that we were almost reading each other's minds, an uncanny experience. I did my best to seduce her in the mist and the ghostly moonlight that evening but she somehow resisted my charms, despite me telling her that she would probably regret it in the morning.

On the Monday morning I returned to Gütersloh and my real life. As I accelerated along Breitscheid's 500-metre strip in my Harrier I was aware of a figure at the side of the runway, waving a yellow scarf and mouthing the words, 'I regret it!' After that weekend we tried to see each other whenever we could and soon became lovers, albeit at long distance. Sometimes we would not hear from each other for months and then our letters would cross in the post. At other times I would suddenly become unsettled for no apparent reason, only to find that she was going through a particularly difficult time. It was an emotional experience unlike anything I had known previously and one that I still count myself very lucky to have had.

I had last spent time with Antje the previous September and she had since met someone in London, also called David; they were planning to get married in the autumn. I was sorry that I would be losing her as a lover but I believed that we would remain soulmates.

LOADING CONTINUED through the night and the following morning, until the old ship was bursting at the seams. Up on deck were ten of our Sea Harriers and a dozen Sea King helicopters – some anti-submarine

Mark 5s and some commando Mark 4s of 846 NAS. While we prepared for an all-encompassing brief on ship operations, the rest of the ship's company took up their positions around the deck edge and in the catwalks to leave harbour at Procedure Alfa.

The Royal Navy has always been very keen on ceremony and can provide a stirring spectacle at the drop of a hat. That morning the ship was a sight to stir Drake from his hammock in Nombre Dios Bay. Some 1800 crew lined the ship's side to say farewell to a massive crowd of well-wishers gathered around the entrance to the harbour: a crowd that contained wives, families, girlfriends and many who had no real connection with the task force, save that they wanted to wish us Godspeed.

Down on 2 Deck we were half an hour into our operations briefing when I noticed that the overhead projector screen had started to sway almost imperceptibly back and forth. We were at sea.

CHAPTER 2

OFF TO WAR

BY THE TIME OUR briefing was complete we were out of sight of land and I had missed my opportunity to bid the coast of England farewell. It was a peculiar feeling leaning on the rail of the catwalk, staring north towards the horizon that obscured the Dorset coast and Lyme Regis, with its Cobb made famous by the film *The French Lieutenant's Woman*. I had planned a date there with Antje when I was eighty years old and she was seventy. I couldn't help wondering if we would make it. Only a few miles north of Lyme Bay lay Yeovilton and my family. They, together with the rest of the country, were very much caught up in the massive surge of patriotism that accompanied the task force's departure from UK waters while we were caught in a surreal limbo.

By the hour, we were getting news of more ships sailing, not only warships but the STUFT ships, (ships taken up from trade), a very apt acronym. These varied from large passenger liners to North Sea tugs and all were prepared in amazingly short order, including the addition of flight decks to some of them to allow helicopter operations.

Most of that Monday was spent cruising slowly west, as the ship sorted out the chaos in the hangar and prepared for flying operations. In the afternoon 'Hands to flying stations' was piped and we turned into wind to receive our final Sea Harrier from Yeovilton. Bertie Penfold was the pilot and I got the distinct impression that like me he would far rather have stayed behind and kept the home fires burning. The arrival of this aircraft meant that we now had every single serviceable Sea Harrier in the country embarked with the fleet and British Aerospace had been instructed to complete those on their production line as a matter of the utmost urgency.

That evening there was a good party in the wardroom bar. Many of the ship's officers made it a policy not to drink at sea, as they tended to work 'watch and watch' – eight hours on duty followed by eight hours off. This rarely applies to aircrew and we can usually drink in moderation most evenings. There was an undercurrent of excitement that evening. Everyone was debating whether we were actually going to war, or whether there would be a diplomatic settlement with us being the big stick which the government would use to back its demands. It was my view that we must assume the worst and plan accordingly. To this end I had a long discussion with Commander Chris Hunneyball, the staff aviation officer (SAVO). He was a former fixed-wing pilot and had a fairly good grasp of our requirements. I was interested to know what sort of tasks we were likely to have to undertake when we arrived off the Falklands.

He stated that our first task would be to deny the use of Stanley airfield to the Argentine Air Force. This sounded a very easy proposition but I knew from my time in Germany that to render a runway unusable for any period of time was very difficult. It appeared that the runway at Stanley had been built on a solid rock base, which would require a weapon with the ability to penetrate the surface and explode deep underneath, causing a large amount of 'heave' around the crater. Bombs dropped at low level would simply bounce off, causing little or no damage. To do significant damage to the runway surface we would have to drop 1000-pound bombs in a steep dive, which might not be a good idea if there were significant ground defences.

I suggested instead that we use the BL 755 cluster bomb, one of the weapons planned for use in the central European theatre against tanks and aircraft in the open. The 'custard bomb', as it was colloquially known, was a devastating weapon that could be delivered from a height of only 150 feet. Once clear of the aircraft, its casing split and 147 bomblets were scattered over an area on the ground the size of two football pitches laid end to end. Each bomblet was about the size and shape of a baked bean tin and consisted of a high-drag tail unit with an armour-piercing warhead. The nose of the bomblet contained a very sensitive detonator and the casing fragmented into thousands of razor-sharp fragments. Each bomb could destroy anything within its footprint, armoured or soft skinned. Aircraft and personnel certainly came within the definition of soft skinned. I thought that with this weapon we would be able to make a hell of a mess of an airfield and probably slow down any attempt to repair it by virtue of the fact that about 10 per cent of the bomblets would probably not explode, leaving between ten and fifteen very effective anti-personnel mines per weapon. SAVO needed little persuasion and disappeared off to send some signals. I felt pleased that my experience was being acknowledged so quickly and that I seemed to be making a positive contribution to the grand plan.

Shortly after my conversation with Chris Hunneyball I became aware of a disturbance at the bar. A slightly dishevelled-looking civilian with large glasses was struggling to climb onto the counter with a pint of beer in his hands. He stood up, his head bent under the steel deck-head, and called for quiet. When he had achieved a slight lull in the conversation, he looked around the sea of faces and said, 'Gentlemen, for those who don't know me, I am Brian Hanrahan from the BBC. I would like to introduce my cameraman Bernard Hesketh and John Jockel my soundman. We will be coming with you on *Hermes*. Now, I know you are not very keen on the press but I hope that as you get to know us you will come to trust us. In the meantime I would like to buy a round of drinks.'

Brian certainly knew the way to our hearts and was quickly surrounded by eager young men with empty glasses. Treating others is normally frowned upon in the navy as it can lead to excessive consumption but the chance of a free beer from the BBC could not be declined. It was in fact a clever way of breaking down the normal distrust with which the services regard the media. Over the next few months I was to become close friends with the BBC team and there would never be a single occasion when they did not treat us with scrupulous fairness and honesty.

THE FOLLOWING morning found us some ninety miles south-west of Land's End, steaming in circles and awaiting the arrival of the rest of the task force. The weather had clamped in and we had a cloud base of only 200 feet in light drizzle, not an ideal day for my first deck operations, but I had to cut my teeth sometime.

In the event, my first operational ski-jump launch went without a hitch. The sea was relatively calm and deck movement very limited, which made it much easier to judge when to start the take-off roll. Unlike a steam catapult take-off, where the pilot has no control over his launch, a Sea Harrier free launch is entirely under the pilot's control once the flight deck officer has given him the green flag. The FDO on *Hermes* was Tony Hodgson, a hard-working officer probably a little older than most of us who had started life on the lower deck and ruled his team of yellow shirts with a benevolent rod of iron. He was great fun socially and an absolutely dedicated professional on the flight deck. His final visual check of aircraft before launch saved many a pilot a red face or even worse.

Before launch it was essential that the pilot be given sufficient information to align his navigation, heading and reference system (NAVHARS). This not only allowed the pilot to navigate successfully without reference to the ground but also performed the calculations required for accurate weapons release and stabilisation of the Blue Fox radar. Unlike most systems, it did not need a stable period of eleven minutes to align the platform; all it required was a position defined in latitude and longitude and an accurate heading. The heading was derived from an automatic readout positioned below Flyco but the position had to be copied onto a large board and shown to each pilot in turn by a 'board man', who wove his way across the deck, board held high, trying to get a thumbs-up from each cockpit.

The flight deck was a very dangerous place when operating aircraft. Imagine an area of steel the size of two football pitches, surrounded by a drop of sixty feet into the sea. Place on the right-hand edge a steel tower another sixty feet high, covered in masts and radars. Add piles of bombs, missiles, rockets and torpedoes, half a dozen Sea Harriers, their engines producing an ear-splitting whine even at idle and a couple of helicopters with rotor blades slicing the air six feet above your head. Sprinkle this scene liberally with men cocooned against the noise and weather in various coloured jerseys denoting their functions moving purposefully around their charges. Add, finally, several hundred ringbolts and lashing chains to trip the unwary and a thirty-knot wind to unbalance you. Truly not a place for the untrained. To this end, only essential personnel were allowed on the flight deck while flying was taking place.

Having launched, I immediately plunged into the base of the cloud, which stretched all the way up to 31,000 feet. I spent the next hour flying around in the layers of cloud, attempting to get the radar to work. I managed to catch a quick glimpse of Land's End and the Isles of Scilly way to the north-east of us before the Blue Fox gave up the ghost completely and I had to rely on directions from *Hermes* to find the target at the end of each practice interception. This was not a very satisfactory way of spending £10,000 of taxpayers' money, but at least it allowed me to carry out my first proper deck landing.

The method used to recover to the ship in poor weather differed considerably from that used ashore. The precision approach radar approach, used universally by shore bases, consisted of a controller interpreting a radar return and giving the pilot advisory information to enable him to achieve the runway centreline and the correct three-degree glide path. This allowed the pilot to break cloud at 200 feet exactly on the centreline and carry out a successful landing at about 120 knots on the runway threshold.

At sea the problem was slightly different in that after breaking cloud the pilot had to decelerate the aircraft to a hover alongside the ship, before transitioning sideways for a vertical landing. This required the approach to be flown slower than normal, putting the aircraft very close to the aerodynamic stalling speed. To facilitate this, the nozzles were lowered to sixty degrees at the commencement of the descent and power increased to allow the airspeed to be reduced to 140 knots. This produced a very unstable flight regime in which the slightest movement of the tail plane or power setting caused rapid pitching. As a result, the approach felt as if it was being flown balanced on the head of a pin, with the constant danger of falling into the abyss. In addition, the high power meant that the cockpit noise level was increased dramatically, making spatial disorientation a very real possibility. Disorientation, as any pilot knows, can cause the most peculiar conflict between the body and the brain, leading to overpowering but erroneous sensations. It has been the cause of many accidents in the past and will continue to claim lives until someone can find a way of desensitising the brain to spurious physical inputs.

Thus the carrier-controlled approach (CCA) resulted in a very heavy workload and a high stress environment, with a controller working an ancient navigation radar which suffered from poor definition and a minimum range of about half a mile – altogether not what a chap needs at the end of a difficult sortie on a dark night with not much fuel remaining.

I had only attempted two CCAs prior to this first sortie, both in the relatively civilised environment of Yeovilton, and I was not looking forward to my first poor-weather approach at sea. Luckily we still had a shore diversion available, which eased the pressure slightly, and the approach went fairly well, allowing me to break cloud just under a mile astern. From there it was just a case of judging the deceleration to arrive alongside with the speed under control. Once in the hover, things were fairly straightforward. A series of lights had been jury-rigged at the back of the island to give an indication of height above the deck and fore and aft position. These were referred to as the 'Christmas tree' and did a remarkably good job in the daylight.

The technique was to line up the Christmas tree lights and then move sideways across the deck to position over the centreline. Once stabilised there, power was reduced to commence the descent and almost immediately reapplied to cushion the touchdown. It was important to judge the ship's movement, however, as the deck had a nasty habit of moving as you started your descent, which could result in a heavy touchdown or one with a sideways motion. Either of these could damage the undercarriage and would certainly cause a wave of bawdy comment from the 'goofers' who lined the side of the superstructure. Goofing was a Fleet Air Arm tradition, whereby anyone without anything better to do would find a vantage point on the island and watch the aviators make fools of themselves. On *Hermes* the favoured place was on 03 or 04 Deck, in the area of the funnel. This activity was not entirely without hazard, as when aeroplanes crash they tend to send a lot of metal flying through the air. The danger of being hit by debris was, however, outweighed by the possibility of witnessing someone else's embarrassment. It has to be said that even without the occasional drama the flight deck in full operation is an impressive sight and goofing gives the ship's company as a whole the chance to appreciate the ship's raison d'être. Never more so than then, when we were quite possibly on our way to war.

One potential source of embarrassment for me on that recovery was that I was required to back-taxi for the first time. This was a manoeuvre rarely used ashore because of the danger of sucking in engine-wrecking debris (FOD), but the flight deck was supposedly kept completely clean, so back-taxiing was not unusual. The Harrier's exhaust nozzles could be rotated from the fully aft position to nearly twenty degrees forward of the vertical. This was designed to enable the aircraft to be slowed down in the air or on the runway after a conventional landing, but could equally be used to drive the machine backwards, both on the ground and in the air. The technique required a fine balance of power and speed. Too little power resulted in the aircraft refusing to move and a rapidly rising jet pipe temperature; too much power resulted in a rearward speed that was difficult to control. Add to this that neither the pilot nor marshaller was practised at the manoeuvre, the rudder pedals worked in the reverse sense and the deck was surrounded by a drop of sixty feet into the water and you can see the problems. Fortunately, I was only required to taxi backwards in a relatively straight line for a few hundred feet and managed it without loss of dignity.

Later that afternoon I climbed up to 03 Deck to goof as waves of helicopters arrived from Culdrose, some of them bringing last-minute joiners and others laden with stores. One of the late arrivals was Lieutenant Commander Des Hughes, an ex-Phantom observer who had been teaching radar intercept theory on 899 at Yeovilton and had been drafted to us as our operations officer. Des was an experienced aviator with an elfin sense of humour and was respected by us all for both his knowledge of the aircraft systems and his ability to cut through the bullshit and make things happen, even if it meant pissing off senior officers.

In among the stores received that afternoon were large numbers of brown crates covered with explosive markings. The cluster bombs had arrived in the nick of time before we were out of range of land.

We also disembarked some personnel. A team of dockyard workers had volunteered to sail from Portsmouth with us to complete the rebuild of the mast, this despite them having been told the previous week that they were to be made redundant. They had worked flat out for the previous three days and completed the job just in time. Before they flew off to Culdrose we threw a party for them in the wardroom and then poured them onto the helicopter without a care in the world and clanking with duty-free bottles. Also to leave was Andy McHarg, one of our junior pilots. Much to his chagrin, he had developed a serious eye infection and was sent ashore to recover.

With all our transfers complete, we now headed off to the southwest at speed. The Bay of Biscay is notorious for its rough seas and the next twenty-four hours were no exception. The vast Atlantic rollers have

3000 miles of unbroken ocean in which to gather momentum. What starts as a mildly choppy sea off the coast of New England develops into a series of long, greasy, powerful swells by the time it reaches Biscay. Add to these waves strong winds completely unobstructed by any land mass and you have the recipe for some very uncomfortable weather.

That night I experienced the worst discomfort I had known since my short period in a minesweeper when I was a cadet at Dartmouth. Even though the ship was by far the largest in the Royal Navy, she was tossed about like a coracle. The seas were running in a westerly direction with up to thirty feet between trough and crest. This gave the ship a peculiar corkscrew motion, which made it very difficult to forecast what was going to happen next. With my cabin being a long way aft, I experienced some of the worst of the motion, although not as bad as those poor souls trying to sleep in the forward mess decks. Each time the ship crested a wave, the stern rose rapidly some forty-odd feet, pinning me to my mattress. A few seconds later, as she slid down into the trough, there was a floating sensation as the stern dropped away. This was not too bad when lying horizontal but made walking about the ship extremely tiring and very hazardous. It also resulted in a large amount of spilt beer. I hardly slept at all that night. Not only was the ship's motion not conducive to sleep but the noise of the sea rushing past the hull and the vibration from the propellers turning at high revs also combined to keep Morpheus well and truly at bay.

Over the next few days the ship steamed steadily south at around twenty knots while we started to prepare for our various roles. We also practised bringing the ship to action stations. On hearing the pipe 'Hands to action stations, hands to action stations. Assume State One, Condition Zulu', everyone immediately reported to his station and all defensive positions were fully manned. *Hermes* had very little in the way of defensive armament, two Seacat missile systems and a couple of machine guns, but all ops room functions and damage control headquarters had to be manned with the utmost speed. The result of this was that hundreds of men burst into the passageways heading in various directions, all carrying gas masks and life jackets and pulling on anti-flash hoods and gloves. As if this chaos were not enough, all the water-tight hatches and doors were also slammed shut and fully secured.

The first attempt resulted in a thirty-minute reaction time from the pipe to being fully closed up. This was obviously far from acceptable when we might have only a few minutes notice of an incoming missile. Commander John Locke, the executive officer, left us in no doubt that this was a poor result and repeated the exercise ad nauseam for the next few days until we were reacting in less than fifteen minutes. Even this time was later halved, with the added incentive of a real attack.

By 8 April we were some 400 miles off the Portuguese coast and settling into the routine fairly well. We flew fairly intensively, including a forty-eight-hour period while closed up at action stations. We honed our intercept skills, practised our combat manoeuvres and started to develop techniques for attacking Type 42 missile destroyers. This was important as the UK government had previously sold the Argentine Navy two of these ships with fairly effective anti-aircraft missile systems. I studied the details of the Seadart radar and came up with a series of manoeuvres which I believed would allow two Sea Harriers to penetrate its defences and sink or disable a Type 42. On Good Friday we put the theory into practice and completely confused one of our Type 42 escorts. I can remember feeling happy that we now had a good chance against the Argentine destroyers if the need arose.

That evening the weather was beautiful. A large area of high pressure was stationary over the Azores, giving us light winds and a calm sea. The flight deck was opened for recreation for forty-five minutes between day and night flying and I took the opportunity to stand on the ramp, looking west, watching the glorious oranges and pinks of the setting sun as it sank towards its shimmering reflection on the ocean's surface. I have always considered aviators to be particularly fortunate; not only do we see more sunsets than most of humanity but, if you judge it right, you can experience the incredible beauty of a ground-level sunset and then slip your earthly bonds and soar into the evening sky to watch a second sunset from high above your earthbound colleagues.

My reverie was however rudely broken by the call to action stations and I was forced to dive through the nearest watertight door and head back to my troglodytic existence.

By now we were heading due south towards Ascension Island and had settled into a routine of eating, flying and sleeping, with a few beers thrown in for good measure. There were a few incidents to relieve the boredom. A Sea King suffered a tail-rotor control failure but managed to carry out a very nice running landing on the aft end of the flight deck, and Bertie Penfold was marshalled backwards into the side of the island. He was incandescent with rage but we pointed out that it would have been slightly worse, and a great deal wetter, if he had been marshalled backwards over the side of the deck. As it was, the damage was limited to a slightly bent tail-plane tip and was soon repaired.

I carried out my first live intercepts during this period. One was a Spanish Navy Atlantique maritime patrol aircraft snooping around some way north of the task force. At this stage we were not sure whether the Spanish were on our side and didn't want to risk our progress being communicated to Buenos Aires. After a couple of slow passes alongside him, he seemed to get the message and turned away from the fleet towards his home base. The second was a twin-engined light aircraft that was showing far too much interest in us. He also turned tail and headed back towards land as soon as I showed up on his wing.

Preparations for war continued and a great deal of time was spent repainting the aircraft. The Sea Harrier's normal colour scheme was an attractive dark grey with a white underside, all very nice for air displays but not very good camouflage in the conditions we were anticipating in the southern ocean. The remedy was large numbers of men with four-inch paintbrushes and gallons of grey paint. After covering all the white surfaces, we then painted out the white circles in the roundels, although I reckoned that if the enemy got close enough to see those, we would probably be in deep guano. The result was actually very easy on the eye and certainly considerably more warlike. We also painted out the pilots' names on the sides of the cockpits, with one exception, that of Major Willard T. McAtee USMC. Willy was the archetypal US Marine, ready for anything, but much to his disgust had been forbidden from taking part. As he said, 'Who the hell can have a war without inviting the marines?' His name remained on the side of his aircraft until the night before the first raid on the islands, the least we could do for a great aviator and friend.

13 April

Got up at 0440 for an 0620 six-ship launch. It was pitch black and frightened me fartless. I ended up with no radar, no radar warning receiver and no head-up display. All in all, not the most enjoyable sortie I have ever flown. Tried out some loft bombing profiles and they seem to work OK, so we are into toss bombing now. Defence stations all day. Action stations today took four minutes for weapons systems and nine minutes for State 1, Condition Zulu. Getting better!!

The morning of 15 April dawned bright and clear. We had now passed through the south-east trades and were well into the doldrums. The outside air temperature had climbed into the twenties and whenever the flight deck was opened for recreation, lines of lily-white bodies could be seen stretched out on towels, soaking up the sun. Today, however, was different; we were about to cross the equator and this was cause for celebration. In accordance with long-standing naval tradition, King Neptune was to hold court.

Neptune and his court were played by a bunch of hairy-arsed senior ratings, some representing mermaids with long wigs made from lengths of string. In the wings lurked Sweeney Todd, the demon barber, with his huge pair of scissors and massive cut-throat razor. In attendance also were a number of 'enforcers' whose job it was to round up those unfortunates who had not crossed the equator before and drag them before Neptune. Once there, they were forced to kneel and given a drink, before being roundly abused, covered in flour and water, given a shave and haircut and thrown with great ceremony into a tank of water. There they were repeatedly ducked, with each ducking accompanied by a round of raucous applause. This was followed by the presentation of a certificate which read:

A Proclamation

To all mariners and lubbers alike wherever they may be, be it known by his royal proclamation that His Gracious Majesty King Neptune, ruler of the Seven Seas and Six Oceans and all underwater terrains, did after all due consideration, admit to his realms one…

Flt Lt MORGAN RAF

who on the 15th day of April 1982 did sail across latitude 0 degrees.

In committing this offence the aforementioned mariner did undergo the penalties laid down and passing the same to the satisfaction of His Majesty and his court, did then pay homage and become a humble servant to his majesty from that time on.

Neptunus Rex

SPECIAL FALKLAND WAR EDITION

This was a very welcome day of relaxation before we carried on with the work-up.

That evening we were told that there would be a mail run leaving in the morning, so I sat down at my writing desk and wrote my first letters home.

HMS *Hermes*
15 April

My dearest little wife,
How are you? I hope things have settled down somewhat after my rather precipitate departure. You probably saw all the coverage of our departure from Portsmouth. I was in a briefing at the time and missed it but I gather it was a spectacular send-off. I can't tell you much about what we have been doing, for obvious reasons, but

we have been working hard to prepare for all eventualities, although we did have a rest on Easter Sunday and on the day we 'crossed the line'. It being my first time across the equator, I was hauled up before Neptune's court and found guilty, forced to drink an awful concoction and then covered in flour and water before being thrown into a tank of seawater. I am still trying to get the paste out of my hair!

I expect you have been getting all the news back home, as we have a TV team on board, who have been sending copy back via satellite. In fact you will probably have seen some film by the time you get this letter. Morale is pretty good at the moment and we are all set to give these guys a whopping if they don't wind their necks in pretty rapidly.

Thank you for the pictures and the drawings which you packed for me; it was a lovely surprise when I opened my logbook for the first time. I've got them on the inside of my writing desk, as we are not allowed any loose paper or materials around the cabin, because it may foul the pumps if the cabin gets flooded. My cabin is just on the waterline, above the props on the port side, which makes it a little noisy when we are going fast. Almost like an express train but it is not too bad otherwise. The rest of the bunch are a good crowd, including Spag, Ted Ball and Tony Penfold. Also Fred Frederiksen who was at Dartmouth with me and was recalled from Boscombe Down.

I bet Yeovilton is a bit quieter now, with all the noisy Harriers gone and most of the helicopters. I hope you have a nice Easter and I hope the kids weren't too grotty. I felt a bit low for the first couple of days out but I'm feeling a bit more cheerful now that we are getting stuck into the preparations. I don't think that we have too much to worry about from the Argies, especially with a couple of nuke submarines in the area. In fact it sounds from the news as if they are getting cold feet about the whole deal, so we may not have to go all the way after all. You can always hope.

You know I miss you and the kids something rotten. God knows why. I must be getting sentimental in my old age. Talking about old age, I am attempting to keep a diary so that you can get an idea of what happened when I get back. I don't think it will be up to Pepys' standard though. I am also trying to cultivate 'out of body' experiences, so if you suddenly find someone with you one evening, don't worry; it will just be my ka!

I've just been told that the last post leaves in a couple of hours, so I'd better get this in the box. I don't know when I'll be able to write again but you'll be able to follow my progress from the TV reports, unless we unload the team. If you get desperate, it is still possible to get a signal to me through Yeovilton, by the way.

Give the Boggits a big hug for me (and the cat, hamster, fish and tadpoles!) and I'll write when I get the chance. Take great care of yourself my love. I love you very much indeed, even if I do get ratty sometimes.

Lots of love

    D

I also wrote to Antje.

My dearest disciple,
I must admit that I never thought that I would be on my way to war with the navy before I had even finished my conversion to the Sea Harrier! As you can see, I am at present on board *Hermes* as she rushes off south. I cannot tell you precisely where we are or what we have been doing for obvious reasons but we have been working quite hard and playing quite hard as well. It is rather different flying from a runway which keeps moving around!

I was rather depressed to start with, especially as we were about to move into our cottage and everything seemed to be working out really well. I had even started seriously considering leaving the RAF at the end of this tour and settling down in Somerset, it is such a peaceful and friendly area. I am feeling a bit better now, however, as I come to terms with the new situation. I have every hope that we will be back in the UK within a few months, once we have waved the big stick at these bloody people.

If things do not go quite so well, then I still have the knowledge that I have learned a lot more about life – and death – over the last couple of years than I ever knew previously, thanks to a large degree to you, my dear Ant. Should the worst happen, which is highly unlikely, do not forget me because I have no intention of forgetting those I love and I have every intention of looking for them again as soon as I am able. So if in a few years time you find a small boy who falls desperately in love with you, don't be too hard on him!

I didn't have much time before I left to put my life in order but I have asked Carol to let you know if anything happens to me. Actually, I expect you will know anyway, if the past is anything to go by. I believe we will be back in a few months without too much trouble, in which case you must both come down and help us celebrate, as I am sure there is going to be one hell of a party!

For the first time in my life I am trying to keep a diary, so that I can look back in years to come and remember. Actually, my memory is awful these days. It must be old age! I hope that you are still enjoying life as much as you were when I got your last letter; you deserve to be happy because you are so full of love.

I have just heard that the last post leaves in three hours, so I must finish quickly and get this letter in the post. I do not know when I will be able to write to you next but I will be thinking of you, that I can promise. Take great care of yourself and above all, be happy. Tell David he is a very lucky man and I still intend to meet him and check him out!

In times when bullets prove, when deeds decide:
Nor the cool laughter of the youthful corn
Nor the brief hot poppies hide
Earth trodden and torn.

In times when smiling eyes and lips tell lies,
And only dead men tell no tales, no tales
Casting their last disguise,
Love alone avails.

Hold hard to the dear thought. For courage less
This tenderness is but a dress worn thin
Against the cold. Love's dress
Is blood-deep under the skin.

JOHN PUDNEY

Auf wiederschauen Mäuschen,

All my love
David

The next morning it was business as usual with a dawn launch, loaded for the first time with live weapons. It had been decided that we would trial one of each of our weapons, both as a check that all our procedures were correct and as a morale-boosting demonstration for the rest of the ship's company. Nothing amuses sailors more than watching pilots make very loud bangs, except perhaps the possibility of them making cockups. A firepower demonstration of this type has great potential for both, so Andy Auld, the commanding officer, decided to lead the sortie himself. Andy was a quiet, rather serious Scot who had previously flown Phantoms and had considerable experience in the low-level attack role.

My weapon for this exercise was a retard 1000-pound high explosive bomb. This had a high-drag tail which opened as soon as the bomb was clear of the airframe to enable the aircraft to escape the debris from the subsequent explosion. It was quite hazardous doing the pre-flight walk round in the dark with only the aid of a small pocket torch, not made any easier by the fact that half the aircraft was hanging out over the side of the ship and it was the first time I had ever flown with a live weapon. Under the fuselage was the large olive-green shape of the bomb, nestling between the Aden gun pods. Yellow rings around the nose showed that it was filled with 186 kilos of RDX, enough high explosive to do some serious damage. I crouched down and checked the arming vanes on the back of the bomb and the security of the fusing wires. I think that all six of us that morning were very aware that this was another step towards the war which was becoming more likely with every passing day.

Black Section launched and successfully delivered their weapons onto a smoke float astern of the ship. The first three aircraft tossed 1000-pound bombs fitted with airburst fuses, the next three dropped retard bombs and numbers seven and eight launched two pods each of 2-inch rockets. All functioned correctly and every one was close enough to the target to cause major damage. We then watched the final two aircraft carry out an even more spectacular evolution. They initially ran in parallel to the ship in a couple of miles trail. Once the lead aircraft had passed the ship, he pulled up and threw a Lepus flare high into the air. The Lepus was designed as a night reconnaissance aid and consisted of a three-million-candela magnesium flare suspended beneath a parachute. The second Sea Harrier, flown by Lieutenant Martin Hale, one of our junior pilots, then locked a Sidewinder onto the flare and launched.

The missile streaked across the sky, accelerating to over three times the speed of sound before homing perfectly and destroying the flare. It was a very satisfying demonstration for all the pilots but left the ship's company slightly disappointed, as there wasn't a very large bang from the warhead. It was pointed out that even a small bang close enough to your arse would certainly ruin your day. We had at least proved that all our weaponry worked and that we could deliver it when the time came.

The next morning saw us riding at anchor a couple of miles to the west of Ascension Island. This tiny British outpost rises precipitously out of the ocean approximately halfway between Brazil and Angola, a full 1000 miles from the coast of South America. It was formed, together with St Helena some 600 miles further south, by an ancient volcanic eruption and was a particularly bleak place. The only sign of vegetation was a tiny green cap of rainforest perched precariously on the top of the mountain. The rest of the island was covered in a black volcanic dust, which also formed the black sand beaches with their forbidding rollers.

The only advantage that Ascension possessed was Wideawake airfield, a landing strip 10,000 feet long able to operate the largest of aircraft. Wideawake was to become our nearest resupply point for the next two months and was to allow many hundreds of RAF personnel to claim their Falklands campaign medals while remaining 3900 miles from the action. Now that would have been my kind of war! While we waited for orders, Andy McHarg returned to the fold, fully fit and raring to go, having been flown to Ascension by VC10. In his pocket he carried a C60 tape which had been pressed into his hand by the Smiths Industries rep before he left Yeovilton. The only clue as to its possible use was 'Falk Loft 82' printed on the label.

Falk Loft 82 turned out to be a new standard of software for the weapon aiming computer. The back-room boys in the UK had been working day and night to give us a number of additional capabilities. The result was a system of throwing bombs onto a radar-defined target from a range of up to three miles. In addition to this, they had designed a method to give us a distinct advantage in a dogfight. This was called Superscan and it allowed us to lock our Sidewinders onto an enemy aircraft even though we couldn't bring our noses to bear on it. In actual fact, when we tried it out we found that there had been an error in the programming which meant that it worked a treat when the wings were level but if you entered a left-hand turn the missile scanned out of your right ear. A great try given the enormous time constraints involved, but not quite a coconut.

THE FOLLOWING morning at 0900 our lives suddenly changed. Someone on the Royal Fleet Auxiliary *Olmeda* spotted a periscope. We were brought to action stations and were under way within eighteen minutes. *Hermes* had Sea Kings in the air very quickly and they picked up a target moving south but were unable to say whether it was a submarine or a whale. Whichever it was, it had finally precipitated our move towards the Falklands and our tryst with destiny. After a couple of hours Admiral Woodward made a broadcast to say that we were now on our way to war and that everyone should do everything possible to prepare themselves for the coming conflict. This finally silenced those who had been sure that Margaret Thatcher was bluffing and a new sense of purpose could be felt about the ship.

The following day we formed ourselves into three planning teams, one to examine the problem of attacking the Argentine Type 42 frigates, one to examine air-to-air tactics and the final team to develop tactics for the ground attack mission. I teamed up with Clive Morrell to consider the ground attack options, the most important of which was Stanley airfield itself. Clive was a very experienced aviator who had flown Buccaneers and Starfighters before spending three years in Germany with me flying the Harrier. He was very tall and thin, with a rather Mediterranean complexion, hence his nickname Spaghetti Morrelli. He had a wonderfully laid-back outlook on life and I had never seen him flustered or upset, despite the many and various tribulations of life in the Germany Harrier Force. I remember him causing consternation on one occasion when he was due to take a spare aircraft to an air display at his old German Navy air base in Schleswig-Holstein. Shortly before he was due to take off, his girlfriend arrived from the UK in the back of a Hercules. Adana was an air traffic controller at Lyneham and had decided to come over for the weekend on spec. Spag was faced with the difficult choice of seeing his old German mates or spending the weekend with Adana. In typical Spag style he persuaded the squadron to let him have the two-seat Harrier and took her to the air display as well. Not only did he overcome his thorny problem but he also amazed German air traffic control by having Adana handle all the radio traffic for the formation. For quite some time it was believed that the Brits had a fully qualified female Harrier pilot, something unheard of in the early 1980s.

Within a couple of days we had come up with a number of plans for the airfield attack. The first entailed an operation in the dark using night vision goggles to achieve high-angle dive attacks with 1000-pound bombs, which could achieve the desired result of cratering the runway. The use of these goggles was very much in its infancy and had been limited to helicopters until then. We discovered, however, that the definition with them was quite adequate for weapons delivery and the cockpit could be made compatible by the judicious use of masking tape over a few bright lights. I was amazed that sitting in my cockpit on deck on a very black night I could still see the detail of the waves up to half a mile away. I am sure that this plan would have worked well but it was abandoned a few days later when we received further intelligence on the defences around the target. In addition to visually aimed anti-aircraft guns, the occupying forces had installed 35-millimetre Oerlikon guns linked into Fledermaus radars. This would enable them to fire accurately by day or night and would make high-angle dive-bombing very hazardous. In addition we were told that there was a Roland missile system based at the airfield. This was a highly effective point defence system which could engage targets at altitudes between 50 and 11,000 feet. There were also a number of older missile systems which all combined to make dive-bombing a very unhealthy option.

We also considered using a loft profile, which entailed aircraft running in at very low level before pulling up and throwing the bombs in from a range of a couple of miles. The problem with this attack was that it was impossible to achieve the accuracy or the grazing angle required to damage the runway. We therefore decided that the best way to inflict serious damage was to attack at low level with cluster bombs and concentrate on airfield facilities and aircraft in the open. If we could create enough havoc, the enemy would be very reluctant to risk basing any fast jet assets at Stanley.

Having decided on the low-level option, we set about designing the geometry of the attack so as to give ourselves the best chance of achieving our objective with the minimum of losses. We were very aware that our total assets were only about 10 per cent of those which the Argentine forces could bring to bear, and it was very important that we conserved aircraft. Without aircraft, we knew that the conflict would be lost, a sobering thought. Our plan of attack was reworked several times before we agreed that it could not be further improved. Even so, I had privately decided that we could expect to lose two or three aircraft during an attack on such a heavily defended target. This being the case, I resolved to put myself in the number two slot, which I considered to be the least hazardous position.

That night I wrote a letter which I hoped would never be delivered, as had so many servicemen before me:

> Well, my love, I'm afraid it has happened. I am leaving this letter with Andy George, to be forwarded to you as soon as possible after my death. Please try not to be sad, I know that dying will not hurt me and I am equally sure that I will see you sometime, somewhere. All things are possible if you want them strongly enough.
>
> If you read *Jonathan Livingston Seagull* and *Illusions* and also *The Little Prince*, I think you might understand. Those three small books meant more to me than all the other books I have ever read put together. I am sure that what they say in them is true. Death is an unfortunate but necessary method of passing on to a new level of consciousness. Not a gateway to heaven but a chance to improve your knowledge and awareness and get a little closer to the concept of total love. It is only in the last year or two that I have really understood, or started to understand the meaning and power of love. It has to be spontaneous, selfless and all embracing. I am afraid that I wasn't really very good at it and it is a bit annoying that I didn't get the chance to practise a bit more. However, don't think you have seen the last of me! I intend to spend a lot of time with those I love; every time you think of me, I will be there, that is a promise. Please try to explain that to the kids, I will always be there in their thoughts to help them and look after them when they need me.
>
> Please, none of you feel any bitterness towards anyone who was responsible for my death, they could not touch the real me and pain is only there if you allow it to be. Likewise, please do not hesitate to find someone else you can share your love with, you will most certainly have my blessing.

I would like to give you a final explanation of my feelings for Antje. I was, at first, attracted to her sexually but discovered within a matter of a couple of hours that there was an uncanny bond between us. We could literally read each other's thoughts. I must admit, it confused and puzzled me and I could not explain it to myself, let alone you, although I desperately wanted to. I thought that if I tried to explain, I would only hurt you and that you might leave me, which I could not stand the thought of. Not because of pride but because I was beginning to realise how much I really did love you, despite the problems we had gone through.

Well, the rest you know really. The only way that I can explain our relationship is that it feels as if we have known each other for thousands of years, which maybe we have, and when I met her again in London, it was just a natural progression to go to bed together. You may find it hard to believe but my relationship with Antje made me even more aware of my love for you than I was before. Probably because I became so much more aware of my own emotions and began to learn so much more about life and death. I was no longer frightened to say I loved you and I understood what I meant. Even if I showed it in funny ways sometimes! *Illusions* says it all really.

You know, we really did have some good times together and I don't think I would change much if I had my time over again, except perhaps to try a bit harder not to be ratty! Give Elizabeth and Charles a great big hug and a kiss for me. I will always love you all and I intend to look after you, if you need it, until we meet again.

> Don't be dismayed at goodbyes
> A farewell is necessary before you can meet again
> And meeting again, after moments or lifetimes
> Is certain for those who are friends.
>
> RICHARD BACH

Take care, my love

D

On the 20th we took the next step towards war and loaded all the aircraft with live missiles. It was fairly nerve-racking the first time I flew with a live Sidewinder. In peacetime you could wait for years to get the opportunity to carry one and the process would be surrounded with the trappings of awe associated with such unusual events. Normally, numerous precautions would be taken to guard against accidents and you would never point the weapon at another aircraft. Here we were flying normal intercept practices against each other with two live missiles and I found myself being almost paranoid about safety. I could only hope that everyone else was as cautious.

The following day a high-level contact was picked up by *Hermes'* long-range radar and Simon Hargreaves was sent off to investigate. He discovered it was a Boeing 707 airliner at 35,000 feet and on closer inspection was amazed to find that it was in the markings of the Argentine Air Force. He closed in and flew in formation with the 707 for some time while they took photographs of each other, before the Argentine pilot turned away for home. There was great excitement on the ship at this unexpected first sight of the enemy and I detected a definite change in attitude. The enemy was no longer a vague intangible concept; we had seen him and had been in a position to shoot him down.

That afternoon I was sitting in my cockpit at five minutes readiness to fly with two live missiles and two hundred rounds of 30-millimetre ammunition in my guns. War in all its reality seemed very much closer than it had done at breakfast time. I was wearing the life jacket with the number three on the back. I had noticed that the number thirteen jacket had been renumbered and we now had two with the lucky three stencilled on the back. Someone else was obviously hoping to convince the fates that we should be looked after.

I had only been in the cockpit for half an hour or so when I was scrambled. I hit the start button and as soon as the generator was on line, turned on all the electrics, typed in the launch position, ran rapidly through my checks and was given the green flag to launch. As my wheels left the top of the ramp, I noticed that the stopwatch was showing just five seconds short of three minutes since I was given the order to start. This was the fastest I had ever got airborne and the adrenalin was flowing fast, the blood rushing through my body, as I turned to the south and climbed for the target.

At forty miles I found a radar contact, well above me and tracking east some one hundred miles to the south of the ship. As I closed to twenty miles, heading south-east to intercept the small green blip on my screen, I picked out a vapour trail against the brilliant blue of the subtropical sky. I armed both my missiles and my guns and made sure that I had a decent f-stop set on my gunsight camera; I didn't want to miss filming this one! At about ten miles I put the radar into standby and shortly afterwards identified the aircraft as a Boeing 747, cruising at 38,000 feet. I stayed 5000 feet below the airliner and closed to a couple of miles abeam, where it became obvious that it was not an intruder, but merely a scheduled civilian flight plying its lawful way between the two continents. With a peculiar mixture of relief and disappointment, I made my guns safe and turned north-west to return to the ship.

That evening we heard that the operation to retake South Georgia was under way but that we had lost two Wessex helicopters in bad weather on the Fortuna glacier. The story was initially very confused but it eventually filtered through that they had crashed in 'white-out' conditions while trying to pick up an SAS patrol which had got into difficulties. It seemed that Operation Paraquat was not going smoothly and we all hoped that this was not a bad omen.

Our morale was not helped the following night when Flight Lieutenant Bob Grundy ditched a Sea King astern of the ship. He had been operating on night vision goggles when the weather had deteriorated to the point where he considered it hazardous to continue on his own and was returning to pick up a second pilot. The aircraft impacted the water hard but Bob was able to scramble out of the cockpit, minus a couple of teeth, and was picked up by another helicopter. His crewman was not so fortunate however and was never found. The mood in the bar that night was sombre, especially among the helicopter pilots. Things did not seem to be going well.

That evening, I wrote my final letter to Antje.

HMS *Hermes*

23 April

My dearest disciple,

You will know by now what has happened to me. I am writing this letter to leave with Andy George, my cabin mate, to be sent on to you after my death. Please do not be sad, my love, you and I both know that death is only a gateway to a new level of consciousness. When I was young, I used to be scared at the thought of dying but it holds no great horror for me now. I expect it will be mildly unpleasant for a short period but pain and distress can only affect you if you want them to.

I really want to thank you for changing my life. I have learned so much about love and living over the last couple of years and I owe most of it to you. I am certain we have met before this life and I am equally certain that we will meet again. I certainly intend to look for you next time. It is actually rather exciting to be on the brink of a brand new experience of such tremendous proportions. I am certain that I can carry my knowledge with me into my next existence.

What I want you to do right now is to promise me that you will be happy for the rest of your life. You are the only person who can affect your happiness and I won't have you being sad. I will always remember your face in the moonlight and your hair streaming in the wind, and talking the night away in the clubroom at Breit-scheid and the thrill of your touch and the deep longing for your body and the intoxicating smell of your hair on my shoulders. And the dried flower and the sauna and the swimming pool. I think you were my most perfect illusion. I only wish I had created you earlier! In my next life, I will surround myself with imitation Antjes until the real one is available.

Will you tell David all about me now? I am glad that I told Carol about us before I left and if you have held anything back from David, now is the time to tell him all. It was such a relief not to have to pretend to Carol any more, after I told her. I was silly not to come clean before and she was very understanding. Why do I always underestimate women? You must excuse the shaky hand-writing, as the sea is very rough tonight and it is difficult to write.

There is little more to say really, my love, you know my thoughts and words are superfluous. I have been very lucky in life; I have two children, whom I loved very much, a wife whom I also loved dearly, although it took me a long time to realise how much, and of course, you, my dearest disciple, who helped me under-stand. Think of me when you read *Illusions* or *The Little Prince* because every time you think of me, I will be there with you.

Bis gleich Mäuschen,
David

On the 25th, however, things began to change. We received permission to harass the 707 if it returned, including firing live ammunition across its bows to persuade it to keep clear. At last we felt that things were beginning to move forward, although we still did not know in which precise direction. Later on that morning rumours began to fly around the ship that we had made some serious gains in South Georgia and soon the commander came on the tannoy to announce that we now had control of the island. Not only that, but we had attacked and crippled an Argentine submarine in the process.

That evening we all gathered in the wardroom to listen to the BBC World Service and a great cheer went up when the details of the action were announced. The anti-submarine Sea King boys were over the moon, as this was the first A/S kill since 1945. The ship's general demeanour suddenly took a huge change for the better, despite the memorial service for Bob's crewman that afternoon. That evening I wrote in my diary, 'Morale is <u>very</u> high. All we need now is an Argie jet or two!'

Listening to the World Service soon became a nightly ritual and was a way we could feel in touch with our loved ones back home, knowing that they too were listening. Some years later I became friendly with the Wasp pilot whose missiles hit the conning tower of the *Santa Fe*.

Lieutenant Commander Tony Ellerbeck was a larger-than-life character who would have probably been an explorer had he been born a couple of generations earlier. He was a great hunting and fishing man who possessed an impressive array of sporting guns and took every opportunity to use them. A few months previously he had been on a courtesy visit to an Argentine naval port with HMS *Endurance*. While there, he had been out for a day's sport with a local naval officer and the two had got on very well.

The *Santa Fe* had limped into Grytviken harbour and grounded herself alongside the jetty. The crew had been taken off and were huddled on the shoreline some way from the submarine when Tony arrived in his Wasp to survey the damage. As he walked past the sorry knot of Argentine sailors, one jumped to his feet and shouted, 'Tony! What are you doing here?' When Tony didn't answer immediately, the Argentine sailor suddenly realised and groaned, 'Oh no! Not you!' It was his fellow sportsman, who had been in command of the submarine. Such are the contradictions of war.

26 April

A depressing day. Rough weather, heavy showers and three and a half hours at five minutes readiness in the cockpit without getting airborne. Could do without too many of those. Missing Carol and the kids a lot. Didn't get to sleep until after midnight last night. One glimmer of hope in the darkness: we have a change in the rules of engagement. We can now shoot down anyone within forty miles of the fleet, after standard warnings.

The following day was equally unpleasant and we began wondering if this was the norm in southern latitudes. I spent several hours on alert again and discovered it was possible to get some fairly good sleep by jamming your elbows into the demisting ducts around the canopy and resting your helmet on your fists. This formed a very effective geometric lock and if your smoked visor was lowered no one knew you were not awake. All that was needed was to brief the plane captain to slap very hard on the side of the cockpit if the order to scramble was given.

The rest of that afternoon was taken up discussing with the engineers a method of dispensing chaff for aircraft self-defence. We had access to packets of these aluminium-coated fibreglass filaments designed to produce large radar returns when deployed into the airstream. I had already discovered that it was possible to squeeze two packets between a 1000-pound bomb and the weapons pylon. This allowed the chaff to deploy as soon as the bomb was released and would offer some protection to aircraft carrying out a loft delivery against a target defended by radar-guided weapons systems. What I now tried to do was design a system that could also be used against an airborne fighter threat.

The obvious place to put the chaff was in the airbrake. Unfortunately, on the Harrier the airbrake remains partially deployed when the undercarriage is down, to improve low-speed handling. My initial idea was to use speed tape to secure chaff packets to the rear of the airbrake but this proved very unreliable and tended to shower the aircraft behind with chaff as you launched. Lieutenant Phil Hunt, the squadron deputy engineering officer, came up trumps and designed a suitable system of welding rods, split pins and string which allowed six packets of chaff to be secured in the airbrake well. This protected them from the airflow as soon as the gear was up but allowed them to be deployed by a piece of string, tied to a drilled-out rivet hole in the airbrake, when the airbrake was cycled in flight. Heath Robinson would have indeed been proud of the result and within twenty-four hours all the aircraft were equipped with a workable chaff capability. When we tried the system out, we found that the resultant chaff cloud appeared on radar as a target the size of a frigate, which we hoped would be more than enough to confuse the radar-guided missiles carried by the Argentine Mirage fighters.

HMS *Hermes*

28 April

Hello again, love,

We have just been told that there will be a mail run tomorrow morning, so I will just scribble a quick note to bring you up to date. We had quite a pleasant trip down with quite a lot of flying and lots of action station practice. The last couple of days have been fairly rough but not too bad. The bad news is we might run out of beer! We have a self-imposed limit of two pints per night at present.

Spag and myself have formed a ground attack planning team, in case we have to 'do the Argies over' and we have been checking out all the kit and inventing the odd goodie to surprise them.

You will have heard about the *Santa Fe*, I expect. That made their eyes water a bit. We now have a really good team here (except for the captain, who is a doddering old Seahawk pilot who thinks he is still at Suez!) and we are all pretty confident. We had a nasty the other day, as I expect you heard. Bob Grundy lost his crewman when his Sea King went splash; he is OK though, just cuts and bruises.

Thanks very much for the letter; it was super to hear from you, although I don't think we'll get much mail for a bit now, as we are outside Nimrod range. I expect that this will take seven or eight days to get back to you but we can send the odd 'shipgram' now; forty words only. So don't worry if you get a telegram, it will just be a shipgram from me.

Do you know what I really miss? The walks in the country, bottles of wine in front of the fire, gardening together, warm, snuggly Boggits, just lying there holding you. All sorts of soppy things like that. Never mind, I will make up for it when I get back.

Keep the bed warm for me till I get back, my love, and I'll have a bottle of the '76. Actually we are already thinking about parties. One in Port Stanley next week and the other when we get home!

Take care, love. I miss you dreadfully.

All my love

D

DREAMS OF A FAR PLACE

Tonight I lie awake and dream
Of sun-kissed, dewy mead
And fiery eves.
Of gnarled oaks gargantuan
And sweet, scrubby pine,
With deep needle-littered brambles
All ablaze with autumn's fullness.
And rhododendron blossom fair
And lissom, paying no heed to deeds of beast or men.

Of love's sweet touch,
Of words unsaid that need no explanation
Within the commune of the heart.
Tonight I hear the cries of children,
Calm their fluttering hearts and
Comfort distant souls.

For though my earthbound body rest
Amidst the wild and storm-tossed
Mountains of the sea,
My heart and soul, my love, tonight
Lie cradled home with thee.

On the 29th HMS *Brilliant* rejoined us from South Georgia. With her came over ninety special forces personnel, who proceeded to make themselves at home wherever they could find a bunk or camp bed. One of our pilots got to his cabin to find a fierce-looking guy asleep on the deck, cuddling a crossbow. That evening, on my way back from the crewroom to the wardroom in the red-lit semi-darkness, I tripped over a sleeping body in the passageway and sent an object rolling across the deck. When I bent down to retrieve it, mumbling my apologies, I realised that it was a hand grenade. These were good guys to have as friends!

One of the specials in the bar that evening was an old friend of mine, Flight Lieutenant Garth Hawkins. He had been the SAS's forward air controller for many years and was without doubt the best FAC I had ever encountered. He was a giant of a man, in his fifties and with greying hair but still as strong as an ox. He had a thriving business in the Home Counties but stayed with the SAS after he should have retired because they asked him to. I had first met Garth some years before, in Belize. At the end of one exercise he came back with the canvas top of his Land Rover in shreds and his clothing in tatters. When we asked what had happened to him, he just said, 'I don't mind you guys trying to knock me off the top of the Land Rover but I do wish you wouldn't jettison fuel over me!' One of our pilots had to buy him quite a few beers that evening. On another occasion he was conducting an exercise near the Mexican border when a local farmer walked over to him to ask why he had thrown a red smoke grenade into one of his fields. Garth explained that it was so that the pilot of the Harrier could identify his position and therefore find the target. The farmer smiled in relief and told him that this field was his best marijuana crop and he didn't want it bombed.

30 April

Well, today we heard that our baptism of fire is tomorrow. It is a funny feeling really, rather like losing your virginity: feel rather apprehensive about the whole thing but will probably enjoy it when I get started. The plan is to attack Stanley airfield with nine aircraft: four tossing 1000-pound bombs followed by four with cluster bombs and one with 1000-pound retards. The plan is good (must be, I did a lot of it) and there are only a couple of nasties on the airfield. With a little luck we will not have too much trouble. We all have to come back, anyway, because we start a beard-growing contest tomorrow!

The dining room that evening was converted into a planning room and we sat down and plotted our ingress and egress routes in minute detail. We also plotted all the known air defences, both missiles and guns, which was fairly sobering. The Argentines had prepared well and we would be very lucky to come away unharmed.

It had been our intention to run four aircraft into the target from the south, to pull up at three miles and toss three bombs each onto the defences. This we hoped would get all the defences pointing south while the low-level raid hit them from the north. Unfortunately, the captain disapproved of this plan, as he thought the toss-bombers would be too exposed to the Roland missile system. We were convinced that our aircraft stood a very good chance of escaping unharmed behind their chaff screens but we were overruled. This resulted in all the aircraft having to attack from the north, from behind Mount Low – not a tactically sound idea but we had to make it work. It was certainly a bloody sight better than the captain's suggestion that we attack in close formation and drop our bombs on the leader's command.

I pored over my maps for a very long time that evening, memorising every contour and every feature. I realised that there would be no time for map reading once we got close to the target. Officially, our task was post-strike reconnaissance after a Vulcan bomber raid planned to take place just before dawn. Unofficially, we were going to 'kick arse' in true naval style.

CHAPTER 3

BAPTISM OF FIRE

AT 0815 THE FOLLOWING morning Antje left her flat in Stanhope Road to walk to Highgate tube station for her journey into work at the German Chamber of Commerce in Suffolk Street off Pall Mall. Just before she arrived at the station, she had a sudden thought. A check in her handbag proved her fears correct; she had left her copy of *Illusions* at home. I had given her a copy of the little book and for some time she had carried it around with her. That particular morning for some reason she had the overpowering feeling that it was of the utmost importance that she had this small volume with her. Despite her fiancé's objections, she retraced her steps and collected the precious talisman.

As she finally boarded the Underground train, I was making my way to the wardroom to guzzle down a full English breakfast before reporting for the final mission briefing. I was wearing a newly laundered flying suit and, of course, fresh underwear!

Most of the details had been briefed the evening before and everyone was well aware of their individual duties. In addition we had received an escape and evasion briefing, detailing safe houses and giving us some rather bizarre survival hints:

Seal eyes are said to contain enough vitamins to sustain a human.

Shags and cormorants are delicious.

Beware of seal wallows. These are deep muddy-sided hollows in the tussock which can be impossible to escape from. They could also have a form of quicksand in the bottom.

Staats Island, off the west coast, is inhabited by the guanaco, a type of llama. These are wild and have been known to attack humans.

I must remember to avoid the guanacos!

The final briefing was complete by 1000 GMT (0600 local time). The weather was suitable, with a stiff westerly breeze and scattered cloud with a high cloud base. The visibility was in excess of ten miles, with only a slight possibility of rain showers. Altogether, it was a very good day for our mission. As we were completing the briefing, we received the code word 'Superfuze', the indication that the Vulcan from Ascension had delivered its load of 1000-pound bombs onto the airfield. So the RAF had managed its part of the attack, now it was our turn.

Grey fingers of dawn tentatively probed the eastern sky as the twelve of us made our way across the gently pitching deck towards the silent bulk of our fully armed Sea Harriers. We moved with the slightly shambling gait associated with the modern fighter pilot. Each of us was weighed down with helmet, oxygen mask, anti-G suit, maps, immersion suit and layers of thick-pile clothing to enable us to survive in the near-freezing water around the islands. HMS *Hermes*, the old lady of the Royal Navy, which had sailed millions of miles since her commissioning in 1959 and launched hundreds of thousands of aircraft sorties, was in her twilight years about to launch her first ever air strike against an enemy.

It was now 1 May. In Somerset my children would be celebrating the coming of spring with traditional dancing and jollification. In the South Atlantic the autumn storms were gathering and the Sea Harrier force was about to show its mettle. The weeks of meticulous planning and practice were now coming to a head. Each pilot carried a Browning 9-millimetre automatic pistol together with two loaded magazines, probably more of a psychological prop than any practical use, even for a passably good shot like myself. After a few half-hearted jokes, we had taken refuge in our private thoughts and most of us were happy to immerse ourselves in the well-practised and comforting routine of preparing to fly.

My aircraft was lined up on the flight deck centreline behind Andy Auld's, with three 600-pound cluster bombs hanging from the weapons pylons. Having carried out the initial safety checks in the cockpit, I walked slowly around the aircraft, checking that it was in all respects ready for flight. I also checked that both guns were loaded and connected, that all the arming leads and lanyards on the bombs were correctly fixed to the pylons and that all the safety pins had been removed. The bombs looked rather less warlike than the 1000-pounders, their thin skins being built more for aerodynamic function than to cause damage. I was in no doubt, however, that these weapons would wreak havoc once they were deployed against targets on the ground. Nick Taylor had carried out a very impressive practice drop of the bomb a few days previously and the resultant area of beaten water was a sobering sight. So too was the bomblet that detonated prematurely and sent a white-hot slug of copper whistling past his tail.

I mentally ran through my part in the plan as I carried out an extremely thorough check of my Martin-Baker 'bang seat'. It was essential that everyone carried out his individual role as perfectly as possible to preserve the integrity of the attack. We had only allowed three seconds between aircraft over the target, so there was little room for error. As I strapped myself into the seat I was acutely aware that the odds were very much against us all returning safely. The temptation was to look over at the others as they settled into their cockpits just to catch a final glimpse, to preserve a final picture of each of them as some sort of insurance against them not making it through the day. I double-checked all the armaments settings in the cockpit and set up the head-up display aiming data, adding two chinagraph pencil marks on the sight glass in case I suffered a display failure. These marks coincided with the weapon aiming point – one seen from my normal sitting position and a further one seen from a position crouching down behind the gunsight camera, where I suspected I might be during the final stages of the attack. The marks were calculated for a delivery at 480 knots (550 mph) and a height of 200 feet.

At 0640 the order came booming over the flight deck broadcast system: 'Stand clear of jet pipes and intakes; start the Sea Harriers.' I held up five fingers to my plane captain to show that my ejection seat was now live and he replied with the signal to start as I heard the other eleven Pegasus engines winding up around me. As my engine stabilised at ground idle, I began my post-start checks and after a few minutes the flashing anti-collision lights showed that all twelve fighters were ready to go. There was time for a quick glance at the en-route map before *Hermes* turned into the prevailing westerly wind and the chocks and chain lashings were removed leaving the aircraft ready for take-off.

As the hands on my watch moved, oh so sluggishly, towards ten minutes to the hour, I inserted the ship's heading into my inertial navigation kit and rechecked: flaps down, armament master switch live, nozzle stop set at 35 degrees, trim 3 degrees nose up and ejection seat live. Exactly on time, the red traffic light below the window of Flying Control turned green, and Tony Hodgson dropped his green flag to launch Andy Auld ahead of me. My machine was buffeted violently by Andy's jet efflux as the grey bulk of his aeroplane threw itself off the end of the ski-jump. I taxied quickly forward to the take-off point. Tony, braced against the jet wash, gave me the green flag and with a final nod I slammed the throttle open. Within one second the power of the engine started to drag the locked wheels across the deck and in two seconds the jet was accelerating at a terrific rate towards the ramp, driven by the ten tons of engine thrust. As the end of the deck disappeared below me, I rotated the nozzles and leapt into the air some seventy knots below conventional stalling speed, accelerating rapidly into forward flight. Within ten seconds of launch the wheels were up and I was in a tight left-hand turn to join up with the leader as the other aircraft got airborne at five-second intervals behind us.

As we carried out a lazy orbit I watched the other aircraft cut the corner to join us and by the time we overflew *Hermes* we were all together and starting to take up our defensive formation for the transit to the islands, still well over the western horizon. As we set heading, Andy called to Mike Blissett, the number three, 'Three, you have the lead, my nav kit has dumped.' Mike replied, 'Sorry, boss, so has mine!'

Mike was the senior pilot of the squadron, an experienced ex-Buccaneer man who was dying to get to grips with the enemy. He had very fixed ideas as to how fighter pilots should behave and I had already been bollocked for not eating my cheese rind at dinner. To this I had replied that in my view fighter pilots could eat what the hell they liked. It must have been galling for him to have to turn down the lead on this our first mission.

Andy then asked me to take the lead, but my kit had also dumped as I left the ski-jump. Faced with such a catalogue of unserviceabilities, Andy decided to retain the lead and in fact we all managed to realign our systems on the way into the islands.

The initial transit went without incident and we soon settled down into a flexible formation, with everyone scouring the rapidly lightening sky for enemy aircraft. After ten minutes on a westerly heading we turned south towards our planned landfall at Macbride Head, the most north-easterly point of East Falkland. Almost immediately I saw a couple of dark shapes hugging the water and closing rapidly from the east. I shouted, 'Break port! Bogeys left ten o'clock level,' and we all pulled our jets into a screaming left-hand turn to face the threat. As we turned through about forty-five degrees, I realised that the sinister shapes were in fact our three spare aircraft on their way to attack the grass airfield at Goose Green. As Fred Frederiksen hopped his formation over ours, we regained our heading and with pulses racing caught our first sight of the islands.

The coastline crystallised slowly into a dark scar separating the restless sea from the layers of cloud stacked over the high ground to the south.

My first impression was of its similarity to the Scottish coast, which made it difficult to believe that we were not on one of our more familiar exercises rather than bent on an errand of destruction. There was little time to dwell on this, however, as we made our way down the coast towards our initial point near Volunteer Beach. I can remember being struck by the complete absence of trees, the beauty of the white sand beaches and the sight of a lone cow pausing in mid-chew to watch with detached interest as we swept past on our deadly mission.

After a couple of minutes my radar warning receiver emitted a high-pitched rattle. This was an indication that I had been illuminated by a radar-laid gun but after half a second it fell silent and I never found out the origin of the warning. The area seemed completely uninhabited and I saw no anti-aircraft fire.

At Volunteer Point, some ten miles north of the target, Red section detached to the south-east, to set up for their loft attack. Gordie, Oges, Neill Thomas and Spag accelerated and ran into the mouth of Port William, pulling up some three miles out and releasing their weapons in a forty-five-degree climb before banking away hard to the left, diving back down to low level and running out to the east. This attack delivered nine airburst bombs and three with delayed-action fuses. The airburst weapons were fused to explode fifty feet above the target and produced a devastating cone of shrapnel over a wide area, together with a very impressive fireball. We had planned a one-minute interval between the impact of these weapons and the arrival of the low-level attack to ensure that no one caught a 1000-pound bomb in the back of the neck as they ran over the target. To make doubly sure, Spag had been briefed to call 'Bombs gone' as soon as he had completed his delivery.

As we approached the northern shore of Berkeley Sound, with only ninety seconds to run to the airfield, Black formation split into two sections. Mike Blissett, Ted Ball and Bertie Penfold detached to the right in order to set themselves up to approach from the north-west while Andy Auld and myself headed for the east side of the pair of 900-foot mountains to the north of Stanley. I was aware of the increase in tension as I urged my machine as low as I possibly could towards the craggy outline of Mount Low. Right on cue I heard Spag shout, 'Bombs gone!' just before we passed abeam Cochon Island. Ten seconds later and to my amazement Andy Auld suddenly pulled his aircraft into a tight right-hand orbit. This was the manoeuvre that we had briefed to ensure separation from the loft bombs should we not hear Spag's call. Andy was the only one not to hear the call and as I followed him around the orbit I saw to my horror that the rest of the formation was continuing with the attack. As the other three disappeared over the saddle between Mount Low and Beagle Ridge I realised that this put me as the last aircraft across the target. The very place that I had not wanted to be!

There was not much time to worry about this, however; the die was cast and I just had to press on and do the best I could. As we crossed the south shoreline of the sound I was aware of intense concentration as my eyes flicked between engine instruments, the head-up display and the inhospitable rock-strewn tussock grass whipping past at over 500 mph a scant fifty feet below my aircraft. I was flying lower than I had ever done before.

As I rounded the eastern slopes of the mountain, tucked behind and slightly to the left of my leader, the target came into view. At first I couldn't take in the sight that greeted me in the thin grey dawn light. The airfield and the entire peninsula on which it was built seemed to be alive with explosions. Anti-aircraft shells carpeted the sky over the runway up to a height of 1000 feet, so thick it seemed impossible for anything to fly through unscathed. Missiles fired from the airfield and outside the town streaked across my path, long wavering white fingers chasing the previous attackers out to the south-east. Tracer fire criss-crossed the sky and as I watched a number of guns turned in my direction, sending feelers of scarlet probing towards me. The tracer curved lazily down, rather like a firework display and not initially conveying much feeling of imminent danger. I was reminded of Antoine de Saint-Exupéry's description of anti-aircraft fire over Arras in 1944. It was almost beautiful in a peculiar detached way. As the tracer fire got closer, however, it suddenly seemed to accelerate and began whipping past my ears, bouncing off the grey sea all around me. My brain froze in horror for a fraction of a second as I realised that this wasn't a game anymore and someone was actually trying to kill me! The years of training then took over and as I took evasive action I realised that I was automatically flying even lower.

In London, Antje was at her desk, with the all-important, slim volume safe in her handbag.

> Hold hard to the dear thought. For courage less
> This tenderness is but a dress worn thin
> Against the cold.

I hauled the aeroplane hard left and then right, to pass between and below the Tussock Islands and Kelly Rocks, themselves only thirty feet high. This gave me a few seconds of perceived safety before I was once again over the open sea and pressing on towards the airfield below the level of the sand dunes. Inspection of the gunsight film later in the day showed that we were all flying at a height of between five and fifteen feet as we approached the target.

Keep jinking; never be predictable; fly as low as you possibly can.

I became aware of a number of Argentine soldiers firing down at me from the sand dunes on the northern edge of the airfield, their bullets kicking up the water all around me. I raised the guns' safety catch on the side of the stick and squeezed the trigger hard, expecting to hear the roar of the 30-millimetre cannon and see the eruptions of smoke and flame among the enemy on the near horizon. But the guns would not fire. I thought that they must have jammed but realised later that in the heat of the moment I had failed to select the gun master switches – a salutary lesson.

As I crossed over the beach I yanked back on the stick, flattening the defenders on the dunes with my jet wash, and levelled at 150 feet, the minimum height required for my cluster bombs to fuse properly. In slow motion I took in the damage caused by the rest of the formation: the airport buildings billowing smoke and a number of aircraft lolling at drunken angles, obviously badly damaged. The fuel dump to my right was a storm of orange flame under a gathering pall of oily black smoke and huge lumps of debris were still falling from the sky from the explosions of the 1000-pound bombs. The dust cloud from Andy's cluster bombs was drifting slowly away to the east, although I was not aware of his aircraft at all. One aircraft which seemed undamaged was a small civilian Britten-Norman Islander. I quickly lined up my bombsight, raised the safety catch and mashed the release button, dispatching my three cluster bombs. The first bomb separated from the port, outboard wing pylon and after a short safety delay blew off two sections of skin to expose the 147 bomblets. These were in turn ejected to form a cloud of death which rolled over the airfield. One third of a second after the first weapon had dropped, I felt the thump as the second bomb left the centreline pylon mounted under the fuselage and fell away towards the target.

Suddenly there was a huge explosion and the aircraft started vibrating like a road drill. It was impossible to read any of the cockpit instruments to check for engine damage but the aircraft still seemed to be flying. I now had a dilemma. In the GR3, if you interrupted the release sequence, you had to close and reopen the safety catch before the rest of the weapons would release. I wasn't sure of the logic in the Sea Harrier's weapon aiming computer and just pressed the button and hoped. Instantly there was a satisfying thump as the third bomb released and fell towards the aircraft on the concrete pan by the control tower. As soon as the last bomb had cleared the starboard wing pylon, I dived my machine for a large pall of smoke beside the tower. I still have a very clear recollection of passing below the level of the tower windows as I entered the cloud of thick black smoke. (When I returned to the airfield after the war was over, I discovered that the tower windows were only about twenty feet above the ground.) I waited a short while inside the smoke, with visibility absolutely zero, then pulled the aircraft into a maximum-rate turn to the east. I was acutely aware that the ground rose gently to the south of the airfield and I didn't want to become a crater in the side of Canopus Hill.

As I punched out of the smoke, my radar warning receiver emitted a strident, high-pitched warbling note; I had been locked up by a radar-laid anti-aircraft gun. This was no time for gentle flying. I racked the aircraft into a bone-crushing 6-G break to the left through ninety degrees to put the radar at right angles to my flight path and flicked out the airbrake to release a bundle of chaff into the airflow. Despite the Heath Robinson design, it did its job; the radar lost its lock and I was able to haul the vibrating aircraft back onto an easterly heading and run down the beach and out to sea and safety.

As we cleared the target area we changed radio frequency and checked in. To my amazement everyone acknowledged the call. It seemed that we had all survived the attack against all the odds and despite the last minute screw-up in the order of attack. I felt a wave of euphoria sweep over me and realised that I would have held myself personally responsible had anyone died during the attack that was mainly of my design. It suddenly struck me that I had been subconsciously studying each member of the formation before we manned our aircraft in an attempt to ascertain who would not be coming back.

Once safely clear of land, I slowed down and climbed gently up to 10,000 feet; it was now time to pay some attention to my own predicament. I called *Hermes* and informed the ops room that I might need a helicopter to pull me out of the water if my damage was serious. I knew there was a Sea King stationed about forty miles out from the carrier and he could be with me in a few minutes if the need arose. As I reduced speed the violent vibration began to reduce to acceptable levels and I was able to check out the aircraft systems. I was amazed to find that everything appeared to be working correctly except a tiny gauge down by my left knee which showed the position of the rudder trim. This in itself was of no consequence to the operation of the aircraft but gave me the first indication that damage had been done to the tail of the plane. On the way back to the ship I carried out a low-speed handling check, which proved normal, and then began to consider my options.

Once back above *Hermes* I circled at a height of 5000 feet whilst Ted Ball came up to inspect the damage. After a fruitless inspection of the left of the aircraft, he swooped underneath the belly and looked at my right side. After a few seconds he said, 'Ah yes . . . You have got a bloody great hole in the tail.' I moved the control surfaces to and fro and he told me that they appeared to be working correctly but that there was a distinct possibility that the reaction controls, critical for vertical landing, might have taken some damage. This put me on the horns of a dilemma. It was obviously important to recover the aircraft if at all possible, but if I could not control it in the hover I might crash on the flight deck and cause an enormous amount of damage to both men and aircraft. I therefore decided to try a rolling vertical landing. This entails running the aircraft onto the deck with about fifty knots of forward speed and is not a cleared manoeuvre, as there is a distinct danger of running over the side into the sea. It does however reduce reliance on the reaction controls and might give me the option to overshoot and try again if the controls jammed. Flyco accepted my decision and the goofers prepared to watch the first ever RVL at sea.

I waited until all the other Sea Harriers had landed safely and been lashed down securely before starting my approach. I was feeling remarkably in control of the situation as I selected my undercarriage and flaps to the landing position, tightened my lap straps and set myself up for a straight-in approach to the back end of the ship. As I got closer everyone on the flight deck started to creep forward to get a better view of the impending arrival. This worried me somewhat as, if I lost control, I might take a lot of people with me. I pressed the transmit button and called, 'Clear the deck, I'm coming in!' The flight deck crews soon got the message and headed rapidly for the comparative safety of the catwalks on either deck edge.

I stabilised the speed at fifty knots and adjusted the power and nozzle angle to give me a gentle rate of descent towards the stern of the carrier. Slight adjustments were required to compensate for the rise and fall of the deck but I managed to achieve a good firm touchdown about fifty feet past the round down and braked cautiously to a halt before following the marshaller's signals to park at the base of the ski-jump. As the chain lashings were attached and I started my shutdown checks I became aware that I was sweating profusely despite the biting thirty-knot wind whipping in through the open cockpit canopy. The adrenalin flow also made it difficult to unstrap myself and undo the various connections to the ejection seat before standing up on rather shaky legs to leave the cockpit. Outside on the windswept and slippery deck stood a crowd of people staring at my tail. Having given a thumbs-up to Bernard Hesketh of the BBC, I walked a little unsteadily round the tail of the aircraft to inspect the damage. The hole was about six inches across and had obviously been caused by a 20-millimetre shell which had entered the left side of the fin at a grazing angle of about ten degrees and exploded, causing considerable damage to the right-hand side of the fin and tail plane. After a little consideration I realised that the shell had probably passed very close to my head and had been only one of about forty per second coming from this particular gun. Lady Luck had certainly been on my side that morning.

As we signed our aircraft back in there was a mighty roar from outside on the flight deck, as Tartan section returned from Goose Green. After encountering us near Macbride Head they had carried out a photographic reconnaissance run along San Carlos Water before carrying out a low-level attack on the second airfield on East Falkland. They ran in so low that the defenders hardly had time to raise their weapons before they were past. One of the Argentine soldiers said that only madmen would fly so low and one of the pilots was surprised to come face to face with a horse as he ran in for the attack. The cluster bombs dropped by Fred and Martin Hale destroyed one Pucara, killing the pilot, and severely damaged at least two and possibly five others. Andy McHarg also dropped three 1000-pound retard bombs, one of which made a large crater in the grass runway.

Thus ended the first sortie. We had flown a total of twelve Sea Harriers against two heavily defended airfields, delivered a total of thirty-six bombs, destroyed a large number of enemy aircraft, set light to a number of fuel storage sites and buildings and escaped almost unscathed. Euphoria now took over from the concern of the pre-dawn briefing. The first operational sortie, the most important in any pilot's life, was over. The rest would now be easier for everyone.

That evening Brian Hanrahan sent his report of the raid back to the BBC, which ended with a sentence that became famous:

A few hours after the Vulcan attack, it was *Hermes'* turn. At dawn the navy's Sea Harriers took off, each carrying three 1000-pound bombs. They wheeled in the sky before heading for the islands – at that stage just ninety miles away. Some of the planes went to create more havoc at Stanley, the others to a small airstrip called Goose Green, near Darwin, 120 miles to the west. There they found and bombed a number of grounded aircraft mixed in with decoys. At Stanley the planes went in low, just seconds apart. They glimpsed the bomb craters left by the Vulcan and they left behind them more fire and destruction. The pilots said there had been smoke and dust everywhere, punctuated by the flash of explosions. They faced a barrage of return fire, heavy but apparently ineffective. I'm not allowed to say how many planes joined the raid, but I counted them all out and I counted them all back.

We gathered in the briefing room to debrief the sortie, everyone with eyes shining, babbling away to each other as the adrenalin started to subside. The tension of the last few hours now drained away as we ran through the details of the mission and passed all the information to the intelligence officer for onward transmission. It was difficult to know precisely how many aircraft we had damaged on the ground but there was no doubt that quite a few Pucaras would not be flying for a while. We had also inflicted considerable damage to the airfield facilities and Neill Thomas' post-strike reconnaissance photos showed several fierce fires burning around the buildings. Bertie had planted two out of his three retard bombs on the runway but little damage had been done because of the low grazing angle. The pictures also showed the limited extent of the damage caused by the Vulcan raid: the very first of its twenty-one bombs had hit the runway but the rest had marched off into the wilderness. It seemed a lot of effort for one hit on the runway but at least it made it unlikely that the Argentines would be able to use the strip to operate fighter aircraft. As we concluded the debrief I noticed that Oges was looking intently at his watch. Soon a piratical grin creased his face and he just said, 'Bang!' One of his bombs had been fitted with a one-hour delay and had just exploded. We were told later that there had been a number of Argentine soldiers inspecting the hole when it had blown; in future they would give a wide berth to any apparently unexploded bombs.

My part in the day's operations was now over and I made my way down to the wardroom for some lunch. I was glad to see that someone had at last cleared the sacks of potatoes that had been sitting in the 3 Deck passageway since we sailed. I had watched them gradually rotting for some time and in the last couple of days they had started oozing out of the sacks – not really very appetising. Actually, the food on board had been very good up to this point, although I had begun to notice that there was always broccoli on the menu. It turned out that this vegetable freezes better than almost any other and was therefore to become our staple diet. Luckily, I rather liked it.

Back on deck, the maintainers were hard at work refuelling and rearming the aircraft. Sidewinder launchers were fitted to each outboard pylon and missiles slid into place and connected up. Each missile's tracking was checked with an infrared torch and a magnetic protective cap, the 'noddy cap', placed over each seeker head. Protection from the elements was to play a very important part in preserving the serviceability of the weapons in the hostile weather of the South Atlantic. It was not unknown for people to sleep with a missile seeker head in their bunk just to dry the electronics out.

Thirty minutes after we returned from the Stanley raid the first combat air patrol (CAP) sortie left the deck to counter the anticipated reaction from the Argentine Air Force. Our sister squadron on *Invincible* had been flying CAP to the east of the islands since two hours before our raid on Stanley. They had received reports of numerous enemy aircraft to the west but no one had succeeded in getting close enough to engage them. This changed around midday when Lieutenant Soapy Watson and Sharkey Ward were vectored onto three Mentor light attack aircraft about to attack a Sea King in the area of Berkeley Sound. Sharkey managed to score one hit with 30-millimetre cannon before the Mentors ran for the protection of the air defences at Port Stanley. Shortly after this the two were engaged by a pair of Mirages, which ran in at supersonic speeds at high level before firing head-on missiles and departing rapidly to the west. It seemed that the enemy had no wish to come down to medium level to fight with us and we had no intention of trying to climb up high to tangle with them.

Later that afternoon it was our turn. Bertie Penfold was airborne with Martin Hale when the long-range radar mounted on *Hermes'* mast picked up another pair of aircraft. The SHARs turned to take the bogeys head on and found them on radar, some 13,000 feet above them. As they closed the range, a missile was fired from one of the enemy aircraft which headed towards Martin. He immediately carried out the manoeuvre that we had briefed and practised: he rolled on his back and pulled his Sea Harrier into a vertical dive. After a few seconds he pulled back into the fight, dumping his airbrake chaff as he did so. This defeated the missile, which fell away before reaching him. Bertie, meanwhile, had seen the missile fired and the fighter then turn around right in front of him. This gave him a perfect zero-aspect tail shot but at very long range and on a retreating target. He fired his AIM9-L and called, 'Fox two away . . . but it is a bit rangy!' After what seemed a very long pause there was a flash followed immediately by a large explosion and the aircraft was transformed into a cloud of wreckage. The pilot was not seen to eject.

As Bertie and Martin were returning to the carrier, John Locke came on the ship's broadcast and let us know what had happened. A huge cheer ran through the ship. At that time we believed that they had achieved the first kill of the war, although we learnt later that 801 had beaten us to the draw by a few minutes when Flight Lieutenant Paul Barton and Lieutenant Steve Thomas had engaged a pair of Mirages near Pebble Island. Paul had dispatched one with a Sidewinder and Steve had damaged the other, which tried to make an emergency landing at Stanley. This was a bit of a mistake, as the pilot was shot down by the Argentine air defences as he approached the airfield. Luck was not on his side.

Paul Barton was another of the RAF exchange pilots and had been the qualified flying instructor (QFI) on No. 3 (F) Squadron at Gütersloh during my second tour in Germany. He was a first-rate instructor and his knowledge of the aircraft systems had been outstanding. He had, however, been hopeless at air combat manoeuvring (ACM) and was known to be 'easy meat'. Any number of times we had fought each other and the outcome had always been the same. The only thing that changed was how quickly I could get a guns solution on his aircraft. Shortly after I arrived at Yeovilton, he had taken me up for my first 1 v 1 ACM sortie in the Sea Harrier. I had been fairly relaxed about it and as we split for our first combat I was feeling pretty confident in my own ability.

We turned head on at about six miles range and passed very close with a closing speed of around 1000 mph. I immediately pulled my aircraft into a huge loop, topping out at over 20,000 feet. At the apex I unloaded the G and hung there, inverted, searching for Paul below me. Sure enough, I picked up the tiny Sea Harrier, way down at our 5000-foot base height. He was drawing a lazy horizontal arc across the Somerset countryside and showing no sign of threatening me at all. Just like Gütersloh, I thought as I headed towards the point in space where he would be in about fifteen seconds time. As my airspeed rocketed and he started to grow in my sights, I realised that he had not lost sight of me and was pulling his aeroplane up into the vertical to meet me head on. No sweat, I thought, I'll have him on the next pass. My first hint that all was not well was when he started to pull his nose around towards me just before we passed each other. To my horror I realised that he was making angles on me very rapidly and, yelling an expletive into my oxygen mask, I tried desperately to match his turn. But my speed was too high and within seconds I was fighting for my life. It was only a matter of ten seconds before I heard the humiliating words over the radio; 'Fox three! Knock it off, knock it off,' confirming that he had achieved a guns kill on me.

We flew three more engagements that afternoon and he shot me a further three times. I felt like a very chastened rookie pilot as I followed him back to Yeovilton and broke into the circuit to land. As we walked across the concrete pan from the aircraft to the squadron buildings I said to him, 'How the fuck did you do that, Bartoonski?' He replied with a barely suppressed smirk, 'The navy has taught me how to fly combat, Mog. You're with the big boys now!'

Over the next few days I learnt the science of combat. I studied the 'energy egg', obliques and nose-low slices, lead turns and low-speed scissors. I also learnt to recognise missile shots as well as guns opportunities and when to run away and when to stay and fight. What I had once regarded as an art form, I quickly learnt was a definite and well-defined science, and if a QFI could do it, I was certainly bloody well going to do it as well!

We met Bertie in the briefing room and everyone crowded around him, slapping him on the back and shaking his hand. As he was finishing his debriefing, the door to the 2 Deck passageway opened and the admiral's steward put his head around the door. It was Sandy Woodward's birthday and he had sent Bertie some of his cake to celebrate. I was struck by this genuine and human gesture from a man who had the worries of the whole task force on his shoulders in the first twenty-four hours of a major battle. I took my turn to congratulate Bertie and as he consumed his cake I asked him how it felt to get the first kill of the conflict. He looked me straight in the eye and said, 'Actually, Mog, I didn't enjoy it very much.'

The rest of the day passed in a blur. Both carriers launched CAP missions as quickly as they could in order to maintain airborne cover against the probes from the Argentine aircraft. There were numerous air raid warnings and on one occasion we were convinced that an Exocet missile had been fired at *Hermes*. It transpired that this was probably a false alarm caused by another ship's navigation radar but it certainly concentrated the mind. By the end of the day the Sea Harrier force had shot down four enemy aircraft and severely damaged two airfields, all at the cost of one slightly damaged SHAR which was repaired overnight.

The maintainers made a very good job of patching up my aircraft, cutting out the considerable damage caused by the exploding shell and riveting new skin and an external stringer over the holes. That and a little judicious use of speed tape was all that was required to make the machine serviceable for the next morning. I asked that the exit hole be saved as a memento of my first mission and was assured that it would be kept safe for me.

That evening the Sea King boys mounted a major operation to find the Argentine submarine *San Luis*. This was a modern boat of German design which was very quiet and difficult to detect. Three Mark 5 Sea Kings belonging to 826 NAS spent the night of 1/2 May carrying out an intensive search to the north of the islands. They prosecuted a contact and dropped no less than six Mark 11 depth charges and two Mark 46 homing torpedoes before returning to *Hermes*. It was never established whether these weapons were actually dropped on the submarine or the local whale population. The aircraft remained airborne throughout the mission, refuelling and changing crews in the hover over the two frigates *Yarmouth* and *Brilliant*. In the course of the night they established a new record for a helicopter remaining airborne on an operational mission – ten hours and twenty minutes. In the early hours of the morning one of the Sea Kings detected a surface contact and was fired upon when it closed to identify it. This turned out to be the Argentine Patrol Vessel *Alferez Sobral*, which was searching for the crew of a Canberra bomber shot down by 801 NAS that afternoon. The Sea King retreated to a safe distance and called for backup from the Lynx helicopters from *Coventry* and *Glasgow*. They attacked with Sea Skua missiles, which badly damaged the ship, although she managed to get away.

As a result of the first twenty-four hours of action, both *Hermes*-based squadrons were very pleased with themselves but there was some worrying intelligence suggesting that a surface threat was building. Reports indicated that several major Argentine naval units had sailed from their home ports and could be heading in our direction. Throughout 2 May we were braced for an attack by the air group based on the Argentine carrier *25 de Mayo*; it seemed that we might be heading for the first carrier battle since Midway. I can remember looking down from the bridge and counting dozens of bombs, depth charges, torpedoes and Sidewinders lying in serried rows in Fly 1 to the right of the ski-jump. If we had taken a hit on those, I reckon that the front of the ship would have probably blown off. Not a very encouraging thought. The weapons were stockpiled here for immediate use, having been brought up from the ship's magazines by the weapons lifts that ran all the way down to 7 and 8 Decks.

In the afternoon I was tasked to carry out a surface search to the north-west in an attempt to locate the Argentine carrier group. It was a very lonely feeling, heading out 200 miles from the ship with a radar that would, if I was lucky, find a ship at around ninety miles – about thirty miles after she had seen me. As it transpired and rather to my relief, I found nothing but an endless expanse of open sea and returned to *Hermes* after an hour and twenty minutes. Later in the afternoon a Sea King was launched on a similar mission and very nearly didn't make it back. *Hermes* had informed the crew that the ship would be maintaining a northerly track for the duration of their sortie but shortly after they left turned south without telling them. At the end of their three-hour flight they returned to where they confidently expected the ship to be only to find it was a further sixty miles south. Luckily, there was a frigate stationed forty miles to the north of the force and the helicopter had just enough fuel to reach it and carry out in-flight refuelling by winching up a fuel line from the back of the ship. There was a fairly heated discussion between the crew of the helicopter and the ops room when they eventually landed back on *Hermes*.

We were not the only ones searching for the enemy. In the early hours of the morning Flight Lieutenant Ian Mortimer had launched from *Invincible* to investigate a radar transmission from the west. This was in fact a Tracker reconnaissance aircraft from the Argentine carrier engaged in a search for our fleet. He flew up the bearing of the transmission, radar silent, in an attempt to find and destroy the aircraft. About 150 miles out from *Invincible* he was suddenly illuminated by a Seadart radar. He instantly knew that this could not be one of our ships and therefore had to be an enemy Type 42 frigate. To his horror, at that moment he saw a group of lights on the surface a few miles ahead of him. He dived for the sea and pulled his aircraft round to get out of range before tentatively turning back and switching his radar on. There, sure enough, was a group of contacts which could only have been the enemy carrier group. On his return to *Invincible*, he hurried down to the ops room to report his findings, only to find that the ships were already plotted. No one had thought to tell him before he went.

The Argentine Tracker had in fact located us, and the Skyhawks aboard the *25 de Mayo* were preparing for a dawn attack. A second Tracker was launched but had trouble with its radar and could not confirm the position of the British task force. This, together with light winds, caused the attack to be abandoned and the carrier battle did not happen.

SIX HUNDRED MILES to the west of us a BBC correspondent was trying to cover the conflict from the Chilean port of Punta Arenas. Michael Vestey was to become a friend and drinking companion years later and tells a very interesting story. He had got to know a Chilean officer on his arrival in Punta Arenas. He was a charming and well-educated man who spoke perfect English, knew the British services well and like so many Chileans was a keen anglophile. Michael received a phone call from him, asking him to come to his office. When he arrived, his contact passed him a piece of lined paper upon which the following message was written in blue ink:

A1

1 heavy unit, 2 light units. 13–1400 Zulu time. Lat 54 00S, Long 65 40W. Steering course 335 degrees, 18 knots.

'Can you pass this to your people?' he asked. 'The BBC?' Michael replied. The Chilean smiled, 'No, your government.' As a member of a military regime he had assumed that Michael worked for the British government – that anyone employed by the BBC must be a spy. When Michael disabused him of this, he simply insisted that he pass the information on. When asked about the meaning of the note, the officer merely said that it was important and that the British government would know what it meant.

On the short walk back to his hotel Michael considered his dilemma. What did the note mean and to whom should he give it? Would he compromise his independence and objectivity as a journalist by forwarding what was obviously a shipping movement of some sort? He decided that whatever his responsibilities as a broadcaster, his responsibilities as a citizen were clear. Once back in his hotel room he rang the military attaché at the British embassy in Santiago and informed him that he had some 'A1' information for him from the local military. 'Can't you telex it?' the attaché said. 'It's just that we are not the only people listening to this conversation.' The hotel did not have a telex and the diplomat eventually agreed to take it down over the phone and then hung up abruptly.

AN UNCANNY QUIET hung over the fleet that afternoon. I spent several hours in the cockpit at Alert 5 very much aware that we might be attacked at any moment. I just hoped that we would have sufficient time to get airborne before the attack hit. I certainly didn't want to be caught on the deck with bombs and bullets flying around and I had little faith in the surface fleet's air defence capability. The only exceptions to this were the Type 22 frigates with their Seawolf missiles. This was an excellent low-level air defence system but it was designed for point not area defence. To enable them to protect the carrier the frigates had to stay so close that they effectively became one with the capital ship. It was certainly a great morale booster to see *Broadsword* sitting a few cables off the port side, between the threat and us.

My thoughts strayed as I watched the ships manoeuvre back and forth – there had been a few good evenings in the wardroom bar over the last week and a number of popular songs had acquired new lyrics. To the tune of 'Don't cry for me, Argentina':

> Don't cry for me, Galtieri,
> The truth is we will defeat you.
> We'll sink your carrier
> With our Sea Harrier,
> Meanwhile our Sea King
> Subs will be sinking.
>
> Three and a half thousand bootnecks
> Will soon retake Port Stanley,
> So don't delay now,
> Be on your way now
> To Buenos Aires
> You bunch of fairies!

Lieutenant Clive Wood, one of our direction officers, when not controlling our intercepts proved himself an excellent composer of lyrics. One of his prize offerings was set to the tune of 'What shall we do with a drunken sailor?'

> What shall we do with an Argie Mirage?
> What shall we do with an Argie Mirage?
> What shall we do with an Argie Mirage?
> Early in the morning.
>
> Smash him in the face with an AIM9-L
> Smash him in the face with an AIM9-L

Smash him in the face with an AIM9-L
Early in the morning.

CHORUS

Nuke, nuke, nuke the bastards,
Nuke, nuke, nuke the bastards,
Nuke, nuke, nuke the bastards,
Early in the morning.

What shall we do with an A4 Skyhawk?
What shall we do with an A4 Skyhawk?
What shall we do with an A4 Skyhawk?
Early in the morning.

Shoot him up the arse with an Aden cannon,
Shoot him up the arse with an Aden cannon,
Shoot him up the arse with an Aden cannon,
Early in the morning.

CHORUS

The final verse, which covered the fate of the Argentine widows, is probably best left unpublished. It seemed in bad taste even then, but Clive never seemed inhibited by taste. His favourite party trick was to walk into a crowded bar with his stuffed monkey. Clyde, as the monkey was called, had one arm secured around Clive's neck with Velcro leaving the other arm to be fitted over Clive's hand like a glove puppet. It was amazing what this wandering hand could get away with in mixed company.

As dark approached that evening and we stood down from our alert, thick fog began to envelop the fleet. This was a great relief to everyone as the chances of an air attack at night in poor visibility were very slim. It had been a very tense day but the action was not yet over.

In the afternoon, some 400 miles to the south-west of our position, the nuclear submarine *Conqueror* had received orders from Whitehall to attack a group of three Argentine naval vessels close to the position given to Michael Vestey by his Chilean friend. Just before 3 p.m., *Conqueror* fired three Mark 8 torpedoes. The cruiser *General Belgrano* took one hit on the bow and one astern, sinking one hour later. I was sitting in the briefing room when John Locke broke the news over the ship's broadcast. It was greeted with a second of stunned silence, followed by a huge cheer which rippled through the ship. I stood up quietly and put a large chinagraph cross through the recognition picture of the *Belgrano* which we had pinned on the noticeboard. Two down!

It didn't take long for us to realise the proportions of the human disaster that had just taken place. None of us had the slightest doubt that the attack had been the right thing to do and we all felt that we were a little more secure now that the Argentine flagship was no more. There was an awareness, however, that a major warship sinking so quickly was likely to leave many men in the water. Survival time in the waters around the islands was measured in minutes without a survival suit and only an hour or so when wearing one. If the Argentine sailors had not been able to get into life rafts quickly they would be very poorly placed. The thought of a lingering death in a cold, dark sea was a little too close to home and had a sobering effect on everyone.

I think that we were all very happy when the fog lasted for the next twenty-four hours. I spent some time walking around the flight deck with no company save my own thoughts and was intrigued to find a small flock of pure white, pigeon-sized birds roosting on the lip of the ski-jump. As I approached them they shuffled off to one side but did not show any sign of getting airborne. They obviously had no desire to fly in the fog either. There was something very endearing about these little visitors; they had absolutely no fear of human beings and had it not been for their rather bulbous beaks could have been mistaken for doves. It struck me as rather incongruous that in the middle of a bloody war white doves were taking over the flight deck. These birds were soon identified as sheathbills, natives of the Falkland Islands, and were to be our constant companions for the next few weeks. In fact they became a bit of a hazard as they proved to be totally unafraid of the aircraft as well. This resulted in a number of launches being held up while the yellow shirts chased them around the flight deck. Eventually, the flight deck officer took a shotgun to them and earned the very vocal opprobrium of the captain, who equated his actions very forcibly with the Ancient Mariner's slaying of the albatross. Luckily, the FDO was not required to wear a corpse around his neck, but I think it was a close-run thing.

Most of the pilots, although appreciative of the lull, were also frustrated that they couldn't get on with the business in hand. Poor Bertie, after his hectic first day of fighting, had gone down with a stinking cold and by the evening was feeling and looking like death warmed up. He was very despondent despite our attempts to cheer him up and was not looking forward to spending the next few days anchored to the ops desk. I had huge sympathy for his predicament as it was precisely this position that I would have been in had I not been allowed to fly. The idea of being locked inside a tin can with people trying to sink you did not fill anyone with joy.

The weather forecast for the following day was fine, so some of us made the most of a few uninterrupted beers that evening, before turning in fairly early, in order to be bright-eyed and bushy-tailed to face whatever the morning should bring. I had a niggling feeling that it was going to be a busy day.

That night I had a most bizarre experience. I dreamt that I was hovering above my own body as I slept. I was somehow aware that I was having an out-of-body experience and that my ka was able to move around the cabin with complete ease. Unfortunately, I seemed to be much lighter than air and was unable to find a way to get low enough to duck under the frame of the door. I knew that if I could only drop down six inches or so I would be able to leave the cabin, rise up through the passageways to the weather decks and be home within a few minutes. It was a very vivid dream and I can remember being extremely frustrated and disappointed that I could not quite escape from the ship.

EPITAPH

For me
Do not grieve.
I sleep the sound sleep
Of the just.
I cared for nought but life
And those I must forsake.

Death
Was not my wish,
But such was my chosen path
And in that path
I was fulfilled.

Memory
Is all I ask,
However slight, a mere
Whisper in the breeze
Of spring
A silent thought.

CHAPTER 4

FIRST LOSSES

THE RESPITE AFFORDED us by the weather did not last for long and the morning of 4 May dawned bright and clear. The Sea Harriers were in the air as dawn broke, flying CAP and armed reconnaissance sorties over the islands. I was sent to fly a CAP mission to the north-east of Stanley and returned an hour later without having had any trade whatsoever. It was, as Gordie Batt said with his normal black humour, 'as quiet as a Mirage crewroom'. I was back-taxied to a tie-down spot next to the after lift and told to remain in the cockpit and come to Alert 5 once I had been refuelled. The sun was warm on my shoulders in the cockpit and before long I began to feel sleepy. I had already learnt that it was important to grab rest whenever you could, so I told the plane captain I was going to get my head down for a while, rested my helmet on my fists, closed my eyes and let my mind wander. I tried to imagine what my family were doing back at Yeovilton and how they were coping with the fact that the fighting had now started in earnest. I imagined that it would be pretty hard on Elizabeth and Charles because there was bound to be news coverage from the Argentine side which would be shown in the UK before our reports had time to get back. There was no such thing as real-time news reporting in 1982 and BBC film had to be physically loaded onto ships heading north and flown home from Ascension Island. I was sure Carol would be putting on a brave face and just hoped that she would be able to carry on with the mundane but essential daily routine without undue concern for my welfare.

I also mused over what Antje might be doing. I had no doubt she was still able to sense my moods and would be sharing the emotions that I had experienced over the last couple of days. My mind drifted through the mists of our times together – the glorious realisation that there was a person with whom I could communicate without the constraints of language, someone beautiful and timeless who could answer my questions before they formed in my mind, who knew my desires when they were but unruly thoughts coalescing in my brain. I sincerely hoped that she would find the happiness that I was unable to give her.

For a while I drifted in and out of that delicious semi-conscious state that precedes sleep. Life seemed calm, almost languid after the excitement of the last few days. After half an hour or so I opened my eyes and idly scanned the horizon. About five miles away I saw a ship making a lazy turn to port onto a westerly heading. I could see from her profile that it was the *Sheffield* but there was something odd about her which I could not quite place. There seemed to be a bright reflection coming from the side of her superstructure and a small but oddly coloured cloud of smoke drifting downwind from her hull.

As I watched she slowed in the water and stopped. It was now clear that something was very wrong indeed and to my horror more smoke began to billow out of her superstructure, forming a dense cloud which drifted slowly away to the east. After a little while the smoke became very thick and turned black as night as the fire gained hold. I could see figures in orange survival suits appearing on the forecastle and noticed that all her radars had stopped rotating. After only a few minutes it became obvious that the ship was very seriously damaged. Helicopters converged on her and started to winch off survivors as *Arrow* came close alongside in a very well executed but extremely hazardous manoeuvre, in order to allow survivors to jump from one ship to the other.

An Argentine formation of two Super Etendards had been directed towards the fleet by one of their Neptune maritime patrol aircraft and had fired two Exocet missiles from a range of approximately twenty-five miles. This had given the ships around three minutes to react, which should have been enough if they had been on the ball. *Yarmouth* called the raid, fired chaff and turned downwind, thus defeating the homing head of one missile. *Sheffield*, however, was transmitting on her satellite communications, which blocked out part of the radar warning equipment's frequency spectrum. As it happened, that part of the spectrum was exactly where the Exocet homing head operated so their ops room did not receive the warning of an inbound missile. Had they followed *Yarmouth*'s lead, the *Sheffield* might well have not been hit. As it was, the missile was spotted visually from the bridge and the officer of the watch wasted vital seconds trying to alert the ops room rather than initiating avoiding action.

The missile struck amidships, just above the waterline. It not only devastated the centre of the ship but also severed both the main electrical distribution cable and the fire main. This left the ship dead in the water with no communications, no electrics and no way to fight the fires. In addition, because the watertight doors were not all shut, dense black smoke spread throughout the ship within seconds, blinding and suffocating the crew.

Within a few minutes *Sheffield* had ceased to be a fighting unit and the assessment was made that the only option was to abandon ship. The fires raged out of control and began to threaten the weapons magazines. Many acts of heroism were carried out by crew members attempting to rescue their fellows, which undoubtedly reduced the number of casualties. It was decided to move all the remaining spare personnel as far forward as possible, so a band of men sat huddled on the forecastle, with little to do but worry about their immediate future. Here they were organised by Clive Wood, who had been sent over from *Hermes* to help out.

Clive realised that he had to bolster morale and drew on the example of Jack Hawkins in that naval wartime drama, *The Cruel Sea*. A good sing-song was required and the choice of song was obvious. The Monty Python film *Life of Brian* had been shown repeatedly on the ship's CCTV system for weeks and everyone knew one song in particular. Clive began singing 'Always look on the bright side of life' and everyone joined in.

To Clive's great surprise, even the wounded sailors appeared to cheer up and it was amusing to witness the stunned looks on the faces of the aircrew and medics as they were winched down from the hovering helicopters. Arriving on the smoking deck, they were greeted by half the ship's company, sitting cross-legged, singing and whistling as if they didn't have a care in the world. The story was duly reported by the press at home, who described Clive as the hero of the hour, leading his men in the singing of 'hymns'!

As I sat in my cockpit watching the horrific scene unfold, my feelings were now very different from those of sleepy contentment which I had had only a few minutes ago. I was itching to get airborne and do something. Parked on the flight deck was the worst of all worlds; I felt completely impotent and very vulnerable. At the time we did not know whether it had been a missile strike or a torpedo attack from an Argentine submarine. Either case could mean that *Hermes* was next and I really didn't want to be there if that was going to happen.

From my vantage point aft of the island I watched as the helicopters began to bring *Sheffield*'s casualties aboard. There were a few stretcher cases lifted swiftly but with the utmost care out of the aircraft and hurried to the aft lift and thence down to the sick bay on 3 Deck. Medics clustered around the injured, their Red Cross armbands and tabards over their blue number eight shirts and their features obscured by the anti-flash hoods and elbow-length gloves. The fire-retardant cotton gear looked like a cross between a 1930s wedding outfit and a medieval knight's armour but proved remarkably effective in preventing flash burns to the head and hands.

It was clear that many of the injured had not been wearing their protective gear. Many of them had singed hair and the telltale reddening of the hands and face. Their injuries did not seem very serious but would develop over the following forty-eight hours into extremely painful and debilitating burns. I saw one sailor emerge from the helicopter with his hands already encased in burn gloves. His uniform was in tatters, with virtually no material left covering his legs and arms. He had obviously been caught in the direct path of an explosion and was extremely disorientated. The medics sat him on the deck immediately in front of my aircraft and I watched as they poured bowl after bowl of cold water over his exposed flesh in an attempt to cool the burns and prevent further damage to the flayed skin. His face looked just like a bad case of sunburn but his eyebrows were missing and the front of his hair was singed and fused into small lumps. He insisted on standing and walked unsteadily as if in a dream to the lift, and I noticed as he passed me that his hands were slightly clawed, with pieces of flesh already sloughing from the fingers. I had always been scared of being burnt and I watched this poor man with a mixture of pity and horror in the certain knowledge that his injuries were going to cause him excruciating pain and disability, probably for many years to come.

I was reminded of the agnostic's prayer: 'Oh God, if there is a god, save my soul, if I have one.' In my case, I would add, 'And don't let me burn.'

The helicopters bringing in the casualties were loaded with firefighting equipment for the return journey. *Arrow* also put Gemini dinghies in the water with portable pumps to attempt to fight the fire, but with very little success. The fire spread rapidly and after five long hours the decision was made to abandon *Sheffield* to her fate.

When asked by Brian Hanrahan what made him take the final decision, an obviously shocked and distraught Captain Salt replied:

> I think that I started thinking that we were on a losing wicket when we realised that the fire was spreading. The decks were hot. On the upper deck you could feel the heat of the deck through your feet,

with shoes on. The superstructure was steaming. The paint on the ship's side was coming off. Around the initial area where the missile had penetrated, the hull was red, it was white hot and red hot. We could see the flames coming out of the hole. The extent of the damage was such that we knew there was no way, in that class of ship, that you could possibly fight that ship again.

The crew of the 'Shiny Sheff' were relatively lucky. Although a large number suffered burns through not wearing their anti-flash there were few deaths. Probably the worst-hit contingent was the Chinese laundry crew. Most major ships in the Royal Navy have a number of Chinese civilians on board to carry out various functions including laundry, tailoring and making shoes. These men live in the most cramped spaces imaginable, provide their own food and are paid very poorly by the 'Number One Man' in Hong Kong. Most of their pay goes to their relatives back home and their boss makes a very good living from the contract. Rumour had it that the Chinese had become uneasy about going to war and had sent a telex to Hong Kong requesting permission to leave at Ascension Island some weeks before. The reply to this was succinct: 'Dragon has long tongue – you stay!' I only hope that their families received some sort of compensation but somehow I doubt they did.

The laundrymen on *Hermes* seemed a jolly enough crowd and were quite happy to barter. It was quite usual for sailors to drop home-made fishing lines with inflated condoms as floats over the side in harbour and take their usually unhealthy-looking catch down to the Chinese and swap it for a week's free laundry. They were also not without a sense of humour. One of our officers, heartily fed up with having his shirt buttons crushed in the laundry, pierced four holes in a tin lid, painted it white and sewed it onto his uniform shirt. The shirt duly came back from the laundry beautifully starched and pressed, with a neatly finished off three-inch buttonhole in the appropriate place. The tailor could complete a very good suit within a week and the cobbler would produce a lovely pair of hand-made shoes in a couple of days from a tracing of your foot on the page of an exercise book. In fact, even after you had left the ship, you could ring him up and order a pair of shoes purely by giving him your mess number and the style required – a very civilised system.

As the last of the casualties came aboard, Gordie Batt launched to carry out a further attack on the airfield at Goose Green. He took with him Nick Taylor and Ted Ball, their intention being to drop cluster bombs on any Pucaras they found and then to plant 1000-pound retard bombs on the grass runway. Fred's team had used the best attack direction on the first raid three days previously and they took the very reasonable decision to attack from the east, running up Choiseul Sound. This attack direction afforded some cover in the form of a number of small islands in the sound and would allow them to acquire the target visually at a reasonable range.

I completed my alert by lunchtime and was stood down without flying a further mission. I was disappointed not to have a chance to avenge the *Sheffield* and uneasy about the possibility of there being a submarine in the area. Nevertheless, having signed my aircraft back in, I made my way down to the briefing room to hang my Mae West in the safety equipment compartment and return my pistol and magazines. I realised that the wardroom staff would be very busy, as the stewards were also trained in first aid and were used to help deal with casualties, and there were certainly a few of those today, so I went next door to the ACRB and sat down to a burger. The previous few hours had been harrowing and everyone was fairly introspective. The Sea King pilots had been in the thick of the rescue of *Sheffield*'s crew and had also been hunting for submarines. An attack had been made on a contact but no confirmation of a kill had been obtained. This, together with the 826 NAS extended anti-submarine search a couple of nights earlier, prompted a further song, to the tune of the Welsh national anthem:

Whales! Whales,
826 sink fucking whales!
When there's no submarine
To be found at the scene,
826 sink fucking whales!

I felt very sorry for the A/S guys who were busting their guts to protect us from the threat and getting no positive results. We subsequently discovered that no submarines were sunk during the conflict but I am sure that their activities caused the enemy to think twice about pressing their attacks on the fleet. Despite the lack of positive evidence of a submarine threat, it was decided that afternoon that we should all sleep above the waterline in future, just in case. A happy thought!

As I finished my brief lunch I heard the roar of Sea Harriers landing on and was in the briefing room in time to greet Ted Ball as he walked in.

'Hi, Ted,' I said. 'How did the attack work out?'

There was a slight pause before he answered, 'OK, but we lost Nick.'

For a second I was completely stunned. 'What are you talking about?' I asked.

'They got him – and he didn't get out,' said Ted in a voice that reflected both fatigue and the realisation that we were not immortal after all. He had already spent forty minutes with the certain knowledge that Nick was dead and was psychologically a step ahead of me. A chill rippled over me, the feeling of emptiness and loss which I had felt so many times before when colleagues had died. This was soon replaced by anger and a sense of guilt that I was still alive.

There is probably only one constant when you fly fighter aircraft: pilots die. They die at the most unlikely times, in the most benign of circumstances. It doesn't matter what type of aircraft you fly, whether you are young or old, experienced or a rookie, whether it is peacetime or war. It is the constant that everyone is aware of and no one dares contemplate, except perhaps in the quiet of your cabin or in the drunken camaraderie of the mess dinner sing-song around the out-of-tune piano in the early hours of the morning. Here you can sing of death and flying in the same breath and it all seems like a harmless game played by overgrown schoolboys.

> They say in the air force a landing's OK
> If the pilot gets out and can still walk away
> But in the Fleet Air Arm, the prospects are dim,
> If the landing's piss-poor and the pilot can't swim!
> Cracking show, I'm alive,
> But I've still got to render my A25.

The A25 was the report form required after every serious naval flying accident.

A few of us gathered round as Gordie and Ted debriefed the sortie. All had gone well initially and the three of them had arrived at their initial point in good order and without encountering any opposition. The first sign of trouble occurred when they were only thirty seconds or so from the target. Gordie's radar warning receiver had burst into life, emitting the shrill warning of a gun radar lock. He broke right, directly in front of Nick and flicked his airbrake out to deploy chaff. This broke the radar lock and he was able to pull hard left again and continue his attack. Nick carried on towards Goose Green and was hit by a 35-millimetre high explosive round. Ted's gunsight film showed his aircraft in the latter stages of the attack as it crossed the airfield boundary. A large explosion shattered the fuselage just aft of the cockpit and the aircraft became an instant fireball. As we watched the film frame by frame, the fuselage began to disintegrate and ploughed into the ground. It was obviously not survivable; no one could have escaped from that blazing trail of debris.

There was a long silence punctuated only by a quiet 'Shit.' We had lost our first pilot.

I did not know Nick very well. He had finished his Sea Harrier course shortly before I arrived at Yeovilton and had been appointed to 800 NAS for his first tour of duty. He was an ex-helicopter pilot like myself and was married to the Wren officer on 707 NAS, the commando Sea King training squadron, also based at Yeovilton. His wife was one of a team who had volunteered to break the news of any casualties to their families. Unfortunately, the first name to come through was that of her husband. I can only guess at the horror she must have felt when she read the signal.

Carol heard that a Sea Harrier pilot had been shot down and was desperate to find out who it was but no one at Yeovilton would tell her. She eventually phoned RAF Wittering, the UK home of the air force Harriers, where they were able to confirm that it was not me. She was greatly relieved but knew that this might only be a temporary respite from bad news in the future.

We ran through the fatal attack in detail to try to ascertain what had caused Nick's demise and decided that the most likely reason was that his aircraft was not fitted with a radar warning receiver. The airframe had been allocated to British Aerospace at Dunsfold so that they could carry out trials of the Sea Eagle anti-ship missile. This missile promised to be a potent addition to the Sea Harrier armoury and was far more effective and sophisticated than the French Exocet. Unfortunately for Nick, the trials equipment had been mounted in the space normally used for the RWR, which meant that he was blind to any electronic threat. We were fairly sure that Nick had flown through Gordie's chaff cloud as he manoeuvred against the gun radar and been locked up without knowing it. The rest was inevitable. Nick had flown very close to the weapon and was easy meat for the Argentine gunners. He was buried on the edge of the airfield where he fell and his grave is tended to this day by the grateful residents of Goose Green, who regard him as very much one of their own. He will never be lonely.

The wreckage of Nick's cockpit yielded up the Sea Eagle aiming panel to the Argentines and it was subsequently concluded that this was another factor in their decision to order their naval vessels back to port.

That evening we held a wake in the bar. It was a serious affair and many of the ship's officers made a point of offering us their condolences.

It soon became obvious that there was a distinct divergence of opinion. Our squadron to a man were talking only of avenging Nick and were even more determined to do whatever it took to triumph in this conflict. On the other hand, many of the seaman officers were wringing their hands and saying that we couldn't afford to lose ships and men and that we would have to rethink the whole thing. I formed the opinion that the surface navy was very good at arranging cocktail parties but seemed bloody useless at fighting a war. It was only in the cold light of day that I decided I was being unduly harsh on them. We had the dubious advantage of having lost many friends in the air over the years and were well rehearsed in the skills required to put on a brave face and carry on. Incidentally, we were relieved to discover that Clive Wood had survived unharmed but alas Clyde had perished with the *Sheffield*. He was later replaced by another monkey, named Cyril. It was no coincidence that this was the *Hermes* commander's middle name and that John Locke was not a fan of the puppet.

That evening twenty or so of us settled down to sleep on the floor of the wardroom bar on rows of camp beds placed at intervals along the bulkheads. I must admit I was not looking forward to spending the rest of the conflict in a large dormitory and was very grateful when John Locke gave some of us permission to use the captain's day cabin, aft on 4 Deck. This was an airy space with the luxury of a square porthole overlooking the wake. We shared it with some of the commando Sea King pilots, an arrangement which worked well as they tended to spend a lot of time flying during the hours of darkness and returned to sleep as we were getting up. Fortunately, the Argentine pilots seemed to share our lack of enthusiasm for flying in the dark and we only reacted to positive intelligence of raids or to carry out the odd harassing attack on the islands.

THE WEATHER THE following morning was very different. The clear skies and good visibility were replaced with a shroud of low stratus and fog patches. My only sortie of the day was a CAP mission to the north-east of East Falkland to cover any possible Super Etendard attacks. We believed that the Argentine Navy still possessed at least a couple more Exocets and would certainly attempt to attack us again if they could find out where we were. The only excitement of the whole sortie was the recovery, when I finally saw the ship through the murk at a range of 400 yards and a height of a mere ninety feet. I was more than happy to sit in the crewroom and read for the rest of the afternoon.

The next morning was, if anything, rather worse. Fog swirled around the ship, blanketing the superstructure and stifling all the normal sounds of activity on the flight deck. The sea slid past grey, oily and rather sinister, almost flat calm. Down below life went on as usual and it was quite possible to lose track of time and the passing of day and night. We were lucky in that we at least had the opportunity to see daylight several times a day, even if it was not always particularly nice weather. On our journey south the met officer, a schoolmaster by trade, had briefed us on the weather conditions we could expect to experience. We were prepared for gales and rough seas but hardly any mention was made of fog. We discovered later that most of the observations had been made from Stanley itself, where it was rarely foggy, but a few miles out to sea it was a very different story. The sea temperature hovered a few degrees above freezing for most of the year, which meant that as soon as a slightly warmer and more moist air mass moved in, the whole area became covered in fog and low cloud. Moisture dripped continuously from the aerials on the island and the aircraft became covered in condensation, inside and out.

It was not possible to keep all the aircraft in the hangar as space was at a premium and as a result we started to have some very annoying electronic unserviceabilities. The NAVHARS control panel was positioned directly below the cockpit canopy rail, which meant that moisture was always dripping onto it, inducing numerous failures. One bright spark had the idea of removing the panel cover, covering it in cling film and refitting it. Amazingly this worked and reduced the number of failures dramatically. A similar problem was experienced in the nose of the aircraft, where the radar started to suffer moisture ingress through the hinged joint of the radome. This was fixed by tying rubber tourniquets around the joints when the aircraft were not on immediate readiness to fly.

By far the best fix, however, was the one designed to prevent the engine fan rotating in high winds; this could have caused excessive wear to the engine bearings. It was stopped by feeding a broomstick down the front of the engine after it was shut down. This required an engineer to first stop the fan using the flat of his hand, a rather hazardous evolution when suspended inside a slippery air intake. Once the handle had been placed in position, an entry had to be made in the aircraft's Form 700 to that effect, so that no one would start the engine with a lump of wood stuck in it. This entry was worded: 'Broom handle inserted in LP fan to prevent rotation,' and subsequently cleared with: 'Broom handle removed from LP fan.'

Later in the morning there seemed to be a slight improvement in the weather and I set off once more to the east of the islands, to hunt for the Super Etendards. Once airborne, we discovered that the cloud was solid from 100 feet up to over 1000. Once on top, however, it was crystal clear, with an unbroken blue sky as far as the eye could see. We set ourselves up on an east–west track in order to make best use of our Blue Fox radars. In such conditions it was possible to pick up low-level targets at a range of fifteen miles or so but it required a great deal of heads-in work on the radar scope. After some twenty minutes on CAP I picked up a very small, fleeting blip at a range of about fifteen miles. I imme-diately selected narrow scan, to increase the data rate, placed the target marker over the area of the return and searched very slightly up and down in an effort to refine the contact. After a few seconds I saw another fleeting blip now about fourteen miles ahead and slightly to the right. The fact that it was still under the target marker told me that it was not an aircraft but that it could possibly be a ship or even a helicopter.

I called the contact to Gordie, who was a couple of thousand yards to the north of me, and slipped down into the fleecy tops of the cloud. As

I descended through the stratus the cloud became darker and I lost all sensation of movement. I was focused 100 per cent on trying to maintain contact with the will-o'-the-wisp radar return which now reappeared tantalisingly at ten miles, right on the nose. I attempted to lock the radar in order to use the radar cross in the head-up display to help see the target. Initially the radar locked on but after a second or so the lock indication reeled drunkenly to the bottom of the screen, taking the radar scanner fully down and forcing me to recommence my search. I had just reacquired the target when I had a sudden sensation that something was dreadfully wrong. I quickly scanned my instruments and saw to my absolute horror that I was descending rapidly through 200 feet.

I snatched back on the stick and levelled off at 100 feet above the ocean with the adrenalin pumping. I knew that the target must be very close now and forced myself to let down, very slowly and cautiously, to fifty feet on the radio altimeter. At this height I could see nothing but the grey blanket of cloud: no sea, no ship, no horizon – nothing. With great reluctance I decided that the contact might well have been spurious. In any case, the conditions were such that I had very nearly flown into the sea. The low stratus had merged with the sea fog to form one contiguous layer from 1100 feet all the way to the surface. Flying in these conditions was hazardous at the best of times and I had nearly wasted a valuable Sea Harrier, let alone myself.

This was not the first time either. I had nearly made a large smoking hole in the North German Plain some eighteen months previously. It had been a frustrating morning in the middle of an autumn exercise. Our off-base site was a small strip of grass secreted away in the middle of a large area of pine forest to the north of Senelager. The sky was a vast canopy of blue but, being the season of mists and mellow fruitfulness, the Weser valley was covered in a gossamer blanket of low-lying fog. Through this fog advanced the 'enemy' and it was our job to stop them.

After several hours of waiting, the fog had burnt off and two of us we were tasked to join up with two Harriers from another site and attack a column of German armour in the area of a river crossing north of Holzminden. We started up and taxied out of our camouflaged hides down the tree line to the take-off point. The acceleration was phenomenal as I slammed the throttle open and within five seconds I had reached the marker boards at the side of the strip and rotated the nozzles to leap into the air. Grass strips are never very smooth and this one was so rough it was impossible to read the cockpit instruments during the take-off roll. Once airborne, we set off for our contact point and there met up with the rest of our formation. We took down the attack brief from the forward air controller and set off in a well-spaced 'card' formation towards the target area. As we approached the river, the FAC called that he had lost sight of the target and as I flashed over the area at 450 knots, I glimpsed a row of Leopard tanks in a firebreak in the forest below. I called them so that the rear two aircraft could try to attack them and commenced a hard climbing turn to the right to clear the target area. At this moment the FAC asked if I had a note of the target's position.

A cautious pilot would have waited a few seconds before replying but I immediately transferred my attention to the map and read off the target coordinates for him. When I looked out of the cockpit again, only five seconds later, I was inverted with the nose of the aircraft buried nearly thirty degrees down towards the German landscape. I wrenched the machine upright and pulled straight to the buffet in an attempt to coax the maximum lift out of the inadequate wing. There was a sudden realisation that I was going to die. I could not see how I could possibly recover from the dive without hitting the ground and I knew that it was too late to eject as my rate of decent was undoubtedly outside the seat's design parameters. The whole world seemed to slow down and I became completely deaf. I did not hear the FAC and the other aircraft shouting at me to pull up and became completely mesmerised by the approaching ground. I noticed that the field in front of me had been recently ploughed and as I got closer I could see short pieces of stubble sticking out of the furrows. Looking ahead, I saw a fence with several hawthorn bushes dotted along it and remember hoping that I could fit between the two immediately ahead of me. I was still thinking quite logically and reasoned that my only chance of living was to try to survive the inevitable impact and eject on the bounce before the aircraft broke up.

I sat there for what seemed an age, watching the ground rushing up to meet me, and then suddenly I was climbing away between the hawthorn bushes and back into the still autumn air. I could not believe that I had survived and was quite sure that I must have scraped the ground during the recovery. It took several minutes before my adrenalin returned to a manageable level and my hands stopped shaking. I was still dry-mouthed and rather light-headed when I landed back at the site ten minutes later. I spent a good five minutes on my back under the aircraft after shutting down but could find no evidence of hitting the ground. A few days later I developed a crawling sensation all over my body. It felt like small caterpillars creeping over my skin and was obviously a psychosomatic reaction to the incident.

Thoughts of this brush with death were very much in my mind as we continued our lonely vigil. My reaction was much less marked this time, however, and by the time we were recovering to *Hermes* it was mostly just another experience to tuck away in the back of the mind.

My recovery to the ship was quite uncomfortable. I had always had an aversion to instrument flying and the CCA configuration, with its high power setting and instability in pitch, was as usual very disorientating. I fought the aircraft down the imaginary slope towards the deck, locked onto the head-up display and trying desperately to match the height calls and heading changes being passed to me by the controller. I was aware that the cloud base was well below the normal 200 feet minimum and at a range of about two miles I decided to drop below the glide path and try to pick up the surface of the sea visually; at least that would remove one variable from the equation and I knew that there were no ships between me and the carrier; I had made a careful sweep of the area with my radar before starting the approach. The grey surface of the ocean started to appear at around 100 feet on the radio altimeter and this gave me a great psychological boost. Somehow it made the approach seem far less difficult if the surface was in sight. This technique was obviously desperately dangerous ashore, where there could be unknown and unseen obstacles, and was equally frowned upon at sea by the purists. It was however a widespread and accepted practice among the Sea Harrier community, if you were caught out by the weather with no possibility of a diversion. The RAF would never contemplate flying without a suitable diversion but in the Royal Navy such things were routine.

I saw the ship's wake at about three quarters of a mile, took the breaking stop, and achieved a reasonably stable hover abeam the island. Luckily the calm seas meant that the deck motion was virtually nil and a few seconds later I had transitioned neatly right, positioned over the double tramlines painted on the deck centreline and landed on. As I slammed the throttle closed and taxied cautiously forward over the greasy deck into the 'graveyard', I was aware of an intense feeling of relief and a sudden numbing tiredness which seemed to originate from deep inside my psyche and flow out to the very tips of my fingers. The chain lashings were attached to my outriggers and after confirming my seat was safe I was given the signal to shut down. I closed the HP cock, switched off the electrics and slid the canopy back on its rails. For a few moments, I just sat there. We had been at war for less than a week and yet I could hardly remember what it had been like before. I realised I was getting very tired both emotionally and physically and was glad that I now had a few hours off before starting the alert cycle again.

I flopped in the corner of the briefing room and looked around at the other faces. Gordie was looking strained; he had obviously not enjoyed the last few minutes of the trip either. Ted was busy preparing a briefing and Bertie was arranging for the next two pilots to take up the alert in the two aircraft that Gordie and I had just brought back. We were all looking considerably more tired and introspective than a week ago. Bertie was doing remarkably well considering his dislike of enclosed spaces but the strain was starting to show on all of us.

I was not the only one to have problems with the weather that day. In the afternoon we heard that two aircraft from our sister squadron on

Invincible were missing. A search was mounted but no sign of them was ever found: no wreckage, no radio calls, no emergency beacon, nothing. They had been vectored to investigate a possible contact and had simply disappeared. I immediately thought of my experiences a few hours earlier and I am convinced they were victims of the same set of circumstances that nearly claimed my life. It is possible they had a mid-air collision but I believe that less likely. Whatever the reason, it was a tragedy that had a profound effect on the rest of us that evening. I hardly knew Lieutenant Al Curtis but the other pilot, Lieutenant Commander John Eyton-Jones, had been a buddy for years.

I had heard of John by reputation some time before I met him. He was someone who believed that you should squeeze every last drop of enjoyment out of life. He was an excellent pilot and a truly charismatic leader of men. Having flown both Sea Vixens and Phantoms, he was sent on exchange to No. 1(F) Squadron at Wittering, to fly the GR3. This he did with his customary flair and was soon accepted by the air force as a first-rate operator. I first met him in Belize, where we maintained four GR3s as a deterrent force against the bellicose ambitions of the Guatemalan military government. One sweltering afternoon I drove a Land Rover across to the tiny ramshackle building that served as an airport terminal with a view to collecting E-J from the weekly VC10 flight from Brize Norton. There was some consternation when we discovered that he was not on the flight. Later in the day we were told that he would be arriving the following week – all very mysterious.

Sure enough, the following Wednesday E-J arrived. After he had unpacked his kit in the terrible Nissen huts that we called home I asked him why he had been delayed for a week. He looked very sheepish and related the bones of the story. He had decided to stop off in London to see an old friend before taking the train to Swindon, where the RAF would pick him up. Unfortunately, he imbibed rather too freely during the course of the evening and fell asleep. By the time he awoke from his alcohol-induced slumber, the aircraft was already on its way. That was the official story but we all wondered if there was a little more to it than was released for general consumption. E-J was a great party animal and certainly lived life to the full.

His loss affected me greatly, and that evening in the relative quiet of my cabin, before I climbed up to 4 Deck to sleep, I wrote the following poem with him very much in mind:

REMEMBRANCE

Somewhere today a skylark sings
With joy, above the field and coomb
Where once he walked, soft-footed
'Cross the deep spring-scented leys,
Where chuckling brook, cold crystal
Clear, tumbles and trills twixt
Banks of peppermint and thyme.

Where once his voice laughed out
In praise of field and sky,
And body swam the heady main
Of nature's sweetest scents
Upon the passing of the rain.
And languid willows trail
Their fronded fingers through the stream.

Forever stilled now lies this voice,
Hard by some far, forbidding shore,
In grave unmarked, 'neath seas
That roam from Horn to Africa.
Yet lives his spirit still in spring,
And song of birds, and scent of
Cleansing rain, in this green land.

E-J's family lived close to mine in the married quarters at Yeovilton and I could only guess at the feelings of shock and despair that must be rocking that tight-knit community as the news spread. There would be many families dreading the knock at the door. We had now lost three of our pilots in the first week of fighting and it was not a record that bore too much examination. It was important to me to be able to express my emotions in poetry, as it would not have been acceptable to air my doubts and concerns to my fellow pilots. We all had to maintain the outward appearance of disdain for the dangers that we faced on a daily basis. If we did not, I feared that the fabric of our tenuous existence would quickly crumble. Most of us allowed ourselves the luxury of harmless superstitions. I had already decided that I was not going to change my lucky flying suit but a change of underwear every day was essential. Another of our number knew that if he was handed the right shoulder-strap first, when settling into his seat, he was certain to die. To avoid this happening, he would reach back and grab the left strap himself before the plane captain had time to hand him the other one.

The following day was once again a complete wipeout, with even the sheathbills refusing to fly. We kept two aircraft at five-minute readiness throughout the hours of daylight but most of the Sea Harriers were given to the engineers for essential maintenance. At sunset the alert status was reduced to twenty minutes readiness and most of us made for the bar for a quiet pint of Courage Special Brew. Here we discovered to our absolute horror that the beer was running low. The lack of women we could tolerate as part of the price of war but a threat to our beer supply was unthinkable! Luckily there was still a plentiful supply of spirits, including some whisky which had been donated by British Airways. I tried a dram of this free hooch and decided it would be better to go without!

HMS Hermes
7 May

Hello, my love,

We have just been told that there will be mail going off today, so I had better put pen to paper. I expect you have been following the news fairly closely, so you will know roughly what has happened so far. We had a fairly uneventful run down here and as soon as we got here, we hit Stanley airport. I was No. 2 in the raid but because of a slight alteration in plans I became the last one over the target. The flak was horrendous by the time I got there, the sky was full of explosions and tracer was flying everywhere. I had briefed all the guys very carefully on the plan (Spag, Bertie's and mine) and on the best evasive action to take and everyone did very well. We obliterated the airport facilities, set fire to the fuel dump and knocked out a few aircraft into the bargain.

Bertie P also put two more holes in the runway. I zapped an Islander (aircraft) on the grass and was hit myself, as I did so. There was a solid thump followed by rudder vibrations, which I discovered were caused by a 20-millimetre HE round exploding in the middle of my fin. I ran out something below ten feet above the ground at 550 knots until I was clear and then headed for home. The lads are mounting the hole for me, so you can think of somewhere to put it!! (It's about 8 inches across.) At the same time we took out Darwin airfield successfully. A couple of days later, Gordie Batt, Ted and Nick Taylor went back to their Pucara step-up site at Goose Green and Nick was shot down. It was his first raid and he got hit by something pretty big and just ploughed in. Still, the other two got back OK. Yesterday E-J and Al Curtis disappeared. We think they either had a mid-air, or flew into the sea.

Still, on the plus side, Paul Barton and Bertie Penfold have both got a Mirage and we have got at least one Canberra. Morale is pretty good, even though *Sheffield* took a bad hit two days ago and will have to be sunk. The weather has been shitty for the last two days with 100 feet cloud base and poor vis, so we haven't done a lot of flying. The beer is getting a bit low but the spirits are holding out!

I miss you dreadfully and when I get back I promise not to be ratty anymore. I hope the kids have been good. I expect the weather has been fairly warm; good weather for seed sowing. I wish I were home to start planting some vegetables and dig the garden.

Did you get a message from the Press Association by the way? One of the press guys on board offered to get his secretary to give you a ring, to let you know that I was OK. I hope it got through.

We are sleeping on camp beds at the moment (those with cabins below 4 Deck) because of the slim possibility of a sub being around. I have found a slot on the floor of the captain's cabin and it's reasonably comfortable but I'm looking forward to my double bed!

Well, not a lot more to say really. I have been very good and not been out with any girls since I last saw you.

Take care, my love and give the Boggits a hug for me.

All my love
   D

7 May

Dear Charles,

Hello, old lad. I hope that you are being good and looking after the girls for me. We have been doing quite a lot of flying since we got here, including bombing the airport at Stanley. My Harrier was hit by a bullet but it was easy to mend.

We have shot down three of their aircraft and they have shot down one of their own! There are some huge birds around the Falklands called albatrosses. They are up to two metres from wing tip to wing tip! How are your goldfish? I hope you are looking after them well.

Take care and give the girls a big kiss for me.

Lots of love
   Daddy

The following morning the weather seemed little changed but around mid-morning there was a sufficient gap to justify launching a CAP mission. I was grateful to be able to get off the ship, even though we spent about fifty minutes boring holes in the sky with no trade whatsoever. On the ship I was beginning to feel desperately claustrophobic and found myself imagining the devastating impact of a torpedo below the waterline or the fireball from an Exocet rolling down the passageways. At least the war seemed cleaner in the air, more chivalrous, more gentle-manly. We were also supremely confident of our own abilities and had proved our mettle against some of the world's best fighters. And if death came, it would be swift, not a scorching scream of tangled metal and blistering bulkheads but an instant snuffing out of life, with hardly time to know what had happened – a far better end, a warrior's end.

I had time to appreciate the deep azure canopy of the sky, the stillness of the air, the strength of the bond that aviators feel with the natural world. I imagined myself in the body of an albatross, soaring the crests of the waves for thousands of miles with hardly a wingbeat, skimming, gliding, wing tips caressing the spume-flecked waves; masters of their world, beholden to no one but fate. This is why I will never stop flying; the mystical feeling of oneness with nature cannot be denied or ignored. Even in the midst of a bloody conflict, the beauty of flying shines like a beacon leading the mind back to normality. It is a balm for the soul; it makes sense of the nonsensical.

The recovery to *Hermes* was a nightmare. The weather had deterio-rated since we took off and the ship was reporting a cloud base of below one hundred feet and very poor visibility. 'Oh God,' I said to myself, 'Here we go again.' There is nothing more certain to pull you back to reality than the prospect of fighting your aircraft down through layers of crud to a landing in appalling visibility.

I set myself up for a CCA and was still in thick cloud at a mile and a half and 150 feet. We had planned to land with 800 pounds of fuel, which was not enough to have another shot at the approach, so there was only one chance. I decided to let down until I saw the surface, and as I descended through ninety feet I caught my first glimpse of the sea. With a mere half a mile to run, the controller informed me in a very alarmed voice that the ship had turned sixty degrees to starboard. I expressed, rather succinctly, what I thought of the fatherless dickheads on the bridge and strained my eyes into the murk to try to see the ship. Warships are of course painted grey to enable them to merge into the sea and I had little chance of seeing 'Mother' in these conditions. I did however see a flash of white in the curtain of grey ahead and called, 'OK, I've got a visual on the wake!'

I aimed towards the life-saving patch of foaming water and slammed the nozzles into the hover stop to kill my speed. As the speed decreased through 100 knots I realised to my absolute horror that I was not pointing towards the stern of the ship, but the bow! What I had seen was the bow wave, not the wake. This presented me with a major problem. I didn't have enough fuel to try another approach and I couldn't land on the deck from the starboard side because there was a bloody great island in the way. In addition to this, the Harrier became directionally unstable between thirty and ninety knots and would roll and crash unless you exercised great caution. A number of pilots had killed themselves by mishandling the aircraft in this flight regime and great emphasis was placed on a careful, straight deceleration phase to avoid this danger.

Unfortunately, I did not have the luxury of choosing my approach path. I had to get my aircraft onto the deck somehow, even though the cloud was actually obscuring everything from 2 Deck up. I therefore gritted my teeth and aimed in front of the ship, passing ten feet or so below the bulging mass of the ski-jump. I remember noting with detached interest the rust-streaked anchor passing by level with my head as I jockeyed my machine around to the left in a desperate attempt to position myself on the port side of the deck. The captain saw my tail pass in front of the bow and rushed through to Flyco, asking Wings in no uncertain terms what I was doing. Wings' reply was reported as being a laconic 'I think he's crashing, sir.' Despite this vote of confidence I wrestled my aircraft around in a hair-raising 270-degree turn and came to the hover alongside the forward lift. After a few seconds I applied a little power and slowly climbed up into the base of the cloud and transitioned across and landed heavily on the deck. I had never been so happy to land back on, despite the very untidy arrival.

After signing my machine over to the maintainers, I made my way up to Flyco and told Wings that I considered the weather unfit for flying. He gave me one of his infectious grins and said, 'Don't worry, Moggie, I'm not going to send anyone else up in this stuff.'

That evening we gathered in the bar for a couple of beers, secure in the knowledge that the Super Etendard pilots were also unlikely to be able to fly. The weather forecast for the morning was for fresh winds, a slightly higher cloud base and better visibility. We all knew that the quiet of the last couple of days was unlikely to last and our mood was fairly introspective. The death of three of our fellow pilots within the first week was something none of us wished to contemplate too closely. We had lost 10 per cent of our strength and 14 per cent of our desperately needed aircraft. Neither could be readily replaced although a number of pilots had been recalled from various parts of the world and were in the process of forming 809 NAS at Yeovilton.

On 6 April, Lieutenant Commander Tim Gedge had been appointed to command this hastily formed unit and he was joined by a motley collection of pilots from various sources. Lieutenant David Austin arrived from the Sea Harrier simulator, Lieutenant Bill Covington and Lieutenant Commander David 'Brave' Braithwaite were recalled from exchange tours in America; Lieutenant Commander Hugh Slade was called back from Australia and Lieutenant Commander Alisdair Craig from his exchange with No. 1(F) Squadron at Wittering.

Brave I knew only by reputation but I was privileged to become close friends with him after the conflict. He was a larger than life character in all senses, with a boyish sense of humour, a total intolerance of fools of any rank, an immense wealth of experience and an uncanny ability to bullshit when his knowledge ran out. He had flown both Vixens and Phantoms and had acquired his nickname after a particularly nasty incident in the air when he stayed with the aircraft far too long when he had indications it was on fire. His observer's seat would not eject, so he risked his own life by landing back on the ship.

I was reminded of this trait many years later when I visited him in Yeovil hospital after he had ejected at about fifty feet from an engineless Hunter. He had landed extremely hard with a partially open parachute in a field a few yards from the Ilchester bypass and suffered massive bruising and dislocation of his pelvis. He had been very lucky indeed to survive his ejection and was unable to walk properly for a very long time. It transpired that when his engine had failed halfway around the final approach he had been pointing towards the married quarters. He turned left to avoid them and found himself pointing at the village school. He managed to avoid the school and then found himself heading towards the bypass, which was full of summer holidaymakers heading west.

When I remonstrated with him and said he should have ejected much earlier, his reply was: 'I couldn't, Moggie; the aircraft would have crashed on the traffic jam.' As it was, the aircraft hit hard at about 140 miles an hour, lost its wheels, bounced though a hedgerow and across a narrow road immediately in front of a coach full of soldiers, and ended up buried in a midden underneath an elderberry bush.

Al Craig and I had met in Belize a year or so previously. He was fairly small and wiry with a ready smile, twinkling eyes and an impish sense of humour. We had got into a reasonable amount of trouble together in that tropical paradise but one particular incident which sticks in my mind happened on one of our visits to the offshore islands. These tiny cays are mostly uninhabited and stand on the second-largest barrier reef in the world. We often hired a boat and took a Sunday barbecue out to one of the cays but on this occasion three of us rented a Cessna and flew out to Cay Chapel, where there was a very small single-storey hotel perched on the edge of the coral sand beach.

Once there, we had a very relaxing couple of days, swimming, snorkelling and drinking the local Belican beer and Caribbean rum. As the alcohol levels rose, I decided that it would be a good idea to have some coconut milk to go with the rum and proceeded to start up the nearest palm tree. I was spurred on by drunken shouts of encouragement from the others until I suddenly realised that I was quite some distance from the ground and my grip was beginning to fail. I tried to make a slow descent back to safety but my feet slipped and I ended up in a giggling heap at the base of the palm. Al came over to check that I was in one piece and discovered that I had skinned my right ankle fairly comprehensively. Despite the anaesthetic effect of the booze, this wound soon began to sting and Al very kindly offered to take a look at it for me. He pronounced it non-life-threatening but requiring antiseptic. Before I could stop him, he poured a generous shot of rum over the ankle. I let out an agonised scream and spent the next five minutes hopping around on one leg, unable to see anything because of the tears in my eyes. The wound did heal well, though.

In addition to these six, we heard that two pilots from my old squadron in Germany had volunteered to fly Sea Harriers. They were Flight Lieutenants Steve Brown and John Leeming, both ex-Lightning drivers and experienced air defence men. It was good to know that we had a few guys in the pipeline to reinforce us, as they would certainly be needed if the attrition continued at its present rate.

CHAPTER 5

SINKING OF THE *NARWAL*

9 May

An eventful day!

I WAS VERY RELIEVED the next morning to discover that the met man had not told his usual lies. The visibility had increased dramatically although the cloud base was still only around 500 feet above the ocean. It had been decided that we should conduct a campaign of harassment of the Argentine troops based at Stanley airfield. We knew that they were still operating Hercules flights into and out of the damaged strip and wanted to make this more hazardous for them in an attempt to cut off these resupply runs from the mainland. By night we were sending frigates close inshore to bombard the area with 4.5-inch gunfire, and during the hours of daylight the intention was for us to drop 1000-pound bombs from high level in order to keep them on their toes. This would, we hoped, also cause them to waste a lot of anti-aircraft ammunition. It was a tactic not totally without hazard, as we planned to attack from 18,000 feet. This height put us well above the threat from the Roland missile system but was still within the range of the radar-laid 35-millimetre Oerlikon guns. These weapons were not desperately accurate at this height but they could track an aircraft fairly well on a stable attack path and a hit from one of their high-explosive rounds was more than enough to spoil your whole day, as we had seen a few days earlier over Goose Green.

I realised, as I taxied forward to the take-off point, that I would be very glad to get off the ship and back into my element. I had a great deal of sympathy for the ship's company, who had to spend the whole time locked in this huge sardine tin just waiting for a missile or torpedo to come through the side. We were the only ones who actually knew what the enemy looked like, the only ones who had actually seen the islands and experienced the gunfire. All those who supported our efforts on the ship had only our word that anything was happening out there above the clouds beyond the hazy horizon. The only contact they had had with the enemy, save for the sinking of the *Sheffield,* had been through us. Unlike the Battle of Britain, where the criss-cross of vapour trails in the sky bore constant witness to the drama being played out above their heads, these men had to rely on our tales and the looks on our weary faces to build a picture of this conflict.

This was helping a particular bond to develop between us, the knights on our grey chargers who rode off to do battle in another dimension, and those who could only do their own jobs to the very best of their ability so that their work would not be found wanting at the critical moment. For years I had been absolutely pedantic about checking every aspect of my aircraft's serviceability, from the signatures on the Form 700 through the physical state of the machine to the safety equipment. Before each flight I religiously checked every possible item and switch, panel and screw and I had never contemplated it being otherwise.

Over the previous week, however, my attitude had undergone a sea change. If I was not under pressure I would still check everything in minute detail: paperwork, airframe, weapons and seat. If there was a little less time I would check the weapons and the seat. If even less time was available I would just check the seat and if it was essential that I launched immediately I would just jump up the ladder, leap into the cockpit, throw the seat straps on and hit the start button. Much of this was driven by necessity but what amazed me more than anything was that I never felt the slightest concern about short-cutting the routine that had served me so well for the previous fifteen years of flying. I realised that I now had complete and absolute trust in my ground crew. These guys, some of them only in their late teens, had responded brilliantly to the challenge. Sure, they were scared and tired and some of them were homesick. Very few of them were finding it an enjoyable experience but they had pulled out all the stops and had won my complete confidence, cementing us into a great team. The plane captain of XZ 455 was already basking in the glory of his aircraft being the first on the squadron to achieve a kill and we sensed that the other plane captains expected us to help them catch up without delay.

The FDO dropped his green flag; I waited for the bow to start to drop into the next trough and slammed the throttle forward. I felt the mighty surge of power from the Pegasus as I hurtled towards the ramp and three seconds later I was in the air, nose pointing skywards, clawing for airspeed. As the speed rose above 120 knots I started to move the small silver lever next to the throttle, in order to move the nozzles aft into forward flight. To my great consternation I discovered that they were still at the pre-take-off setting of ten degrees; in the heat of the moment I had forgotten to lower them as I left the ramp. This could have been a fatal error, as with the nozzles at less than twenty degrees there was no pressure to the reaction controls and therefore no way to control the attitude of the aircraft until the airspeed increased to above the conventional stall. Luckily it had been a clean, stable launch and a few seconds later I was flying happily away with just a slightly elevated pulse rate to remind me to be more careful in future. This was just another little warning that we were getting tired; I would have to be much more aware if I was going to avoid becoming a statistic.

Shortly after launch Gordie came up on the radio and informed me that his navigation kit was unserviceable. This seemed to be becoming a common and very annoying occurrence, although, hopefully, the clingfilm modification would help to improve the reliability of the hardware. I took over the lead and headed west towards Stanley, climbing up to 36,000 feet in order to save fuel.

The transit to the islands passed without incident. We maintained radio silence and flew a wide battle formation so that we could check each other's 6 o'clocks with ease. No matter how good a fighter pilot might be he will always be vulnerable to someone who sneaks up behind him, the 'unseen Fox two'. With ninety miles to go to the coastline, I gave one sweep of my radar and froze the picture. This enabled me to pick out Cape Pembroke, a prominent headland a couple of miles east of the runway at Stanley. I placed the radar marker over the promontory and updated the NAVHARS so that I would be able to position myself precisely over the lighthouse on the point. We had calculated that if we dropped our weapons there on a heading of 265 degrees at an indicated airspeed of 450 knots they would impact somewhere close to the centre of the runway. This was not a very accurate way of delivering the bombs but would ensure that the runway would be cratered if we did manage to hit it. Our main object was to cause a nuisance, but if we could cause some damage so much the better.

As we approached the coast it became obvious that a layer of low stratus was covering the area around Stanley. Before we left Captain Middleton had made it clear that we were not to drop unless we could see the target, as he was very concerned to avoid civilian casualties. I had every confidence that we could manage to avoid bombing the town, given that it was the best part of a mile to the west of the target, but the captain was insistent. Not for the first time I disagreed with his assessment of the options but we reluctantly turned away from the airfield without releasing the bombs as the black mushrooms of anti-aircraft fire started to pockmark the sky around us. We called *Coventry* and were directed to take up CAP station to the east of Stanley. I scanned the ocean with my radar and found the little green contact that was *Coventry* some ninety miles further to the east. I knew that their radars would have a very good picture of any targets at high level out to about 150 miles but this coverage would gradually shrink until a low-level target would be unseen until it was within fifteen miles or so of the ship. They were placing us up-threat and it was our job to intercept any inbound bogeys before they could threaten the fleet.

As we approached our nominated station I turned to the south to clear the area and found a very small target at a range of about fifty miles. I immediately started to assess the return. It was not a fast mover but it was a very definite target and was there on every sweep. By moving the scanner up and down very slightly, I confirmed that it was either a surface contact or a very low-level slow mover. Given the size of the return I reckoned that it had to be a ship of some sort and *Coventry* soon confirmed that there were no task force units in the area. My pulse started to quicken as I called Gordie into close formation to penetrate the cloud. With him tucked in nicely a few feet off my starboard wing, I let down cautiously into the white blanket of cloud. I was extremely wary after my experience a few days earlier and made very sure that all my instruments were functioning properly and that my descent was well under control. I certainly didn't want to lead us both straight down into the waves.

The cloud was several thousand feet thick and started to thin a little as we passed 1000 feet in the descent. I caught the odd glimpse of the nose of Gordie's aircraft out of the corner of my eye as we passed through a couple of layers before we finally broke out into the clear at about 600 feet. As soon as we were clear I called him out into battle formation on my starboard side and saw the underneath of his aircraft as he pulled away, the bronze-green shape of the 1000-pound bomb still nestling between his gun pods. I now had the target dead ahead at a range of ten miles and decided that the best way to check it out was to use a standard straight-in attack profile. This profile had been designed to run two aircraft through a target area from different directions a few seconds apart. In this way the target's defences would be split, giving the attackers the maximum chance of a successful weapon delivery coupled with the best chance of survival.

I called, 'Target on my nose, eight miles, straight-in attack for vis-ident only.' Gordie double-clicked his transmit button to acknowledge the fact that we were only going to identify the target and not attack it and took up the correct formation position.

At six miles I saw a dark shape on the horizon steaming slowly west. I was disappointed that it did not look like a warship and as I got closer it became obvious that it was some kind of ocean-going trawler. With four miles to go I shouted, 'Buster!' and we both went to full throttle, accelerating to 500 knots. I had no idea whether we were going to encounter any defences as we overflew the contact and didn't want to expose either of us to unnecessary risk. The grey surface of the sea was now whipping past in a blur only fifty feet below us as we both strained to take in the details of the ship ahead. With two kilometres to run I called, 'In visual,' the prompt for Gordie to start his manoeuvre, and saw the plan view of his aircraft as he turned hard towards me with ribbons of vapour trailing from his wing tips.

I aimed to fly over the target just aft of her white-painted bridge, between the funnel and the large A-frame on the stern. My eyes scanned the decks for any sign of movement which might indicate resistance but found none. As I flashed over the well deck however I saw something which totally amazed me: fluttering from the stern was a large blue and white striped flag with a golden sun at its centre. This was my first sight of an Argentine flag; the ship was hostile.

I shouted over the radio, 'It's an Argie. Maintain visual. I'm climbing up to report.' I pulled back on the stick and was soon above the clouds once more and back in radio contact with *Coventry*. I told them it was an Argentine trawler but that there was no sign of it having been engaged in fishing; in fact its nets were all laid out neatly in the well deck. *Coventry* told me to stand by for a reply, meanwhile Gordie flew close under the stern and called back to me, 'It's called the *Narwal* and it's got a bloody great Argie flag on it.' I was expecting to be instructed to shadow the vessel and imagined that a helicopter would be sent to investigate but after a couple of minutes *Coventry* called with a short and to-the-point message: 'Red leader from Command, engage!' Christ, I thought, they really want us to sink it!

I relayed the message to Gordie and told him to hold off to the north while I let back down below cloud. He like me was rather loath to attack a seemingly unarmed ship and put a burst of 30-millimetre cannon fire across its bows. The *Narwal* ignored this obvious sign of our intentions and continued to steam slowly west, so sealing her fate.

I decided that we would initially attack her with our bombs. We would have had to jettison them before we returned to the ship in any case, so we might as well lob them at the *Narwal*. Because the weapons had been set up for dropping from high altitude, the tail fuse was set to arm after eight seconds. This meant that we would have to release them as far away as possible, to give the arming vanes the required time of flight. Without this safety feature, the aircraft would be within the debris hemisphere of the weapon when it exploded, with potentially disastrous results. A 1000-pound bomb not only causes a huge blast but also sends out a mass of steel fragments up to four inches across which can fly up to 500 yards. One of these could really spoil your morning.

I agreed with Gordie that we should try a sort of mini-loft manoeuvre, pulling up at about a mile and releasing the bombs just before we entered the cloud base at 500 feet. Using this technique might just give the fuses time to arm but we would still be perilously close to the explosions. As we set ourselves up for the attack I was aware that my brain had entered 'attack mode'. I was concentrating 100 per cent on the task in hand: calculating distance and time, wind and cloud base, airspeed, drift and sight picture. The sense of excitement tinged with apprehension had been replaced by a cold determination to perform to the very best of my ability. I was very aware that we had given the target every opportunity to prepare any defences it might have and that the crew would be in little doubt that our intention was now to sink their ship. If they had means of defence then they would certainly use them now.

As the ship grew larger in my windscreen I made a final check of my weapons switches and concentrated on the decreasing range. With a mile and a half to go, I called, 'In visual,' and a few seconds later pulled the nose up sharply and hit the bomb release button. I felt the satisfying thump of the explosive release units firing, ejecting the slick shape of the bomb from the centreline pylon. I immediately rolled to the left and pulled away from the target. After a couple of seconds I reversed my turn and tried to sight the bomb. As I watched I saw a flash of green over the well deck followed by a very large splash about sixty feet beyond the ship. It was with a peculiar mixture of disappointment and relief that I realised that my weapon had passed a few feet above the ship and landed harmlessly in the sea. The size of the splash told me that it had not had sufficient time of flight in any case and had not fused.

I turned hard left and called Gordie to follow me round for a strafe attack. I double-checked that my gun master switches were selected on – I didn't want a repeat of the embarrassment of the Stanley raid ten days earlier and reset the head-up display depression for fifteen mills, the sight setting for guns. I half hoped that the ship would realise the futility of trying to escape and would heave to before we attacked, but it just kept on ploughing west at ten knots without any attempt at manoeuvring or stopping. It was almost as if there was no one on the bridge. They must have realised that we meant business but gave no sign that they were willing to surrender. I felt a great sense of reluctance as I manoeuvred into position for the next attack run. Part of me felt as if I were about to attack the canvas panels set up in the sand dunes at our local air-to-ground range at Pembrey in South Wales – calm, calculating, assessing drift angles and range, checking that the airspeed was a perfect 450 knots. Another part of me, the man within, was filled with misgivings at the chaos I was about to unleash. The target appeared completely undefended and the high-explosive rounds would create absolute havoc against the thin upper works and hull of the ship, a hull that had been built to withstand the pounding of the southern ocean but not the effect of twenty rounds per second, each with the explosive power of a hand grenade.

I pulled the nose of the aircraft up and rolled left towards the target as I approached the base of the low cloud. Normally I would have aimed for a ten-degree dive but I had to make do with a very much shallower attack because of the weather. I held the gunsight high, above the ship's funnel, until I was about 1000 yards away. I then squeezed the trigger and gently bunted the sight onto the centre of the hull. As I ceased fire with about 500 yards to go I saw my rounds start to impact the sea just short of the target and then walk slowly up the side of the yellow stripe painted on *Narwal*'s hull. It was not a pass that would have earned me many marks on the range at home; not many of the rounds would have holed the fifteen-foot square of canvas and I would undoubtedly have received a 'low warning' and had my score discounted. It was however 'good enough for government work' and I could imagine the explosions slicing through the thin plating of the hull and superstructure.

I was just starting my recovery in order to avoid flying through the debris from the exploding rounds when something odd caught my eye. Beyond the ship just above the superstructure was a small black dot. As I watched, fascinated, it started to grow rapidly in size and suddenly started to twinkle. It was such an unexpected sight that it took me a couple of seconds to realise what was happening: Gordie had lost sight of me and was attacking from the opposite side of the target! It was far too late to do anything about it, so with 30-millimetre rounds flying all over the place we both pulled up and broke left in a manoeuvre that the Red Arrows would have been proud of. I doubt whether the crew of the ship had a chance to appreciate the impromptu air display though, as I imagine that they were trying to avoid the flying splinters.

The near miss had frightened both of us somewhat and I called Gordie in behind me and repositioned for a run from ahead of the target, which was still heading west towards the relative safety of the islands. I emptied my guns into the port bow and pulled off to the right as Gordie started his attack. This time we had a safe separation and I was able to watch as he stabilised his shallow dive and opened fire. Despite the low cloud he managed a brilliant pass, and as he pulled out of the dive the whole of the front of the rust-streaked bridge erupted in a hail of sparkling explosions. I pressed the R/T button and yelled, 'Jesus, Gordie, good shooting!' Immediately, the *Narwal* turned to starboard and slowed to a standstill. She had eventually decided to give up. With lack of fuel now a major factor, we reformed into close formation, pulled back up through the cloud and headed for home. We carried out the return flight in silence, using hand signals to indicate our intentions. I relayed the *Narwal*'s position to *Coventry* and settled down to think about the recovery to *Hermes*. I was very thankful that the weather had improved somewhat from the last few days and that we were able to carry out an independent let-down and visual recovery below the cloud, breaking into the circuit at 300 feet and landing ten seconds apart in good order.

I had mixed feelings about the attack. I accepted the plaudits of the rest of the guys (although the phrase 'fish in a barrel' was mentioned) but privately I was rather unhappy that there had been no return fire and no obvious hostile intention on the part of the target. It was not until the following day that we learnt the full story. The *Narwal* was a 1300-ton stern trawler owned by the South American Fishing and Exploration Company. She had been requisitioned by the Argentine Navy at Mar del Plata a few weeks previously and been pressed into service as an intelligence gatherer. Just before the first raids on the islands she had been warned to leave the area but had not done so. Unfortunately, by staying at sea for a few extra days she had run low on fuel and was taking a short cut through the Total Exclusion Zone on her way home when we spotted her. She was crewed by some thirty fishermen, a few of them well past retiring age, but also had on board a lieutenant commander of the Argentine Navy. He was a very worried man and was convinced that he would be shot as a spy because he was in civilian clothes and carrying his service pistol.

Sea Kings full of SAS troops were dispatched from *Invincible* to capture the vessel and they discovered that one sailor had been killed and several injured during the attack. The only death had apparently been caused when Gordie's bomb had hit the forecastle, travelled down two decks and come to rest in the heads, where the victim had been relieving himself. It had taken off both his legs and he had died almost instantly. When Gordie heard about this he said in a rather detached way, 'Good job it didn't go off; it would have spoilt his whole day!' Black humour was a good way of camouflaging your feelings, but this comment was greeted by a series of heartfelt groans.

The *Narwal*'s crew were evacuated to *Invincible* where they were looked after very well by the British sailors even though they refused to believe that the *Invincible* was still afloat. They had been told that the carrier had been hit three times and sunk without trace. The Argentine naval officer was so certain he was going to be executed that he asked for writing materials to compose a last letter to his family. In an attempt to put his mind at rest, the Roman Catholic padre was sent to talk to him. The sight of a man of God coming through the door only made him more certain that his time had come and it was a while before he could be convinced that we meant him no harm. The casualty was buried at sea the following day and the rest of the crew repatriated a few days later.

That would have been the end of the incident were it not for a post-script which could have been very unfortunate. Shortly after our return to *Hermes* Brian Hanrahan left to file a report using the satellite communications on one of the Royal Fleet Auxiliaries. At the end of his report he was told that Argentine radio was reporting that the Sea Harriers involved in the attack on *Narwal* had strafed the crew in their lifeboats. He saved my reputation by replying that he knew the pilots involved and that they would never dream of doing such a thing.

Unknown to any of us, the next two CAP aircraft had taken it upon themselves to investigate the now helpless vessel and had then proceeded to attack her. During this attack they had damaged the lifeboats tied up under the *Narwal*'s stern. It seemed like an unforgivable piece of indiscipline and I was absolutely livid. I found myself being protective about 'my' ship and indignant that anyone else should have the nerve to attack her when she was dead in the water. It transpired later that the second mission had received permission to attack from *Coventry*.

When the boarding party arrived they found that the engine room had been severely damaged by my first attack and that the ship was taking in a lot of water from the strikes along the waterline. A plan to use her for operations against the islands was therefore abandoned and she was allowed to sink. In the meantime a search of the accommodation revealed a copy of the Argentine naval codes, which were to prove very useful to the 'spooks' busy intercepting the Argentine radio calls.

That evening the fog returned and the wind started to increase, whipping the sea into a frenzy of white water. The combination of high seas and low visibility meant that we were very unlikely to get a visit from the Exocet-carrying Super Etendards, so we gathered in the wardroom for a debrief of the last few days' operations and a well-deserved beer. I noticed that to a man we were looking tired and drawn; the last ten days had certainly taken it out of us and there was no sign of the pressure letting up. We were all very disappointed to hear that the doctors had decided that Bertie had become psychologically unfit and was to be sent back to the UK on the next available ship. He was devastated by the news and we all felt absolutely wretched that he was going to be returned under such a cloud. I could only guess the torment he was going through and every one of us hoped he would be able to make a rapid recovery once he was home. We all recognised him as a first-class Harrier instructor and knew that his skills would be desperately needed to train our reinforcements on 809 NAS at Yeovilton. I also wondered what the future held for the rest of us; my feelings after attacking the *Narwal* had not been those of unrestrained joy. I had trained for years to achieve the highest possible level of efficiency in the various facets of modern warfare but never considered the psychological aspects of killing, or of someone trying to kill me. I sensed that some of the other pilots were having the same nagging doubts but it was not something that any of us felt we could discuss freely without opening a large can of worms. We would all carry on and complete this task to the best of our various abilities and sort out our personal feelings at a later date.

Perspective
Use It or Lose It
If you turned to this page,
You're forgetting that what is going
on around you is not reality.
Think about that.
Remember where you came from,
where you're going and why you created
The mess you got yourself into in the first place.
You're going to die a horrible death, remember.
It's all good training and you'll enjoy it
more if you keep the facts
in mind.
Take your dying with some seriousness, however.
Laughing on the way to your execution
is not generally understood by less-
advanced life-forms and they'll
call you crazy.

So read the page at which *Illusions* opened that evening. Food for thought indeed.

CHAPTER 6

THE LEAD-UP TO THE LANDINGS

THE NEXT FEW DAYS were very frustrating as the South Atlantic weather tried its best to keep us from flying. The westerly gales built up to a crescendo, with winds of sixty knots accompanied by thick fog, a combination rarely seen in the waters around Europe. We sat in the crewroom reviewing the conflict so far and attempting to guess what would happen when the skies cleared. To pass the time David Smith developed an uncanny knack of completing the Rubik's cube puzzle in an ever-decreasing time. The Uckers board was also pressed into service. Uckers is a traditional naval game which can only be described as Ludo with attitude. It can be played by up to four people and usually has a crowd of noisy onlookers who cheer at every vicious move. The board is a couple of feet square and the pieces are coloured circles of wood. It is an excellent way to pass an hour or so and allows everyone to let off steam without causing offence.

The highlight of the 11th was the arrival of mail. Mail takes on huge importance when you are away at sea, even in peacetime. It is a link with friends and family and the home life that is missed so terribly by most. It is, however, a bitter-sweet moment when the arrival of mail is piped. Part of you wants to rush to the mail rack to check for those all-important missives and another part tries to play it cool just in case your mail slot remains empty. This time I was lucky and had several letters, including one from my sister and her family near Dartford.

HMS *Hermes*
BFPO Ships

11 May '82
Dear all,
Many thanks for the letter, it was a nice surprise indeed. Life here is fairly hectic; at the moment we have 60 knots of wind, a very rough sea and fog. Not very nice flying weather!

The passage down was quite good and things have gone our way most of the time since we started operations. I was No. 2 on the Port Stanley airfield raid, which was quite an eye-opener. The ground fire was horrendous, with 40+ anti-aircraft guns and several different missile systems all having a go at us. However, we wellied it a treat and took out several aircraft into the bargain, all for the price of one hole. Unfortunately, the hole was in my tail! (Bad news.) But I was OK and the aircraft was fixed within one day. (Good news!) We have shot down quite a few of their Mirages and Canberras and only lost one guy to their ground fire. Unfortunately we had a couple spear in the other day for no particular reason but that's the way it goes.

Yesterday – sorry, the day before yesterday – I sunk a boat. You will probably have heard it on the news. The *Narwal* was its name and we found it spying on the fleet and hit it with 30-millimetre cannon fire (400 rounds) and then the SAS captured it. Unfortunately, it was badly holed and later sunk. It was a big one too, 1300 tons. Would have been a good prize!

Morale is good notwithstanding the loss of *Sheffield* and all we are waiting for now is the invasion proper.

Our main problem at the moment is beer rationing! We can only have two pints a day, so I'm onto the horses' necks.

Well, duty calls. Look after yourselves till I get back.

Love

David

Down below in the hangar the maintainers used the lull in the fighting to carry out vital work on the aircraft. The conditions were appalling and great care had to be taken to avoid being injured by being thrown against machinery in the heavy seas. In the wardroom, the scene of so many evenings of pageantry and elegant dining, the heavy mahogany tables and chairs were upturned and secured to the deck with rope lashings. The large mirrored back wall of the bar had been covered in plywood to avoid splinter damage and now sported stencilled outlines representing our successes so far. People sat around in their blue action dress, white overalls or flying suits, their highly coloured cummerbunds having given way to webbing belts carrying life jackets, gas masks, survival suits and shell dressings.

Since the sinking of the *Sheffield* the ship had been kept at Condition Zulu, with every hatch and watertight door fully closed. This made moving around a slow and difficult process with every door requiring eight clips to be knocked off and then re-secured. The hatches between decks were too heavy to be easily opened and were fitted with smaller kidney hatches which were tight at the best of times and required anyone wearing their survival equipment to wriggle and squeeze in order to pass through. The heavy metal hatch had to then be pulled back into place and secured with three clips. Many a finger was trapped and many a knuckle skinned passing through these hatches but we all knew that they would be essential to stop the spread of not only water but also smoke and fire if we were unlucky enough to be hit. The rate at which smoke had spread in *Sheffield* had been a salutary warning to us all.

As we entered our second week of conflict it was obvious that everyone was becoming tired. Faces were more drawn and the normal banter of the crewroom was much more subdued. The results of the beard-growing contest were beginning to show and it was clear that some of us were on the way to producing very healthy growths while others were struggling. I am afraid I was one of the strugglers but I was glad to see that Fred and Ted Ball were having even more trouble than I was. Fred had only managed to grow a couple of straggly tufts, which made him look rather like Fu Manchu on a bad hair day.

The weather finally cleared on the morning of the 12th and the war restarted with a vengeance. We were back in the air flying CAP and *Glasgow* and *Brilliant* went inshore to attempt to down the Hercules transport that we knew had been regularly landing at Stanley despite the damage caused by our attacks. This was the moment the Argentine Air Force had been waiting for and shortly after midday they launched a determined attack with two waves of Skyhawks. The first formation of four attacked *Brilliant* from the west at very low level and was met with a devastating salvo of Seawolf missiles. The two lead aircraft were immediately shot down and a third crashed into the sea trying to avoid a missile. Only one aircraft, flown by Teniente Vasquez, completed its attack but the bombs fell wide of their target and caused no damage to either ship.

Half an hour later another flight of four Skyhawks attacked the two warships, three aiming for *Glasgow* and one for *Brilliant*. This time the Seawolf system failed to operate correctly and refused to fire. This was probably caused by the close proximity of the targets, which caused the system to reject them. There was no time to fire the missiles in the manual mode and all four aircraft were able to press home their attacks. Teniente Arraras released two 500-pound bombs, which landed short and skipped over *Brilliant*'s superstructure, landing in the sea beyond without causing any damage. *Glasgow* was not so lucky, however. She attempted to bring her Seadart into action but the missile doors jammed and her crew could only watch helplessly as the two missiles stood smartly to attention and refused to fire.

Primer Teniente Gavazzi hit her amidships with one of his bombs.

He saw an explosion behind him and assumed that he had caused severe damage to the destroyer, but luckily for his target his bomb had passed straight through the ship and exploded in the sea beyond. The damage caused to the ship was however severe. Superficially there were just two holes, one on either side of the hull, but internally it was a different matter. The bomb had skipped off the water, causing a huge splash, and then punched through a fuel tank, spraying fuel oil all over the engine room and those crew members in it. It had then exited through the far side of the engine room, knocking a hole in the engine intakes. This caused four out of the six engines to surge and sustain severe damage to their blades. Once the immediate damage-control actions had been carried out, it was discovered that her speed was now limited to six knots. There was no prospect of changing the engines at sea so she spent the next two weeks as an up-threat radar picket and satellite communications guard ship before setting off on her long journey back to Portsmouth for repairs. One of her engineers carried with him a memento of the incident in the form of a piece of 1000-pound bomb, which showed that it had been made in the UK. I guess that is what you call getting your own back!

Gavazzi was not able to celebrate his success for long, however, as he passed close to Goose Green a few minutes later and was shot down by the same guns that had claimed the life of Nick Taylor on 4 May.

I arrived in the area together with Mike Blissett shortly after the attack and we could only put ourselves up-threat of the ships in the hope that we would be able to protect them as they pulled back to the east towards the relative safety of the fleet. No further attack came, however, and after forty minutes of patrolling we were forced to return to *Hermes*. Both of us were very frustrated at arriving just too late to attack the A4s, although it was definitely comforting to know that the Seawolf system had now proved itself to be effective at very low level.

Our frustrations were made worse when the fog returned that evening. The following morning I was very much aware that everyone was getting a bit edgy; we all wanted to get on with the business in hand and this continual waiting around was not doing our morale any good at all. The day was spent at Alert 5, staring at the fog, counting the sheathbills and grabbing the odd bit of sleep in the cockpit. I began to wish that I had something to occupy my mind. I had started doing an individual staff studies correspondence course before the task force sailed but I had deliberately left all my books behind at Yeovilton. I hated staff work but this course was a prerequisite for promotion so I had forced myself to begin it when I returned from Germany. I now thought it might have helped to pass the time, if I hadn't ditched it at the first opportunity.

John Locke obviously realised that our morale needed a bit of a lift as well and it was announced that there would be a film show in the wardroom that evening. Film evenings were normally a great social event aboard ship and were anticipated almost as eagerly as the arrival of mail from home. Everyone would put on their Red Sea Rig – white shirts with epaulettes and squadron cummerbunds – and meet in the bar for drinks before moving through into the dining room for a civilised dinner with subdued lighting and a nice bottle of wine. After the meal the tables would be cleared away, the projector rigged at the back of the room and the chairs arranged in rows facing the screen. Usually the captain would be invited to join us and the show would start with a cartoon (known as a Mickey Duck) followed by a full feature film. These films were provided by the Services Kinematic Corporation and passed from ship to ship, so it was normally possible to have a film show every week or ten days.

This evening was rather different. Many officers could not attend because we were in defence watches and they had rather more important things to do. Gone were the cummerbunds and crisply starched shirts but there was still something of the usual air of expectancy as we filed through into the dining room in our grubby overalls, one hand clutching a pint of beer and the other trailing our anti-flash and survival gear. The lights were dimmed and the cartoon credits started to roll. The usual roar of 'Good old Fred' greeted the announcement that the film had been produced by Fred Quimby and we settled down to watch Tom and Jerry. There were the usual ribald shouts when the ancient projector started playing up, causing the film to jump, but the cartoon ran its course and we waited patiently for the main feature to begin.

After a few minutes the projector whirred and the image focused on the screen in front of us; it was *Gallipoli*, the film about the ill-fated First World War campaign in the Dardanelles. It was a film I had not seen and I was not prepared for the harrowing scenes of death and destruction that followed. I began to feel uncomfortable after only a few minutes and thought it was probably not the most appropriate film we could have been shown. Before long it came to the scene where the young Aussie soldier leaves his personal possessions hanging on his bayonet stuck in the side of the trench and goes over the top to his death. At this stage I decided that I had no wish to see any more and walked out.

13 May

Foggy again. No Sea Harrier flying but a lot of cockpit alert. Evening 846 spook insertion delayed. *Gallipoli* shown in the wardroom – most inappropriate!

I made my way through the red-lit passageways up to the now deserted crewroom on 2 Deck and sat in silence, listening only to the hum of the air conditioning and trying to get my thoughts in order. I ran my eyes over the names of our pilots on the wall and wondered how many of us would make it through. Nick, E-J and Al Curtis were dead already and Bertie had been sent home. Oges had also gone down with a severe sinus infection. The Argentines had taken quite a few casualties but they had shown they were willing to press their attacks and I had no doubt that we were going to take more losses. The Sea Harriers were our only hope of success in this conflict; without us the Argentines would prevail. The soldiers and ships would attempt to retake the islands but without our air cover they would be picked off by the numerically superior enemy. The Argentines must realise we were the lynchpin of the whole operation and they must surely make us their prime target. The odds were not good but they had shown that their tactics were not up to scratch, which might give us the edge.

14 May

Very quiet day. Had one trip looking for a 'hospital' ship which we think may be a blockade-runner but no success. Starting to get a bit of a cold.

The pace of operations changed dramatically after dark. Having had a very quiet, almost lazy day, *Hermes* dashed north of the islands to launch two commando Sea Kings of 846 NAS to attack the grass airfield at Pebble Island. A large number of enemy light attack aircraft had been deployed there after our raids on Stanley and Goose Green and we needed to get rid of as many as we could before attempting to retake the islands.

It was a foul night with severe gales and high seas. The helicopters approached the airfield at low level, pilots using night vision goggles, and dropped off forty-five men from D Squadron of 22 SAS Regiment. In the space of three quarters of an hour the 'specials' destroyed all the aircraft on the field and blew up the ammunition dump, returning to *Hermes* with huge grins on their faces. Their only casualty was one man with a flesh wound to his foot. Altogether it was a perfect example of what the SAS train for.

Ted Ball and I were briefed to fly over the area and check out the damage the following lunchtime. We did not know quite what to expect as we ran in from the east at something over 500 knots, hugging the contours of the headland. The sky had cleared and the visibility was absolutely sparkling. There was of course no pollution over the islands and once a weather system passed through it left behind the most stunning conditions. Unfortunately, this also allowed the enemy to see you coming unless you planned your ingress route with great care. With this in mind we had routed well north of Stanley as if we were heading for a normal CAP station off the north coast. Once at low level we ran north of Teal Inlet with its small clump of trees, the only ones in the area, and headed for Falkland Sound. I put a china-graph line on the side of the canopy depressed twenty degrees below the horizon to use as an aiming mark for the camera, took a one-second clearing burst of the sky and selected a speed of sixteen frames per second.

We crossed the sound to the north of Fanning Head and less than a minute later rounded Goat Hill, which stands nearly 1000 feet above sea level. From here it was just ten miles to the target, less than two minutes at the speed we were travelling. I concentrated on flying as low as I could over the lakes and inlets and checked that my camera was armed with the correct lights showing on the panel. The main objective of reconnaissance is to gather intelligence visually and this requires considerable training and practice. The secondary objective is to obtain photographic coverage so that the photographic interpreters can tease out even more information using their stereoscopes. Stereoscopy relies on having overlapping images and this requires a large number of frames per second at low level. I had been considered one of the best recce pilots on my squadron in Germany and Ted had been on No. 4 Squadron, the only Harrier unit dedicated to reconnaissance. It was no coincidence that we had been paired up for this mission.

With two kilometres to run to the target, Ted called, 'In visual!' and I started my turn towards the airfield, which I could just make out on the crest of a small rise. Thin wisps of smoke were rising from several locations around the grass strip and as I closed the target I could see a large number of aircraft scattered around the field. In the middle of the runway were three large holes and close to them was a totally burnt-out Shorts Skyvan, recognisable only by the shape of its wings and tail. One T34 Mentor was also burnt out and two others obviously damaged. Of the six Pucaras around the strip, one was severely damaged and three others had smashed canopies. A large area of blackening to the side of the airstrip showed where fire had consumed an ammunition dump. As my eyes took in the detail I panned my camera across the area to record it for the PIs and at the same time checked for defensive fire in case I needed to take evasive action. Luckily, we had made our approach unseen and neither of us was aware of any fire from the garrison at the airfield. I believe we were through the target and away, ducking down over the bay, before anyone had a chance to react.

On our return, we filed our report with ops and the int officer before making our way forward to check our films. The rolls of 2¼-inch-square negatives were laid out on a light table with a PI hunched over them. In a fully worked-up reconnaissance intelligence centre ashore the imagery would be available within minutes of engine shutdown. On *Hermes* this took a little longer but the negatives were normally on the table within ten minutes, which was pretty good going. I grabbed a spare stereoscope and started looking at the black and white negatives on the table. Of the eleven aircraft on the field only one had no obvious damage. The Pucaras that had seemed intact to the naked eye all had considerable damage to either the cockpit area or the engine intakes. Closer examination of the one seemingly intact aircraft showed a large number of bullet holes riddling its port side. We had been able to confirm the success of the mission about which Admiral Woodward later commented, 'In my view, this single operation is easily the best example of a successful all-arms special operation that we are likely to see in a very long while.'

We were certainly taking the fight to the enemy again and the despondency of the last few days evaporated like the dawn mist on a summer's morning.

15 May

Last night the SAS took out Pebble Island. They destroyed the ammo dump and eleven (repeat) eleven aircraft – six Pucaras, one Skyvan and four T34 Mentors.

I went up with Ted to do some recce of the chaos at lunchtime and it was still smoking.

That evening it was obvious that my cold was getting worse. My throat had become quite sore and my nose was blocked. I spent an uncomfortable night on my camp bed dosed up with aspirin and Vicks nasal spray trying not to wake the others with my coughing. At breakfast time, with my sinuses and ears well and truly blocked, I reluctantly reported sick and took myself off the flying programme. I was now resigned to being cooped up in the bowels of the ship for several days but I could not afford to risk damaging my eardrums or sinuses by flying. We would need every pilot we had as the conflict developed.

I was able to make myself useful by acting as duty pilot, which entailed being in Flyco to supervise launches and recoveries. At least this gave me the opportunity to see daylight and feel that I was contributing to the operation. In addition to this, I spent some time with the PIs poring over the large numbers of aerial photographs that had been taken since the first raids. I was looking at some high-level shots of Goose Green when I noticed something that was not there on every pass. A large peanut-shaped object could be seen from time to time alongside the schoolhouse in the centre of the settlement. The shots had been taken from around 20,000 feet and were very indistinct but I eventually came across a series of negatives taken in the late afternoon and could see the shadow of the mystery object on the grass. This showed that it was a Chinook helicopter. We had been looking for the Argentine helicopters for some time, as movement around the islands was very difficult without their use. Now I knew where one Chinook regularly landed we could invite the specials to consider it as a target.

That morning Simon Hargreaves and David Smith were tasked to carry out a recce of the Falkland Sound area, looking for shipping. They came back with photos of two blockade runners, one in Fox Bay and another larger one in Port King, to the north-east. Gordie Batt and Andy McHarg were quickly tasked to attack the *Rio Carcarana* with 1000-pound retard bombs. The ship was well away from any settlement and there was no possibility of collateral damage to civilian property. Unfortunately both pilots managed to straddle the target with their bombs, causing no damage, and had to carry out a number of strafing runs to disable her. The 30-millimetre rounds caused havoc on the upper decks and started a large fire which eventually caused the ship to be abandoned. She was later attacked by Argentine A4s, shelled by one of our frigates and finally attacked by *Antelope*'s Lynx, which sank her on 23 May with two Sea Skua missiles. All this was rather a waste of weaponry, as after the SHAR attacks on the 16th she was a useless wreck.

I was running through the gun camera film from this attack a few hours later when to my horror I found that Gordie's sight was firmly planted in the middle of a fifteen-foot-square red cross on a white background. As he started his recovery you could clearly see the first rounds impacting on this internationally accepted sign for a hospital ship. My blood ran cold as I rewound the film and played it in slow time. There could be no doubt about it: they had severely damaged a ship displaying a red cross, a crime under the provisions of the Geneva Convention. I ran straight up to Flyco and took Wings on one side to break the appalling news to him. He went white and asked me if there was any possibility of a mistake. I replied that it seemed not but that I would check the rest of the film for any other clues. Neither pilot had been aware of any red cross during the attack.

I first checked the recce photographs taken by the morning sortie and found that there was no sign of any crosses on the ship's hull. How on earth then had they suddenly appeared two hours later? I rechecked the film and there could be no doubt about the markings. I then went back to the bomb attacks and found to my immense surprise that there were no red crosses to be seen on the hull only minutes earlier. On the deck, however, were several figures carrying a long bundle of material towards the rail at the exact spot where the markings had mysteriously appeared. By checking back to Simon's recce photos taken that morning, I could easily make out that there was a large roll of cloth lying on the upper deck. I heaved a great sigh of relief and rang Wings with the good news: the crew of the *Carcarana* had prepared a set of red cross flags and lowered them over the side when they were attacked. This in itself was against the Geneva Convention, as a hospital ship is required to be 'clearly marked' before it can claim protection from attack. Gordie and Andy were both very relieved men when they saw the evidence and we now realised that not all the enemy were playing by the rules.

Some forty minutes after the *Carcarana* was neutralised Andy Auld led Simon Hargreaves to attack the *Bahia Buen Suceso* in Fox Bay. This small cargo vessel was tied up alongside the pier next to the Fox Bay East settlement, which presented several problems. We knew there was an Argentine presence at Fox Bay, which meant that there was a possibility of some defensive fire, even if it was only small arms. In addition to this, the ship's proximity to the settlement ruled out the use of 1000-pound bombs or 2-inch rocket pods; either of these weapons might cause unacceptable damage to the rather flimsy houses nearby. The only practical method of attack was with cannon in a shallow dive and this attack had to be made on the ship's beam to be effective.

The pair launched shortly after midday local time and made their attack heading north-west, towards the settlement. They each fired one long burst of cannon fire into the area of the ship's bridge and escaped to the east, returning to *Hermes* with large grins on their faces. Strafing is an exacting method of attack as it can be difficult to judge the open-fire range correctly and to track accurately for the few seconds required to put the rounds on target. If you open fire at 700 yards and cease fire at 300 yards, you can usually see a couple of rounds hit the target before it disappears beneath the nose but most of the rounds impact out of sight. So it was that Andy didn't know where all his rounds had gone until we looked at his film.

As we were preparing to debrief the gunsight film, Captain Middleton popped his head round the door and decided to stay for the show. Simon's film was excellent, with good steady tracking, and I was fairly convinced that he had scored numerous hits on the superstructure and hull. He had not got away with the attack completely, however, as a hole from a 7.62-millimetre rifle bullet was found in his tail. It was a good job that the soldier didn't get his deflection right. We then played Andy's film, which started off very nicely with some good tracking on the superstructure. After a second or so, however, his aim started to ride a little high and the gunsight began to wander over the quay and up into the settlement.

'Are you still firing, Andy?' asked the captain in his clipped South African accent.

'Ah, yes I am, sir,' replied Andy, somewhat sheepishly. Unfortunately the white firing marker at the top of the film is always there when the trigger is pressed, so it was not possible to deny it. But after close examination of the film, it appeared that the only building in danger of being hit was an outside toilet!

16 May
Recce by Simon Hargreaves and Dave Smith this morning found two blockade runners, one at Fox Bay East and another at Port King. Two aircraft were dispatched to each. Gordie Batt and Andy McHarg dropped two 1000-pound bombs each (missed) then strafed the latter. Crew abandoned ship. Boss and Simon strafed the former – no damage assessment but suspect very poorly. Boss put a number of rounds into the settlement but only injured two Argies; one had shrapnel in the bum!

The *Bahia Buen Suceso* was seriously damaged and did not move from Fox Bay for the rest of the war. After the conflict was over it was found to be infested with rats and was towed out to sea. In November it was used for target practice by SHARs of 809 NAS from *Illustrious* and sunk with cannon and rocket fire.

Later in the day I was reviewing the recce film from Simon's morning mission and found a series of lines of blobs in the open just to the east of Fox Bay settlement. When I pointed these out to the PI, he said, 'Oh yes, they are penguins.'

'Penguins?' I replied. 'They can't be. Penguins don't walk along in straight lines, equally spaced.'

I looked closer and was sure that they were not. They were in straight rows of between five and ten, each row separated from the next by forty or fifty feet. Suddenly it dawned on me – they were fifty-gallon fuel drums! The perfect target for a cluster bomb attack.

That evening I made my way up to the briefing room to check the flying programme for the following morning and found Lieutenant Richard Hutchings poring over a set of maps. Richard was one of the Royal Marine helicopter pilots, allocated to 846 NAS and had been flying regular nightly missions over the islands to insert and retrieve special forces patrols. He shared our accommodation in the captain's cabin and regularly arrived back as we were getting up for our day's work.

I walked over to the outspread maps and quipped, 'Hi, Richard, going somewhere nice then?' He gave me a withering look and said nothing. I looked a little more closely at the maps and realised it was not anywhere that I recognised. Certainly it was not anywhere on the Falklands.

The following night Richard and his crew disappeared. Two Sea Kings were transferred to *Invincible*, which took them at high speed to the west of the islands before launching Richard and returning to the task force. Their mission remains classified even today but we were fairly sure that they had been involved in a special forces insertion on mainland Argentina. Several days later Michael Vestey in Punta Arenas received a phone call from his Chilean contact, suggesting he go to a secluded bay at Agua Fresca some twenty kilometres from where he was staying. Michael gathered his television crew and headed west towards the given location. Exactly twenty kilometres from the town, on the shores of the Magellan Strait, he found the partially burnt-out wreckage of Sea King ZA290. When he filed his report for the *PM* programme a few hours later he was told that the MOD was denying that a Sea King was missing. This assertion was soon changed, however, and Michael got his scoop. Several days later Richard and his crew surrendered to the Chilean armed forces and were repatriated to the UK.

The story put about was that they had 'got lost' and had to abandon their helicopter when it ran out of fuel. I don't know of anyone who believed that, especially after Richard, who just happened to be a survival expert, was awarded the Distinguished Service Cross. Indeed, he was invited back to Chile for a 'holiday' the next year. Speculation is still rife over the precise nature of the mission but it almost certainly involved special forces and no specials were ever picked up on mainland Argentina.

There was an unsubstantiated rumour that one of our submarines had sustained some damage in shallow waters a few days later. Whatever the details of the mission, we had to conclude that it must have been worth the loss of a Sea King.

Another Sea King was lost during the night of the 17/18th. One of 826 Squadron's Mark 4 aircraft ditched following a radio altimeter failure in the hover only a couple of miles from *Hermes*. The crew of four were able to scramble clear and were quickly rescued from the freezing water. The aircraft continued to float and a recovery was attempted before it was decided that its load of Mark 11 depth charges was likely to cause a great deal of damage if it detonated. The fuselage was therefore sunk with gunfire and, as suspected, there was a very large explosion as the weapons exploded at their pre-set depth.

18 May
Quiet day. Met amphibious force 300 miles east. Flew on four SHAR and three GR3s including Peter Squire (OC1 (F)), Bob Iveson, Jeff Glover, Mark Hare, John Leeming and Steve Brown. We now have a lot of crabs! Also Hugh Slade and Bill Covington.

To my great relief I woke up on the morning of the 18th able to clear my ears again. My sinuses were still a little squeaky but I was confident that they would not cause me more than passing discomfort in the descent from altitude. Theoretically I should have been passed as fit by one of the medics on board but they had much more important duties to attend to and I considered myself the best judge of my fitness to fly. Although I felt a slight reluctance to expose myself once more to the dangers of conflict in the air, it was infinitely preferable to being locked up inside the ship. No matter how much I reassured myself about the ship's ability to survive a missile or torpedo hit, I could not avoid visualising a projectile coming inboard and the ensuing horrors. I knew that the old lady had an armoured flight deck and a thick hull but we had seen what had happened to the *Belgrano*.

As it turned out, the day was to be a very quiet one. We had steamed to the east of the Total Exclusion Zone and by mid-morning I was airborne with Gordie Batt to provide cover for the join-up with the amphibious force, which had arrived from Ascension Island. One of the ships which joined us during the course of the day was the STUFT container ship *Atlantic Conveyor*. She was a huge, black, slab-sided vessel of the type to be seen every day plying their trade through the English Channel, stacked high with containers. Her cargo now, however, was considerably more important than her normal one and was vital to the success of our mission. Not only was she loaded with stores and weapons of every conceivable type, she also carried a deck cargo of six GR3s, eight Sea Harriers, six Wessex, one Lynx and four heavy-lift Chinooks. After the two carriers, she was without doubt the most important ship in the South Atlantic. It was vital that the *Conveyor*'s assets were distributed as soon as possible and later that morning I was up in Flyco to watch the arrival of four SHARs and the same number of GR3s.

That evening there was a great reunion in the wardroom. My old buddies John Leeming and Steve Brown seemed very relieved to have got to the sharp end at last and downed a few well-earned pints of CSB. Lems had been a particular buddy and we had children of similar ages. Both he and Steve were among a number of pilots from the RAF Harrier Force who had volunteered to join us on the Sea Harrier. They had been chosen because their considerable experience on Lightnings gave them a definite edge over those who had only flown GR3s. Their conversion at Yeovilton had been rapid and frantic, with most of their pitifully few hours on the aircraft being achieved during the flight from UK to Wideawake. In addition, their only experience of deck landing had been embarking on *Conveyor* while she was at anchor off Ascension Island twelve days earlier. The other two SHAR pilots, Hugh Slade and Bill Covington, had originally flown Gannet airborne early-warning aircraft before being sent on overseas exchanges tours. Although Bill had flown AV8B Harriers with the US Marine Corps, neither of them had experience of operating a single-seat air defence fighter. It struck me that evening that we were a very odd bunch of individuals, each with his own particular skills and background but very few with any meaning-ful experience of fighting the aircraft. The only ones who were experi-enced and practised in flying their aircraft were the pilots of No. 1 (F) Squadron, who had arrived shortly after our new SHARs.

Wing Commander Peter Squire, the boss of the RAF squadron, was on his second Harrier tour and had been my next-door neighbour in married quarters at Gütersloh. He was a very experienced and competent pilot with an exemplary record and had been very highly respected as a flight commander in Germany. He was a perfect gentleman with an easy and open manner which commanded respect from all who had anything to do with him and had a well-deserved reputation for his absolute integrity. He was a dedicated family man and treated his squadron as part of his extended family; so much so that we thought that his career would be limited by his inability to participate in the back-stabbing perceived as being a prerequisite for promotion. Luckily the RAF recog-nised this outstanding officer and he eventually rose to the highest level.

The other three pilots who joined us that afternoon were Squadron Leaders Jerry Pook and Pete 'Bomber' Harris together with Flight Lieu-tenant John Rochford. Jerry and Bomber I had met during my time in Germany but John and I had never crossed paths. For all of them it was their first time on board one of Her Majesty's ships and I was glad to help them get orientated and buy them a beer. After all, it was now a distinct possibility that they would take over the responsibility for ground attack missions while we addressed the air threat. Those of us who had seen the ground fire around Stanley and Goose Green had no wish to repeat the experience and were very happy to let the professionals have a go. They, by contrast, would have been happy to have a go at air defence.

Unfortunately, the task force's tasking and reporting system was at best chaotic and was to prove very frustrating for them over the next few weeks. Likewise, the inertial platforms for the GR3 weapons and navigation systems were designed to be aligned on terra firma, not the constantly moving deck of a ship. This resulted in them having very little in the way of either navigation or weapon-aiming information available to them during their missions over the islands. British Aerospace and Ferranti had produced a piece of kit to allow the platforms to be aligned at sea but this box on wheels, the 'wheelbarrow', proved of limited value and the boys of 1(F) usually had to fall back on basic skills half remembered from the Hunter days.

It was very nice to catch up with news from home that evening and to share our feelings with the new arrivals. They were, to a man, raring to go after the long journey down to join us. They did seem rather bemused however by the nightly ritual of calling for silence as the strains of 'Lilly Bolero' issued from the speakers over the bar and everyone listened intently to the flat voice of the MOD PR man relating news of the day's action in the Falkland Islands. This peculiar link with home had started to take on a special meaning for us over the last ten days; it was almost a way of proving to ourselves that this war was actually happening and not just a figment of our imaginations. Even more odd was the fact that some of the Argentine pilots were also tuning in to the World Service to ascertain the effectiveness of their attacks. It seemed that the probity of the BBC was acknowledged as beyond reproach by both sides of the conflict.

Having settled our newcomers into the ship's routine, we spent the next day preparing them for operations from the deck. The arrivals were briefed on embarked operations and introduced to those members of the ship's company that they would need to work with. It was decided that *Hermes* would remain well to the east of the islands for a further twenty-four hours to enable our new boys to fly a couple of practice sorties before committing them to the conflict. I am sure that this decision was well received by them and the practice interception and combat missions were as valuable as the subsequent recoveries to the deck. All turned in very passable first deck landings and arrived down in the briefing room with large grins on their faces.

My first sortie of the day was to find a large tanker, the *British Tay*. She was approaching from the north-east laden with fuel for the fleet and I was glad that we were able to show her that she was not forgotten.

It must have been very lonely for them, making their painfully slow progress towards the comparative safety of the fleet without any escort. We flew past at deck height and were greeted by most of the crew standing on the bridge waving wildly. I certainly did not envy them, sitting on thousands of tons of extremely volatile fuel and heading into a war zone.

Later in the afternoon I was due to launch with Gordie, to fly a CAP mission to the west of the fleet. I was sitting with my engine started, waiting for the NAVHARS to align, when I noticed him getting out of his aircraft. He gave me a thumbs-down and a grimace as he headed back towards the door into the island, obviously fed up that his machine was unserviceable. One of the Alert 5 aircraft was started to come with me and a few minutes later I was blasting off the front of the ramp behind him. As he cleared the deck he jinked left and then right so we were straight into battle formation, and as I accelerated towards cruising speed I saw him start a ninety-degree turn towards me to head out in a westerly direction. We flew on in silence for a few miles before he started a gentle turn towards me. This, one of our minimum-radio procedures, was an indication that he wanted me to turn towards him, and as I pulled my aircraft around to the left he rolled out heading south. This manoeuvre was repeated several times over the next few minutes until I realised that we were no longer heading towards our CAP station but back towards the ship. This confused me somewhat and I was about to break radio silence when the controller on *Hermes* came up on the radio and said, 'Red Leader, check your heading.'

There ensued a long silence during which you could almost see the think bubbles over both our cockpits. Then I suddenly realised what had happened: for five minutes we had been flying around in perfect formation and total silence with each of us assuming that the other was leading! I quickly took the lead and got us pointing in the correct direction. It was a good thing the controller had been on the ball, otherwise we could easily have wandered back through the fleet and given everyone a heart attack.

On our return after an uneventful CAP I discovered that the other pilot was John Leeming, on his first operational mission. We both felt rather sheepish about our mistake and resolved not to mention it to anyone. As the US Marines say, 'Better to die than look bad!'

This was the end of my flying for the day and I started off aft to relax over a cup of tea. I had just squeezed through the kidney hatch and was carefully descending the ladder onto 3 Deck when I saw Garth Hawkins coming along the passageway from the wardroom. Over the last couple of days I had being doing a lot of work with Garth in preparation for the land war. We had been poring over maps of the islands, nominating a series of initial points, or IPs. These prominent features could be used by FACs to bring in close air support against the enemy. Selecting IPs was not an easy task on the Falklands as most of the ground was barren rock but after a few hours' work we thought that we had found sufficient to cover most of the possible routes of advance. Garth had been very upset that the SAS had refused to let him go ashore on their nightly reconnaissance runs. Despite being the size of a house and very fit, they had decided he was too old to be crawling around behind enemy lines.

As he came along the passageway there was a distinct spring in his step and I could see that he was beaming.

'I'm off ashore tonight, Moggy,' he called to me. 'They are letting me go in at last!'

I was pleased he was going to get his chance to see action but I was also sad to see him go; he had a heart as big as a lion's. I promised to brief the rest of the pilots on the IPs we had selected and wished him all the best.

'Talk to you in the air,' he shouted over his shoulder as he headed off to pack his kit.

Later that evening the specials were airlifted by Sea King to various units of the amphibious force. Garth had stayed behind until the last minute and boarded the final helicopter together with twenty-six others. A few minutes later, as they approached *Intrepid*, both pilots heard a loud thump above their heads followed by an immediate loss of power.

The helicopter hit the sea hard, rolled over and floated inverted for a short period before slipping beneath the surface. Of the thirty men on board only nine survived; Garth, the gentle giant, was not one of them. It seemed so ironic that he perished before he had the opportunity to do the FAC job for which he was rightly famous.

The wardroom was a sombre place that evening as we silently raised our glasses to a wonderful man, a true professional and a great friend.

The following morning the boys of No. 1 got their chance at some action. It had been decided that the fuel drums I had found on the reconnaissance photos of Fox Bay were too tempting a target to ignore. Peter Squire led Jerry Pook and Bob Iveson in a three-ship attack with cluster bombs. They came in from the north-west in order to achieve maximum surprise, although we suggested that the main reason for this approach was the name of the two large hills there – The Bosoms!

Peter attacked first with his bombs causing a large number of secondary explosions among the fuel drums and jerrycans. The dump had been dispersed to make it difficult to attack with conventional bombs or guns but the BL755 was perfect for the job. Bob followed a few seconds later, and after he and Jerry had released their weapons on the target, the area was blanketed with explosions and burning fuel. It was a copybook attack and they swept away to the east without a single shot being fired at them.

I met them on their arrival and noticed how their demeanour had changed. Before the flight they had been subdued and serious but now their eyes were shining, they were laughing and joking with each other and revelling in the fact that they had survived their first proper mission over enemy territory. I guess we must have been the same on 1 May, after the raid on Stanley airfield. That seemed so long ago now. One phenomenon I had noticed was that I didn't seem quite as tired as I had been. A week previously I had been dead on my feet and hardly able to function. Now, although I was still feeling tired, I felt that I had reached a plateau and could probably continue at this pace for quite a long time.

That evening we were given the news that the landings were to take place the following morning. San Carlos Water had been chosen as the beachhead. This would mean the troops having to 'yomp' the sixty miles across East Falkland to Stanley but at least the anchorage was sheltered and unlikely to have been mined. We were fairly certain that the beaches around Stanley had been extensively mined.

Everyone was fairly introspective in the bar after sunset. We knew that the next few days would be of crucial importance and had no doubt that the Argentine forces would not let us land without some fierce reaction. If they could throw us back into the sea we would lose any chance of retaking the islands. Received wisdom is that an invasion force requires three times as many troops as the defenders to stand a chance of success. In our case the odds were very much the other way, which meant it was vital that the Harrier force played its part in keeping Argentine air power away from our troops as they consolidated their landings. We were sure that the next few days would see us involved in some heavy fighting and we were bound to start taking losses. We had to hit them hard and often but still try to protect our assets, for without the Sea Harriers the fight could not be won. That was a sobering thought. I found myself wondering not for the first time which of us would survive and who would not be going home.

20 May

846 Sea King found near Punta Arenas in Chile. Hopefully walking trees got to their destination. GR3s attacked fuel dump at Fox Bay – very good! We now have fifteen Sea Harriers and six GR3s.

Tomorrow is D-Day and will be very busy indeed. Hope it all goes well. I love you very much Carol, Charles and Elizabeth. Take care, I'll be with you come what may.

CHAPTER 7

#

OVERNIGHT, AS WE tried to sleep in anticipation of a very busy day ahead, the amphibious force closed the islands. The armada of assault ships, transports and supply ships steamed in close order, protected by their escorts, around the north coast and into Falkland Sound. The weather was perfect for the operation, with a strong north-westerly wind, a sea state of four to five and reduced visibility underneath a low overcast.

Shortly after midnight *Antrim* and *Ardent* broke away and took up positions from which they could bombard the entrance to San Carlos Water, and by the time we were at breakfast, some three hours before dawn, the ships were approaching their final run-in positions. There was a palpable feeling of tension in the wardroom that morning as we were acutely aware that the next few hours would be crucial to the success of our endeavours. If the Argentines were to attack now and disrupt the landings, there would be little we could do to help until dawn broke and the bad weather cleared.

We had also lost our goalkeeper, *Broadsword*, as it was essential to give the landing forces the best possible protection against air attack. I felt distinctly nervous that the only defences we now had against an Exocet attack were two ancient Seacat launchers and a couple of jury-rigged machine guns on the bridge wings. The test-firing of the Seacat, south of Ascension, had resulted in a rogue missile corkscrewing around the sky for a few seconds before hitting the water with a large splash a few hundred yards from the stern, not something designed to instil confidence in the watching ship's company.

All we could do while the drama was unfolding well to the west of us was to prepare for the day ahead. As the eastern sky began to lighten the first pilots manned their aircraft in order to be airborne as soon as it was daylight. The met man had given us the bad news that the overnight cloud cover had evaporated and the sky over the beachhead was crystal clear. We were sure it would not be long before the Argentines realised what we were attempting and would unleash the full fury of their air force.

As the grey light of the southern dawn started to spread across the islands, the assault ships *Fearless* and *Intrepid* had already managed to land many of their men and both marines and paratroops were moving out to occupy the higher ground around the bay. Amazingly there had been no resistance and it seemed that the tactic of sending in dummy raids to various locations around the coast had paid off.

San Carlos Water was a large, fishtail-shaped inlet running north-west to south-east surrounded by high ground which made the approach very difficult for attacking aircraft. It would have been an ideal killing ground however if Argentine forces had been present in any strength. As it transpired, only a small patrol had been in the area but they were able to inflict the first casualties of the land war. There was a brief skirmish between the patrol and British forces which resulted in the downing of two army Gazelle helicopters. These aircraft came down close to the shore and I was horrified to hear reports that the survivors had been machine-gunned in the water by the retreating Argentines. The reports also suggested that the patrol in question had been overrun, had refused to surrender and been wiped out. It was a salutary reminder of the horrors of war and I fervently hoped that such incidents would not become the norm. It might after all be me on the end of a parachute with a bunch of angry Argies below me. I could only hope that normal human behaviour would not be trampled too far into the dust of the conflict. We had already seen Argentine abuse of the red cross to protect blockade runners and ammunition stores. Would there be any further transgressions of the internationally accepted rules of this deadly game?

No. 1 (F) was in action shortly after dawn, with an attack on some helicopters which had been reported by an SAS patrol in the area of Mount Kent. These helicopters had been moved from the old Royal Marine barracks at Moody Brook as a result of the almost nightly bombardment of the area by naval gunnery. Jerry Pook and Mark Hare arrived just after first light to find a Chinook, two Pumas and a UH-1 Huey sitting on the ground. Neither pilot was able to carry out a successful attack on his first run but their subsequent runs left the Chinook and the Pumas burning fiercely. There were in fact over a dozen helicopters in the immediate area at the time they attacked, but the poor light conditions made them very difficult to see against the scrubby grass and heather of the hillside.

As Mark pulled off from his final attack he felt a large thud. On his return to *Hermes* he discovered that he had been hit three times by small arms fire. Luckily none of the damage was serious and the aircraft was repaired overnight and flying the following morning. It was a reminder of the dangers of re-attacks on an alerted target and an indication that small arms fire was still a significant hazard in the low-level environment. It also strengthened our desire to keep the Sea Harriers away from ground attack missions if at all possible.

Jerry and Mark were rightly pleased with their result; the destruction of three helicopters was a significant degradation of Argentine troop lift capability. If they were to be able to maintain their flexibility of movement, they would need to husband their 'helo' recourses.

This raid was but the start of a frantic day. Throughout the hours of daylight the Sea Harriers maintained CAP stations to the north and south of Falkland Sound as well as over West Falkland. It was imperative that we keep any attacking aircraft away from the beachhead until the amphibious force had been able to put their charges safely ashore. Equally, the troops on the ground were desperately vulnerable to attack before they had had time to dig in and consolidate their air defences. The chance of any of the ships picking up inbound raids on their radars was virtually nil because of the high surrounding ground. Likewise, the overland performance of the Blue Fox radar meant that we could see nothing if the enemy was at low level. The result was that we had to fall back on visual CAP techniques, which were hazardous at the best of times.

I flew one mission that morning, as Gordie's wingman. We were positioned to the southern end of the Sound and flew racetrack patterns in wide battle formation at 1500 feet. I felt incredibly vulnerable as we ploughed backwards and forwards across the water separating the two major islands. There was a partial covering of cloud at 2000 feet and had we flown any higher we would not have been able to sight any inbound raids. In addition, we had to fly far slower than we normally would, in order to stay the maximum time on station. We were both expecting to see enemy aircraft at any time and our height and speed would have put us at a potentially fatal disadvantage had they caught sight of us first. The most successful kills are those where the enemy knows nothing until his aircraft explodes around him. The unseen kill should be the primary aim of every fighter pilot and is dreaded by all. Our defensive tactics were designed to make it as difficult as possible for anyone to make an unseen approach but we were forced to compromise safety in order to stand the best chance of stopping any low-level raids.

Our trip nevertheless was completely uneventful, although we heard that ground troops had shot down a Pucara over the landings, so the Argies obviously knew we were there. The Pucara was a rather ungainly-looking ground attack aircraft, unique to the Argentine Air Force. It was powered by twin turboprop engines mounted on rather stubby wings, could carry a range of light bombs and rockets and was fitted with fuselage-mounted 20-millimetre cannon. This aircraft had been designed for use in the counter-insurgency role and was well suited to attacking lightly armed troops. It was highly manoeuvrable but lacked speed and proved very vulnerable to missile defences.

Capitan Benitez had taken off from Goose Green in search of helicopters bringing troops ashore, and after nearly an hour without finding a target stumbled across the British ships in San Carlos Water. As he set up his attack, he was hit by a Stinger shoulder-launched missile fired by a member of D Squadron, 22 SAS in a forward position. The aircraft continued to fly after the missile exploded but after a minute or so the controls began to fail and Benitez ejected at about 300 feet, just before impact, about a mile to the west of Flat Shanty Settlement. Luckily for him he was unhurt and able to escape on foot to the east, away from the landings, finally reaching Argentine lines some ten hours later.

As the morning progressed, a number of our ships took up position in Falkland Sound to provide a last-ditch defence against the air raids on the landings that would inevitably come. Admiral Woodward knew that he had to risk sacrificing some of his warships to protect the landings and I suspect that the crews of the ships concerned had no illusions as to their role and possible fate.

Shortly after 0900 local time a MB339 launched from Stanley to try to gather intelligence on the suspected landings. Teniente de Navio Crippa flew his small light-attack jet up towards Foul Bay and then turned south to run past San Carlos Water and Grantham Sound at low level. He immediately encountered the northernmost warships between Fanning Head and Jersey Point. He continued south and was about to carry out a passing guns attack on a Lynx helicopter when he noticed the frigate *Argonaut* beyond his intended target. His subsequent rather rushed cannon and rocket attack caused very minor damage and a few injuries among the ship's crew but drew considerable fire from the other warships in the area. He ran out to the south-east as low and as fast as he could, jinking to defeat the gunners' aim, and managed to dive behind a ridge of hills before he was hit. The intelligence he was able to report after his subsequent landing at Stanley confirmed that a major assault was in progress and this was not a further feint by the British forces.

Around half an hour before Crippa's attack a series of raids had been launched from mainland Argentina. Lacking Crippa's report, their intelligence was very sketchy. The objective of these flights of Daggers was to arrive in the target area in waves, with little time between each formation, in order to spread chaos among the British ships. They had no information as to the precise location or strength of their targets, only that they were in Falkland Sound.

The first wave of two aircraft arrived shortly before 0930 and ran into the Sound from the north-west. They were presented with a number of warships and selected *Antrim* as their target, attacking her from astern. They strafed the upper works with their 30-millimetre cannon and each dropped two 500-pound bombs fitted with delay fuses. The attack was over within seconds and both Daggers escaped south without being hit. *Antrim* had been caught unawares but escaped with superficial damage. It was now obvious to everyone, however, that the storm was about to break.

BACK ABOARD *HERMES* I had handed my aircraft over to the next pilot and it was being rapidly refuelled and brought back to Alert 5 status. I was just sitting down with a cup of coffee when I heard the pipe, 'Stand clear of jet pipes and intakes. Launch the Alert 5 Sea Harriers!' I ran up the ladders to Flyco and got there as the two SHARs started to taxi forward to the launch point.

Everyone in Flyco was pretty tight-lipped and in answer to my query I received a curt answer: 'Air raid ashore, Moggy.'

So, I thought. This is it. The waiting is over and the hot war has started.

As I stood there, the 'squawk box' from the ops room buzzed and the tinny voice called, 'Further raids ashore. Bring all available SHARs to Alert 5!'

With that I made my way quickly back to the briefing room, passing four pilots in the passageway as they made their way purposefully forward towards the flight deck, pulling on their life jackets as they went. I felt rather as if no one had invited me to the ball but I had had my turn and now I had to wait while the others had a go.

In the briefing room I met Bob Iveson, who was busy talking to ops. Jeff Glover was overdue from his very first mission and concern for his safety was rising fast. Jeff and Peter Squire had been due to launch at 0800 to provide close air support for the landings but the CO's aircraft had gone unserviceable and Jeff had continued on his own. As there were no targets for him in the San Carlos area, he had been tasked to carry out a reconnaissance of Port Howard some fifteen miles to the west. On his first run through the area of the settlement he saw nothing of note. He then cleared the area for some time before running through from a different direction to take another look. Nothing more had been heard from him since.

It had been stressed to me throughout my tactical training that re-attacks should never be carried out because the enemy would certainly be ready for you on the second pass even if they missed you the first time round. Jeff knew this as well as any of us but decided he could get away with it. Wrong! As he ran through for the second time a large number of Argentine soldiers opened fire on his aircraft. He was struck several times by small arms before finally being hit by a Blowpipe missile. The Harrier immediately rolled out of control as part of the wing detached and it was obvious to Jeff that he had to eject. With com-mendable presence of mind he waited until the aircraft had rolled through the inverted altitude and ejected so that he was fired away from the ground and not straight into it. Even so, local residents watched horrified as he hit the water of the creek next to the settlement with a partially deployed parachute. His aircraft crashed in a fireball and the Argentine garrison whooped with excitement and continued firing their weapons in the air in celebration.

Jeff lost consciousness as he hit the airflow on ejection and came to under water. He had lost his helmet and mask in the ejection and had suffered major injuries to his left arm and shoulder. He tried to swim the 200 metres to shore but realised that he hadn't released his parachute.

While he was trying to rid himself of his canopy, not an easy job with the use of only one arm, he saw a boat full of Argentine soldiers pulling towards him. The shock of the ejection at such high speed had made him forget to inflate his life jacket but luckily there was enough air inside his immersion suit to keep him afloat until the rowing boat got to him and pulled him to safety.

Back on *Hermes* we were completely oblivious to this drama but as time wore on it became obvious that Jeff would not be returning from his first mission. The Harrier has an automatic radio beacon that transmits an unmistakable signal on the international distress frequency when the ejection seat leaves the aircraft, but in this case the time between the seat firing and the airframe impacting the ground was so short that nothing was heard by any of the other aircraft in the area. We had to hope that he had survived but all the evidence pointed towards him having been shot down and killed.

SHORTLY AFTER 0930 the next wave of Daggers attacked the escorts in the Sound. Two formations each of three aircraft attacked in rapid succession, leaving *Broadsword* with some cannon damage and *Antrim* with several casualties from 30-millimetre splinters and an unexploded 1000-pound bomb in one of her heads. This bomb had been dropped by one of the final three attackers and had hit the stern, narrowly missing a live missile in the launcher before passing forward through a number of compartments including the Sea Slug missile magazine. *Antrim* was forced to seek shelter in San Carlos Water to effect essential repairs and to defuse the bomb. She had had a very lucky escape indeed; if the bomb had detonated in the magazine the ship would probably have been lost. As it was, her ability to fight had been severely affected and she was withdrawn from the amphibious operating area the following day.

Things were not all one-sided, however, as one Dagger in the first wave was hit by a missile before it could press home its attack. The aircraft broke up immediately and hit the water in full view of the rest of the attackers, killing the pilot instantly. *Antrim* had also caused the

Self-portrait of the author in the cockpit
of a Sea Harrier over the coast of North
Devon in 1983.

TOP Sea King helicopters and SHARs in their peacetime paint scheme on the deck of *Hermes* before sailing on 5 April 1982.

ABOVE Painting over the white areas on the SHAR paint scheme en-route to Ascension Island in early April 1982.

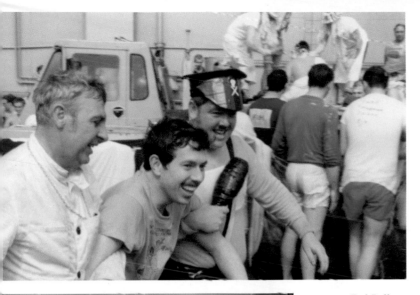

ABOVE Ted Ball being rounded up for a ducking during the 'crossing the line' ceremony, 15 April 1982.

LEFT The 'Heath Robinson' Chaff modification to the SHAR airbrake designed by Phil Hunt. This was very effective at confusing enemy radar and saved the lives of several pilots.

ABOVE The Control Tower at Stanley Airfield, which the author flew past at window height after being hit by anti-aircraft fire during the low-level attack on 1 May 1982.

RIGHT The author standing by the tail of his aircraft moments after landing from the first raid on Stanley Airfield. Some of the damage caused by ground fire can be seen on the starboard side of the fin. (Martin Cleaver, EMPICS)

TOP The Argentine intelligence gatherer *Narwal* after the attack by the author and Gordie Batt on 9 May 1982. Evidence of canon fire can be seen on the starboard side and the hole left by Gordie's bomb is evident on the port side of the forecastle. (MOD)

ABOVE The author with the wreckage of Puma AE-500, damaged by his attack at Shag Cove on 23 May 1982 and destroyed minutes later by Tim Gedge and Dave Braithwaite from *Invincible*.

Andy Auld, CO of 800 NAS, is chaired away from his
aircraft after downing two Daggers in a matter of seconds
on 24 May 1982.

ABOVE Fully armed
SHAR awaiting the
signal to launch from
the deck of *Hermes*
to carry out a CAP
mission at the height
of the conflict.

LEFT Bob Iveson in
the Wardroom bar on
30 May 1982, relating
the story of his escape
and survival after
being shot down over
Goose Green three
days earlier.

OPPOSITE ABOVE *Hermes* with a deck park of SHARs and GR3s towards the end of the conflict. (MOD)

OPPOSITE BELOW SHAR being refuelled at *Sheathbill* (San Carlos forward operating base) on 5 June 1982.

ABOVE *Hermes* in foggy weather on 3 June 1982 with the deck party taking advantage of the lull in flying to scrub greasy deposits off the flight deck.

ABOVE *Broadsword* manoeuvring astern of *Hermes* in heavy seas. The ship's 3-inch chaff rockets can be seen at the top of the picture.

OPPOSITE ABOVE The burning hulk of *Atlantic Conveyor* on 26 May 1982, the morning after being hit by an Exocet missile. (MOD)

OPPOSITE BELOW The wreckage of Peter Squire's GR3 after he lost power and crashed on the strip at *Sheathbill* on the afternoon of 8 June 1982. The aircraft rapidly became a source of spares for both GR3s and SHARs.

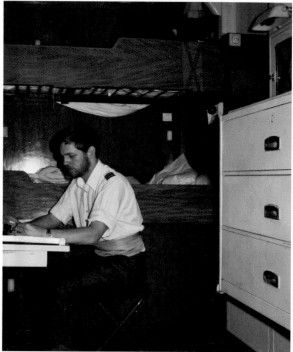

OPPOSITE ABOVE Squadron and ship's officers pose for a photo during the SHAR post-conflict party in Wardroom 2, on 9 July 1982.

OPPOSITE BELOW The author in his cabin on the way back from the South Atlantic. Access to these cabins was restricted during the conflict, due to the submarine threat.

ABOVE The author in piratical pose, showing the dubious results of the beard growing contest. (Fleet Air Arm Museum)

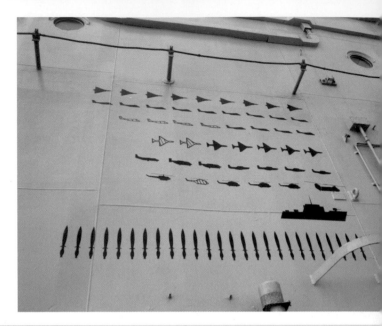

OPPOSITE ABOVE Tally of 'kills' and special forces operations painted on the side of *Hermes'* island.

OPPOSITE BELOW Armada of small ships laden with cheering crowds, escorting *Hermes* through the mouth of Portsmouth harbour on 21 July 1982.

ABOVE The author with his wife and children after receiving the Distinguished Service Cross from the Queen at Buckingham Palace on 14 December 1982.

The author with Hector Sanchez at their
first meeting in London in May 1993.

Argentines some confusion by firing a Sea Slug at low elevation towards the incoming fighters. This missile was a huge weapon, with four solid-propellant boosters which separated after a couple of seconds, leaving the ram jet in the main missile to continue the acceleration. There was no hope of hitting a target at such a level but the display of pyrotechnics and massive smoke cloud must have been very disconcerting for the Argentine pilots. This tactic was referred to as launching the missile in the GASH mode – short for Give Argies the shits! It was probably the best use that could be made of the obsolete system, which had been designed to counter Russian long-range bombers at high level.

As these attackers ran out to the south they came across *Ardent*, which was bombarding positions in the area of Goose Green. The warship immediately swung her 4.5-inch gun around to engage them and sent a Seacat missile skimming over the waves after them, but all to no avail. They had not quite escaped yet, however, as Fred Frederiksen and Martin Hale, manning a CAP station to the south, were rapidly vectored by the controller in *Brilliant* to cut off their escape.

With their bombs gone, the Daggers accelerated to maximum speed, leaving the SHARs with a nigh on impossible task. Fred and Martin picked them up visually as they ran down the eastern side of the Sound at very low level. Martin was closest and achieved good solid missile lock on the closest target. Unfortunately the Sea Harriers were being left behind by the faster Daggers and Martin was forced to fire at very long range. He watched with the utmost frustration as the Sidewinder fell short, despite homing beautifully. The pair continued the chase for a few miles to the west but gradually fell further behind until shortage of fuel forced them to pull up and return to *Hermes*.

While Fred and Martin were in pursuit of the Daggers a wave of Skyhawks from Grupo 5 at Rio Gallegos was approaching from the north. Six of these A4s ran in, in flights of three in quick succession, and found *Argonaut* off Fanning Head. Their attack was swift and well executed, and despite a fury of missiles and gunfire they succeeded in putting two 1000-pound bombs into their target. One bomb hit just above the waterline amidships, smashing its way through the boiler room, and the second penetrated several compartments before coming to rest in the forward Seacat magazine causing a small secondary explosion. Despite the fact that neither bomb exploded, severe damage had been caused to the ship's ability to fight. Her steering and engines were out of action and a number of serious fires were raging below deck. It was only the swift action of Sub Lieutenant Peter Morgan that saved the ship from running aground. When he saw what had happened he dashed onto the forecastle and released the anchor, bringing her to a halt. Later she was towed into the relative safety of San Carlos Water, where the fires were extinguished and the bombs defused.

On their return to *Hermes* Fred and Martin were both spitting blood over having been so close to achieving kills on the Daggers. Even worse, they might have intercepted the Skyhawks if they had not been vectored for the earlier raid. Such is the luck of war. The Argentines were either very lucky or had put a great deal of thought into the coordination of the missions to concentrate their assets.

I had just finished listening in to their debrief and was on my way for a bit of lunch when I heard the roar of a Pegasus as an aircraft came into the hover alongside followed by a whistling crescendo as it descended towards the deck and a whine as the throttle was closed on landing and it taxied into the graveyard. Two minutes later the sequence was repeated as the second Harrier landed. This time the engine noise ceased immediately, causing me to pause in the passageway.

'Crash on deck! Crash on deck! A Harrier has crashed in the port catwalk. Emergency parties close up!'

Oh bloody hell, what now? I thought as I ran around the corner and took the steps of the ladder up towards Flyco two at a time. A crash on deck is always very hazardous and has the potential to be an absolute disaster in wartime, with all sorts of weaponry stacked around the place. We had all seen the horrific footage of the disastrous fire aboard the USS *Forestall*, with live weapons cooking off all over the flight deck and aircraft exploding in huge fireballs.

I reached Flyco in about twenty seconds flat and looked out of the windows to see a GR3 leaning drunkenly to port with one outrigger in the catwalk some six feet below deck level. A number of yellow shirts were scurrying around fixing chain lashings to stabilise the aircraft and stop it going over the side of the ship. There seemed to be no actual damage to the airframe but I could see that the port wing was resting on the outboard weapons pylon, which still had a cluster bomb attached to it. The casing of the bomb was obviously distorted but seemed intact and a very concerned looking John Rochford was still sitting in the cockpit.

Once the aircraft had been secured, John very cautiously emerged from his cockpit and inspected the damage. He and Bomber Harris had spent the last hour searching unsuccessfully for Argentine troops around the beachhead and had brought their weapons back rather than jettison them in the sea. Bomber had recovered without incident but John had landed left of the centreline still drifting left and suddenly got that awful sinking feeling. I felt very sorry for him, as there were a number of comments about 'bloody crabs buggering up the deck'. Considering it was probably only the third time he had landed on a moving deck, I don't think he could be blamed. It was a very public debacle, however, and he was overheard later saying that he 'didn't want to be on this bloody rat-infested rust-bucket in any case'.

Within a few minutes all available hands had been mustered and the aircraft had been hoisted gently back onto all four wheels, apparently none the worse for wear. It was decided that the bomb was unfit for further work and it was lowered gingerly over the side of the ship to ensure that the casings did not open to release the dangerous bomblets inside. To have these rolling around on the flight deck would have certainly got people's attention; they looked quite innocuous, rather like cans of beans, but were extremely sensitive once armed.

AS THE DECK RETURNED to normal things were starting to develop ashore again. Shortly after 1000 a further two Pucaras were launched from Goose Green to search for British troops to the north of the airfield.

After a while they decided to look for targets of opportunity in the area of Grantham Sound. Here they encountered *Ardent*, which engaged them at long range with 4.5-inch gunfire. The pilots turned away to reposition, before running in again for a further, more determined attack. As this was developing, a three-ship formation of 801 NAS Sea Harriers was vectored into the fight by *Brilliant*. This flight consisted of Sharkey Ward, leading Lieutenant Steve Thomas and my old pal, Al Craig. They had been about to leave the area and return to *Invincible* when the raid had been discovered.

Steve was first to spot the Pucaras, from 15,000 feet through a gap in the cloud, and he and Al dived to engage them with guns. One Pucara escaped unseen and returned safely to Goose Green but the other, flown by Mayor Tomba, was not so lucky. Steve and Al both attacked but he was able to use the superior manoeuvrability of his little aircraft to avoid the high-speed SHARs. Sharkey's first attack was more measured and he managed to hit the Pucara on the left wing. Tomba kept flying as low as he could and was jinking hard as the three of them set up for further attacks. Sharkey slowed down and positioned for another pass. More portions of the airframe and canopy flew off as rounds tore into the Pucara and the port engine caught fire. A final, third pass left Tomba with no choice and he ejected a few seconds before his crippled aircraft hit the soft ground and skidded to a halt. After one swing on the parachute, he landed very close to the wreck of his machine and was able to watch as the three Sea Harriers climbed out to the east for their return to *Invincible*, landing very short of fuel.

Sharkey's tactic of slowing down to attack the Pucara was very high risk. The little aircraft had a very low wing loading and could turn very much better than the Sea Harrier. In July 1983 I carried out some air combat trials against a Pucara flown by test pilots from Boscombe Down and we proved that the aircraft was very vulnerable to the Sidewinder missile, even at very low level. This meant that attacks could be made without reducing speed and the missile fired from comparatively long range in perfect safety. Low-speed gun attacks were also evaluated and on the third such pass the Pucara managed to out-turn me and almost bring his guns to bear. An old lesson relearnt – speed is life! It is interesting that most SHAR pilots in 1982 preferred to use guns against a slow-moving target when a missile would actually have done the job quicker and with less danger.

The next cycle of CAPs passed without incident and the ships in the Sound began to relax a little. Aboard *Hermes* we had no illusions that this was anything but a lull before attacks restarted and everyone who launched was keyed up for a fight.

Shortly before midday *Ardent* was still in Grantham Sound. Captain Alan West was quietly pleased with the performance of his ship over the last few hours. They had fired hundreds of 4.5-inch rounds in the naval gunfire support role, together with five Seacats and a lot of 20-millimetre against Argentine air attacks. The air raid warning state had been reduced from red to yellow and his ship's company had been given the chance to have some 'action snacks'. All seemed to be going very well when they suddenly spotted a Skyhawk, very low and heading in their direction. There was no time to manoeuvre and only the 20-millimetre gun managed fire at the attacker before he dropped his weapons and egressed rapidly to the west.

Ardent had in fact been very lucky as Mula Flight had started off from Rio Gallegos with four Skyhawks, losing one when it was unable to refuel from a C-130 tanker and another which failed to transfer fuel from a drop tank. The third aircraft mistakenly attacked the *Rio Carcarana*, which had already been immobilised by Gordie and Andy McHarg five days earlier, and turned for home minutes before the attack.

Forty minutes earlier Neill Thomas and Mike Blissett had launched from *Hermes* and as soon as they called *Brilliant* for control, they were vectored after the retreating A4. They dived down into the mountains to the west of the Sound and to their amazement spotted not one retreating Skyhawk but a formation of four coasting in heading for the landings. This was a section of Grupo 4 aircraft, supposed to be the second element of a coordinated raid on the ships in the Sound following the unsuccessful attack made by the A4 that the SHARs had been vectored against. Mike saw them first and called a starboard break as they passed underneath the Sea Harriers, heading north-east. They obviously spotted the two 800 NAS aircraft and immediately started a break towards them, jettisoning their bombs and drop tanks.

Mike and Neill pulled hard right after the A4s and each achieved a good missile lock against the cool ground beneath the targets. Mike was first to fire and his Sidewinder initially dropped towards the ground before accelerating upwards after the target. He then was startled by the sight of a missile streaking past his left shoulder; Neill had also fired. Mike watched the second missile follow another of the Skyhawks, which had started to climb for a patch of blue sky ahead. This aircraft disappeared behind a cloud with the Sidewinder in hot pursuit. Suddenly, about 800 yards ahead of Mike, there was a fireball as his missile found its target. The A4 blew up in mid-air scattering debris over a wide area. Mike attempted to lock his second missile to another of the Grupo 4 Skyhawks but had his attention caught by something tumbling out of the sky to his left; it was Neill's target with the rear of its fuselage well ablaze. As that aircraft hit the ground with a huge explosion, Mike closed to guns range and fired several bursts of cannon at one of the remaining A4s. Both Sea Harriers were now very low on fuel and were forced to abandon the chase and pull up to high level for the transit back to *Hermes*. The third A4 was left trailing smoke but managed to make it back to base. Although we did not realise it at the time, one of the Argentine pilots had managed to escape from his doomed aircraft and was found dead months later, wrapped in his parachute with two broken legs and a last letter home in his lap.

Both Mike and Neill were highly excited when they landed back on board. Neill took his helmet off and gave us a huge grin. Mike was like a puppy with two tails and I swear that he bounced into the briefing room rather than walked. He was however rather upset at Neill for firing a missile past his left shoulder. Neill assured him that he had a clear shot on his target and all was forgiven. I just sat at the back of the room rather frustrated that all this action was going on and I was stuck on the ship.

Half an hour after Mike and Neill returned, it was the turn of Fred Frederiksen to launch again. It was policy to team junior pilots with one of the more experienced operators if at all possible and this time his wingman was Andy George, our youngest and most inexperienced pilot. Three quarters of an hour later the squawk box from ops buzzed and we were told, 'Red section is returning and they have got a Skyhawk.' A whoop went around the assembled pilots, followed by someone saying, 'Christ, I hope it's Fred and not Andy.'

They were right; if Andy had got a kill and Fred hadn't, there wouldn't be a debrief, there would be a bloody lynching! Fred was keener than anyone on the squadron to achieve a kill and would be immensely pissed off if the squadron baby had beaten him to it.

The whole of the flight deck was on tenterhooks as the two SHARs landed and taxied back into their parking slots to be tied down to the ringbolts in the deck. Once secure, the pilots shut down their engines and opened the canopies before climbing carefully onto the ladders clipped to the right side of the aircraft. One look at Fred's face as he climbed out of his cockpit was enough to reassure everyone; he was beaming fit to burst. He had got his kill!

It appeared that they had been vectored towards an inbound raid which had descended to low level to the west of Jason Island. Once *Brilliant* had lost them off radar, the SHARs were on their own but managed to spot them to the north of Chartres Settlement, heading north-east up a well-defined valley towards the landings. Fred had led the attack and fired a Sidewinder at one of the low-level targets as they wove their way up the valley looking for a way through the clouds that were now forming over the hills. The missile homed perfectly and exploded adjacent to the target's jet pipe, causing massive damage to the control surfaces and forcing the pilot, Primer Teniente Luna, to eject moments before his stricken jet crashed into the floor of the valley. He landed heavily, sustaining injuries to his arm and knee with large pieces of flaming debris from his aircraft raining down all around him. Both

Fred and Andy then carried out unsuccessful guns attacks on two of the remaining members of the formation before being forced to disengage because of their low fuel states.

Fred was quite sure he had engaged a formation of Skyhawks but post-war analysis showed that this was almost certainly a flight of Daggers from Rio Grande which was supposed to be coordinating its attack with similar aircraft from San Julian. The formation was aware one of their number had been lost but they assumed he had flown into the hills during the run-in. Amazingly they were also completely unaware of the subsequent guns attacks as they pressed on towards San Carlos. As they approached the Sound, they encountered *Ardent* and launched a well coordinated attack which resulted in her being severely damaged. The leader's 1000-pound bomb landed short and skipped into the stern while the second aircraft's weapon exploded on impact with the ship's hangar, destroying the Lynx helicopter and Seacat launcher and causing mayhem on the upper deck. *Ardent*'s luck had run out, and as her attackers left the area to the south she headed north-west to join the other warships off Fanning Head for protection.

A PATTERN WAS beginning to emerge, with concentrated waves of coordinated attacks attempting to confuse and overwhelm the British defences. So far the attackers had only attacked the warships in the Sound, exactly as Admiral Woodward had planned, but it was only a matter of time before they realised that the juiciest targets lay beyond, in the confines of San Carlos Water. They had the intelligence by the early hours of the afternoon and would have to act upon it rapidly if they were to inflict serious damage on the amphibious forces.

Less than ten minutes after *Ardent* had been attacked the first three Daggers from San Julian arrived on target and headed straight for the warships grouped near Fanning Head. None of their bombs caused any damage but *Brilliant* was hit by 30-millimetre cannon which penetrated the ops room from where the controller had been doing such sterling work vectoring the CAP aircraft against incoming raids. His information faltered for only as long as it took to wipe the blood off his radar screen and he was then back in business, vectoring the next 801 NAS pair of SHARs.

Sharkey was back in the air with Steve Thomas and they were covering the area to the west of Port Howard in an attempt to intercept any inbound raids. As the wounded controller in *Brilliant* was vectoring them, Steve picked up two Daggers running in head on to them. Ironically, it was the yellow identification stripes painted on their airframes to avoid 'blue on blue' engagements which made them visible against the patchwork of peat bog and scree below. The next couple of minutes was fast and furious as the Daggers dropped their under-wing stores and attempted to outmanoeuvre the Sea Harriers. They had been less than two minutes away from their targets but were now fighting for their lives. All three of the Argentine pilots broke to the south towards Sharkey, who passed head on to the only two he had seen. Steve was able to lock on to the rear man of the pair and release a missile in a perfect stern shot. The heat seeker had no trouble homing on to the afterburner of the fleeing Dagger and the warhead tore the back of the aircraft apart in a huge explosion. The pilot, Mayor Piuma, immediately ejected and his British-designed Martin-Baker seat deposited him none too gently on the surface of West Falkland. Meanwhile Steve had locked his second missile on to the next Dagger, which was now accelerating away to the south in full afterburner. He fired and watched as the lethal rocket chased the receding delta-wing fighter up towards the cloud in a right-hand turn. Both Steve and Sharkey saw the flash of the warhead as it detonated close to its target but neither actually saw the aircraft crash and it was only claimed as a possible until finally confirmed by post-conflict research.

After the initial head-on pass Sharkey had pulled hard right and found himself momentarily out of the fight. While trying to regain position he saw a further Dagger appear from underneath him and fired a missile at it from close range. There was no escape and the fighter blew up and tumbled to the ground. Unknown to Sharkey, this third aircraft had managed to fire a burst of cannon at him before being seen. Luck was on Sharkey's side that afternoon and he had escaped being hit, but he could easily have been a victim of the unseen kill that we all dreaded. This violent engagement had taken place over Green Hill Bridge a mere five miles from the landings, and the final Dagger had been shot down at 1350 local time, their exact time on target for Falkland Sound.

As the pair of SHARs turned south-east to return to the carrier they saw the next wave of attackers beginning their run towards *Ardent* in the Sound. They were too far away and too low on fuel to intercept and watched helplessly as three A4s ran in towards the smoking warship.

On *Ardent*'s bridge Alan West saw the approaching flight of grey naval Skyhawks as they ran up the Sound before wheeling around to attack his ship from the starboard side. In quick succession they released their 500-pound Snakeye bombs. These American weapons were designed for low-level release and had four high-drag plates which deployed after release, giving the bomb fuses time to arm before impact and slowing the weapons so that the aircraft could escape unharmed from the explosions and subsequent debris. The captain watched as the first stick of bombs arced inexorably towards his ship and was thrown to the deck by the huge explosion that told him that they had found their mark. He got to his feet just in time to see the second A4, flown by Teniente de Navio José Arca, running in to deliver his bombs.

John Leake, the civilian NAAFI manager, also saw the Skyhawk approaching and opened fire with his general purpose machine gun, which was now one of the few weapons that remained operational. He continued to fire as the aircraft flew overhead, just missing the mast, despite the fact that another three bombs were heading for the ship. Alan West saw a row of holes appear in the underside of a wing just seconds before another massive explosion rocked his ship. The third Skyhawk was less successful and all his bombs fell clear of the mortally wounded ship as the formation ran out to the south.

Twenty minutes earlier John Leeming had followed Clive Morrell into the air from the ski-jump on the front of *Hermes*. Their destination was a CAP station to the south of the Sound in the area of Swan Island. They heard reports of the attack and saw the explosions as they were letting down to the west of Goose Green. Clive guessed that the attackers would egress to the south-west and headed in that direction at full throttle, hoping to cut them off. A few seconds later he spotted a light grey aircraft through a gap in the clouds and dived down, followed by John, who had seen the enemy at almost the same time.

Clive rapidly overhauled the fleeing Skyhawk, not realising that in the heat of the moment he was attacking the lead aircraft of the formation. The rear Argentine saw him drop out of the clouds and called, 'Harrier! Harrier!' to alert his comrades. All three immediately dropped their tanks and bomb racks and went to full power to try to escape but Clive had already locked his missile and fired it with a massive overtake. The Sidewinder flew straight for the little grey jet and exploded right next to its jet pipe. Instantly the back of the aircraft started to disintegrate. In the cockpit Capitan de Corbeta Alberto Philippi felt the massive explosion and his aircraft pitched up violently. He tried to push the stick forward with both hands but was unable to control his crippled machine. He glanced to the right and saw a Sea Harrier closing rapidly. There was nothing for it; he called to his formation that he had been hit, closed the throttle, extended the airbrakes and pulled the bottom handle of his ejection seat. He heard the canopy detach, felt a huge bang as the seat fired followed by a sharp pain in his neck and then blacked out.

Clive did not see him eject as he swept past, intent on attacking the second aircraft, flown by Teniente Arca. He locked and fired his second Sidewinder but nothing happened: the missile hung up on the launcher. Clive closed rapidly, selected guns and fired all two hundred and forty rounds at the A4, which was now in a tight turn. He didn't see any hits, but as he was rapidly closing the range to his target his second Sidewinder decided to launch itself. He watched in amazement as the missile initially appeared to guide correctly but then seemed to lose lock and fall away harmlessly into the sea below.

Clive was now completely out of ammunition, and as he hauled his SHAR back towards the east he saw a fireball arcing down into the Sound. For one horrible moment he thought this might be his wing man but seconds later John called up on the radio, 'Spag, are you OK?' John had dived down onto the rearmost A4 but had been unable to fire his missiles. He selected guns and carried out a very fast attack from above and behind. Because of his high overtake speed, he found himself well inside the recommended minimum range for firing the Aden cannon. It had been calculated that the probability of self-damage from the exploding rounds, not to mention debris from the target, became unacceptable inside a range of 300 yards. John fired a short burst at about 500 yards followed by another a few seconds later which kicked up spray on the ocean some fifty feet below his target. He was still firing at a range of only 100 yards when he eventually hit the Skyhawk. He saw his rounds impact just aft of the cockpit before the whole aircraft disintegrated in a huge explosion. It is likely that the engine was hit, causing the aircraft literally to come apart in mid-air. John realised he had no option but to fly through the debris and automatically ducked and closed his eyes – not that that would have saved him. His last recollection before he closed his eyes was of seeing the Skyhawk's starboard wing detach from the fuselage directly in front of him.

A few seconds later he opened his eyes and could not believe he was still alive. Not only was he unharmed but it seemed his aircraft had survived as well. He quickly checked inside the cockpit for any indications of failure and cautiously tried out the controls but all seemed well. In fact, against all the odds he had come through the debris completely unscathed and his only concern now was to try to calm himself down sufficiently to carry out a vertical landing back on the ship.

Teniente de Fragata Marcelo Marquez died instantly in the hail of rounds from John's cannon. Alberto Philippi regained consciousness just before his parachute landed in the sea and was able to swim the hundred or so yards to the shore of the Sound. Once ashore, he dug himself a crude hole in the peat in an attempt to shelter from the bitingly cold wind and settled down to await rescue. He had been very lucky to survive the ejection with nothing more than a very sore back. The American-made ejection seat fitted to the Skyhawk was known by the US Marines as the 'Escapac Humane Killer' because of its habit of causing massive injuries during high-speed ejections. José Arca's troubles were not over. He had survived Clive's attack but his aircraft had been hit by a number of 30-millimetre rounds. In addition, John Leake's GPMG fire had punctured his fuel tanks and he did not have sufficient fuel to reach the C-130 tanker to the west of the islands, let alone get back to the mainland. He therefore decided to attempt a landing at Stanley airfield and headed east, astern of Clive and John as they climbed up to high level for the transit back to *Hermes*. On arrival over Stanley he had great difficulty talking to the tower but eventually received permission to land only to find out that his port undercarriage leg would not lower. This made what would have been a difficult landing an extremely hazardous undertaking and he wisely chose to carry out a controlled low-speed ejection over the sea. The ejection was successful and he was quickly picked up by an Argentine helicopter. His aircraft continued to fly and was eventually shot down by anti-aircraft fire, crashing to the south of the airfield.

ARDENT WAS NOW in a parlous state. Her stern had been severely damaged and although her engines were still functioning there was no way to steer the ship and she was heading towards one of the small islands that dotted the Sound. Alan West gave the order to stop engines and slip the anchor and the ship came to a halt. Fires raged out of control astern and an unexploded bomb was lodged in the after auxiliary machinery room. There was also uncontrolled flooding aft and the ship rapidly developed a substantial list. It very soon became obvious that the ship was dying and the order was given to abandon her. *Yarmouth* put her stern against *Ardent*'s bow and the surviving crew were able to step to safety, the captain being the last man to leave. The Argentine pilots had done their job well; it was subsequently discovered that no less than nine bombs had hit her, seven of which had exploded. As darkness settled over the Sound, she slipped beneath the water; we had lost our second warship.

BACK ON *HERMES* Clive and John walked into the briefing room, removed their life jackets and unzipped their immersion suits to let out some of the sweat. Even the taciturn Spag admitted that it had been a fairly exciting sortie, especially when he realised that he had dropped into the middle of a formation of enemy aircraft without knowing that there was someone behind him. We were all rather concerned about his missile hang-up. It seemed likely that there had been a problem with the thermal battery which initiates the whole launch sequence. If this battery had been slow in delivering the required voltage, it might have caused the fault. We never did get to the bottom of this failure but luckily it did not recur.

John was grinning like a Cheshire cat but was still not quite sure how he had survived his trip through the fireball, although he reckoned he had passed through the gap between the fuselage and the wing as they separated. What concerned us more was the fact that he had been unable to get any missile sighting information in his head-up display. He had snagged the system on his return and our weapons electrical experts were checking it out as a matter of priority.

Hermes and *Invincible* continued to launch pairs of aircraft for the next three hours but no further enemy aircraft were engaged. Three Skyhawks managed to break through the CAP cordon as Clive and John were in transit back to *Hermes* but failed to hit their targets. Neill Thomas and Mike Blissett were the last to land on, after dark at 1730 local time. I was just about to go aft for a shower when I got a call from maintenance control to say that they had run all the diagnostic tests available on John's aircraft and could not fault the system. It is always very unsatisfactory to have a 'No fault found' entry in the Form 700 so I dropped into John's cabin on my way to the wardroom and asked him to talk me through the problem as he had seen it.

'Well,' he said, 'I just couldn't get any missile symbology to come up in the HUD no matter what I did.'

'I know that this sounds silly,' I replied, 'but you did have the missiles selected, didn't you?'

John looked at me with a slight frown on his face and asked me what exactly I meant.

'The square button halfway down the panel behind the stick,' I explained.

'Oh, yes, the white one with AAM written on it,' said John.

'Yup, that's the one. And it goes green and says 'select' when you press it.'

John looked confused and then said, 'Oh shit. No one told me that you had to push the bloody button in.'

The problem was solved. There had been so little time to convert him from the GR3 that no one had given him a proper brief on the weapons system. I let the maintainers know and there was a certain amount of mirth at the 'bloody crab's' expense but they were glad they now had a serviceable aircraft for the next day's flying.

It had been a very busy day and everyone was shattered now that the adrenalin was wearing off. I went for my shower before heading to the bar. One of the luxuries of being on *Hermes* was the unlimited supply of boiling hot water. Not only did she produce steam for her engines, unlike the more modern ships which had gas turbines, but she also had redundant capacity from the original steam catapults which had been removed when she stopped operating Buccaneers and Sea Vixens. The only problem with the showers was that they didn't have thermostatic controls so whenever someone turned a tap on the temperature changed rapidly in all the other showers. It was therefore mandatory to call out, 'Turning on!' and, 'Turning off!' at the appropriate time to avoid shouts of anguish from fellow bathers and a chorus of 'Bloody crabs!' The temperature of the water could also vary if the ship rolled violently. This normally resulted in a series of yells followed by a dozen or so half-soaped bodies leaping out of the showers. Despite these tribulations there was something very therapeutic about a good soak in the shower.

I then joined the others in the bar and we conducted a detailed debrief of the day's action. Those who had been involved in the various engagements described them to the rest of us and we attempted to tease out any lessons which might help keep us alive in the days to come. It was clear that the enemy were attempting to coordinate their attacks on our shipping. It was also clear that either their intelligence or their planning was faulty. They had failed to hit any of the amphibious group in San Carlos Water, concentrating instead on the warships in the Sound. *Ardent* had sunk and *Argonaut* had been towed into the relative safety of the anchorage with two unexploded 1000-pound bombs lodged in her vitals. There had been considerable loss of life on the ships but they had done their job of diverting attacks from the landings.

We had acquitted ourselves well in the air but we had had some luck. The only ships with viable radar over land were the Type 22 frigates. The Controller on *Brilliant* had done a first-class job but even so had only been able to give a minute or two's warning of incoming raids. The Argentine attackers were not flying in classic defensive formations as they approached their targets, which made them more vulnerable to attack but also made it very difficult for us to be sure that we had the whole of the formation in sight. This had resulted in two cases of Sea Harriers ending up in the middle of an enemy formation. It did not seem as if the Daggers or the A4s were carrying missiles for self-defence and we had to hope that this would continue. If they started putting missile-armed aircraft among their attack formations we would have to be very careful indeed. We did not have enough aircraft to cover the beachhead properly as it was and could not afford to lose any to enemy action.

I realised that we would have to adopt some pretty risky tactics if we were to stop the inbound raids before they reached their targets. Normally we would not commit to an attack until we had sorted out the enemy formation and were in a position to take shots without being threatened, but the rules of the game had changed here. We would have to attack immediately and hope that we didn't expose our arses too much.

One piece of news which cheered us up a lot was that there were indications Jeff Glover may have survived and been captured. No one knew how we had got this information but in such cases you didn't ask questions. I suspected we had contact with some of the islanders or were monitoring the Argentine radio frequencies. I knew we had a number of Spanish-speaking radio operators who were very secretive about their duties onboard.

I finished my second beer as the steward behind the bar was stencilling the day's kills onto the wall and made my way up to 3 Deck and aft, through the watertight door to the quarterdeck. I stood for a while staring out into the slightly phosphorescent wake – no moon, no stars, the only light the dull red glow of the man-overboard sentry's cigarette. A taut cable stretched off into the darkness, attached to the Type 182 noise maker. This torpedo-shaped decoy made a noise similar to but louder than the ship's propellers, the idea being that any homing torpedo would hit the decoy rather than the ship. *Glasgow* had been saved from a very embarrassing incident a few days earlier when she had attacked what she thought was an Argentine submarine. One of her Mark 44 torpedoes had hit the target and detonated but all that came to the surface were pieces of blood-covered blubber. The second torpedo had continued to run and had homed onto her own noise maker, taking it out with a very large explosion. Had she not had the decoy deployed, she might have sunk herself.

It was quiet, even peaceful on the quarterdeck; the scrubbed mahogany planking vibrated gently in sympathy with the twin screws and the restless ocean slipped past with a gentle sigh on either side of the stern. There was only the smallest pitching and rolling motion as the ship made her way through the waves. War could have been a thousand miles away – or it could be lurking a few hundred yards astern in the form of a *Salta*-class submarine.

It was difficult to think further ahead than the next morning. We had been lucky today but tomorrow everything might change. At least we had shown that we were capable of giving the Argies a bloody nose. God knows what would happen in the morning; the weather forecast was fairly good, which could mean a lot more trade for the SHAR force. On the other hand the Argentines had taken quite a few losses in the Sound, which might make them a little more circumspect. I just hoped that they did not come to the same conclusions as us and make it a priority to engage us in combat. If they targeted us we would start to lose aircraft. If we lost more than a few we would lose control of the airspace over the islands. If that happened we would lose the war.

As I ruminated in the dark an empty *Canberra* slipped silently out of San Carlos. Over 3000 troops and most of their stores had been landed in less than twenty-four hours and the beachhead was becoming more secure by the hour. The most critical phase of the operation was over but there was still a long way to go before we could relax.

21 May

D-Day! Amphibious forces landed overnight and were well established by morning. 1(F) hit a Chinook and two Pumas soon after dawn in the area of Mount Kent and Mark Hare took three 7.62 rounds through the intake, gun and wing, but aircraft is OK. Jeff Glover was shot down on first sortie A.M. (possibly captured). A busy day in the air as we were flying CAPs over the ships in Falkland Sound.

Kills: Spag, 1+1? Lems 1, Neill 1, Mike Blissett 1+1? Fred 1. All A4s. 801 also got 2 Mirage + 1 Pucara. Special forces: 1 Pucara.

Ships: 1 Mirage and 2 A4?

Total losses: 17 plus 3 possibles for the loss of 1 GR3 and 2 Gazelles.

Two AIM-9Ls didn't fire properly. *Ardent* hit badly; later sank.

TOMORROW WILL BE A GOOD DAY TO TAKE CARE!

CHAPTER 8

ENGAGEMENT AT SHAG COVE

THE FOLLOWING DAY was an amazing contrast with the previous gruelling twenty-four hours. We were expecting more waves of air attacks on the beachhead and the first CAP missions were in the air as dawn broke, braced for the worst.

The first Sea Harriers to reach the islands were flown by Fred Frederiksen and Martin Hale. As they passed over Choiseul Sound they spotted the wake of a small vessel as it headed up the exposed stretch of water towards Goose Green. They ascertained from the controller that there were no friendly ships in the area and then attacked using their Aden cannon. Multiple hits were seen and their target, the patrol boat *Rio Iguazu*, was later beached on the north coast of the Sound, near Bluff Creek House. It had been delivering food and ammunition to the Goose Green garrison, together with vital spares for the Pucaras based at the grass strip to the west of the settlement.

Fred and Martin returned to *Hermes* in high spirits. Martin's beard had grown very well over the previous three weeks and he looked extremely piratical as he swaggered into the briefing room with a large smile on his face. Fred was no less pleased with himself as he hung his Mae West on the hook, squeezed himself out of the top half of his immersion suit and headed off for a well-earned cup of coffee and a burger.

The crew of the *Rio Iguazu* abandoned their vessel, which was later found by British forces during their march towards Stanley. Work was commenced to make the patrol boat seaworthy for British use but on 13 June a Lynx from *Penelope* attacked her with a Sea Skua missile and destroyed her, an unfortunate case of lack of communication.

I flew two CAP missions on the 22nd, as Andy Auld's wingman. On the first mission we were capping to the south of Falkland Sound when I heard a PLB transmission on the International Guard frequency of 243.0 megahertz. The personal locator beacon was a small radio transmitter, slightly larger than a packet of cigarettes, located in the left-hand pocket of the Mae West. It transmitted an automatic tone to enable a helicopter to home onto it or could be used to transmit a voice signal to communicate directly with other aircraft. The signal I picked up was the mewing sound of the automatically generated tone. I had no means of homing onto it but by flying first north and then south and plotting where I lost the signal I was able to ascertain that the transmission was coming from somewhere in the area of Port Howard. This was where we suspected Jeff Glover had been shot down the previous day.

My heart leapt! Perhaps Jeff was alive and still free, surviving in the sparse cover of the surrounding hills. I switched to Guard and called, 'Green 2, Green 2, this is Tartan. Come up on Guard if you read me!'

I hoped that he might switch to receive if he heard the unmistakable noise of a Harrier in the area but after a couple of calls it was obvious he was not going to answer me. I told our controller of my suspicions and a Sea King was later sent to investigate. The pilot approached the area with great care, using the coastal hills as cover. He picked up the transmissions and used his UHF homer to confirm that they were in fact emanating from the direction of the settlement. As he cautiously approached the crest of the hills to the east of Port Howard, he saw a large plume of smoke ahead of him and just had time to duck back out of sight as a Blowpipe missile streaked over the top of his rotor disc. The

PLB transmissions had been a trap set by Argentine troops to lure another aircraft into range and it had very nearly worked.

This news depressed me profoundly. Perhaps Jeff was dead after all; either way, his survival kit was certainly in the hands of the enemy and they seemed quite willing to take advantage of it.

Unknown to us, the weather over mainland Argentina remained extremely poor virtually all day and it was not until last light that a pair of Skyhawks managed to get through to the islands. They made a low, fast run through San Carlos Water but failed to hit any of the ships before disappearing over the surrounding hills, followed by ribbons of anti-aircraft fire and missile trails.

Brian Hanrahan and his team had gone inshore with the amphibious forces on the night before D-Day. We had sent them off with a last pint of CSB, a handshake and our sincerest best wishes. Neither they nor us knew what lay ahead and although we had only known them for a few weeks I felt we were losing three friends. The bonhomie on both sides disguised the feelings that no one wished to put into words. Would we meet again? Would we all survive?

Behind the quips of 'See you in Stanley, you old fart!' and 'Leave a couple of sheep for me!' was a genuine affection bred from exposure to a common danger. We were not to see them again for many weeks but each report broadcast on the World Service served as a link between us. It was with even more interest than usual then that we gathered around the speakers in the wardroom that evening to hear Brian's first report from the beachhead, which described the previous day.

It was a brilliantly clear dawn. A beautiful day, a clear one. Clear enough to see the troops climbing up the hillside as they secured the beachhead. Clear enough to see the first settlement to fall back under the British umbrella, their white cottages tucked into the rolling pastures where the sheep were grazing. But it was clear too for the enemy aircraft that came to find the fleet and attack it.

The air attack started an hour after dawn and has continued

right through the day until now. First came the small Pucara bombers' ground attack. Low and surprising. One of them got right into the bay to drop its bombs, but without success. For a few moments the air was full of missiles as the defending ships fired back. I saw one Pucara making off over a hill with a missile chasing it. The captain saw a flash in the sky and debris tumbling down. That set the pattern for the rest of the day. Wave after wave of air attacks came against the fleet. First they had to fight or outwit the Harriers that were between them and the islands. Then they had to go through the task force frigates and destroyers, which were deployed to put up a missile stream, but still some of the attacking planes got through to where we were anchored.

This morning, for example, two Mirages came sweeping down across the bay. We didn't see them at first. We saw the red wake of the anti-aircraft missiles rushing out to meet them. Then there was the roar of their engines, the explosions of bombs, missiles, everybody firing together. One stray missile went off in the air about 100 yards away. Two bombs exploded harmlessly in the hilltops as the planes curved away, diving back where they had come from.

But much of the fighting didn't take place in the bay where we were. It was out in the channel outside. We could see the smoke rising over the hills that cut us off. Three of the ships out there were hit by guns or bombs. Two suffered serious damage but it's not yet clear what the casualties were. The Argentine forces too were suffering losses. The garrison here was cut off. Some, we think, were killed and others surrendered. Then we heard of two Mirages that had been shot down, then another two, a Pucara, a Skyhawk. Another Skyhawk.

As the day went on, more of the attacks came from the Skyhawk fighter-bombers. In one short period, ten or a dozen of them dived down on the ships at anchor, producing the same barrage of fire and counterfire. This time there was a new element.

The anti-aircraft batteries on the shore joined in. Slowly a defensive screen was being built over the bay and the worst period of our vulnerability was over. Throughout the day, beneath the air attacks, the helicopters kept on flying. They stayed below radar range. They left the air above clear for the missiles. But they went on ferrying in men and machinery and all the equipment that the troops need to build a secure beachhead. They also brought in, most urgently of all, the anti-aircraft batteries that are being built on the shores alongside us to secure the beachhead and make it safe for all the troops to move through in their bid to recapture the Falkland Islands.

It was somehow comforting to hear Brian's voice coming over the static of the long-wave radio. His report conveyed the urgency and the terrible importance of the desperate endeavour that we had undertaken. There could be no turning back now; the die was well and truly cast and victory was the only option. The cost of the victory was something which would only become apparent as the conflict progressed but I think we all realised that the quiet of that Saturday was not likely to last unless we had grossly underestimated the will of the Argentine forces.

My thoughts were interrupted by a pipe over the ship's broadcast: 'Do you hear there? Mail. Mail will be leaving the ship at 1100Z tomorrow morning. I say again, mail will be leaving the ship at 1100Z tomorrow morning. That is all.'

HMS *Hermes*
22 May

Hello, love
By the time you get this I expect that we will have our cottage! You seem to be doing a grand job with all the odds and sods and finances. If it will make it any easier, I enclose a cheque so you can get my money into your account. I don't know how much I have got but you can give them a cheque if this is too much. (Does that make sense?) The new addition to the family sounds super, even if

he does chew and shag everything in sight! (And smell!) I'm looking forward to meeting him. I am glad that the cat seems to be coming round and I hope he takes to me and doesn't object to another vasectomised male in the house!

Life here is far from boring, as you will know. Yesterday we got fourteen kills (plus three probables) for one GR3. Not bad odds and the GR3 pilot is possibly a POW. Can't talk about the war because there has been a purge on information getting out but we are not having too much trouble and you will have seen the news anyway. John Leeming has joined us, as have a few other old friends, Syd Morris, Bob Iveson, Jerry Pook, Pete Squire, etc. The weather alternates between fog and brilliant sunshine.

I've had letters from your parents, my father, Sue Smith, Carole and Campbell Bosanquet, Fop, Mike and Lorna, Julia and of course Antje. I've actually done very well. Letters are taking between two and three weeks to get here. The trouble is we only have a couple of hours to get mail off the ship usually; hence the rapid scrawl. It seems a little pointless writing letters when you know they won't go for ages.

I miss you a hell of a lot, you know. I am not afraid anymore but I wish I were back home (either one!) with you and the kids and the cat and dog and goldfish and tadpoles and everything.

By the way, if you don't want the tri-wall boxes, you can collapse them or if they take up too much room, hand them back to stores or give them away, unless you can store them in the farm buildings. If the worst comes to the worst, burn the bloody things!

Well, it's 11.30 so I'd better go to bed. Take care of yourself. I love you very much.

D

Inside the envelope I also placed a couple of short notes to my kids. It was very difficult to decide what to write, or to know how much they knew or understood about the war their dad was fighting on the other side of the world.

Dear Charles,

Thank you very much for your letters, your writing is very good
now isn't it. Beauchamp sounds a super dog, you were very clever
to choose him. I am looking forward to seeing him when I get
home.

I don't think the Argentine planes are very good because we
have shot down lots of them, so you needn't worry.

Give Mummy and Elizabeth a kiss for me.

Lots of love
Daddy

Dear Elizabeth,

How is my favourite daughter? I hope you and Charles have been
good. Is the weather getting warmer yet? I expect you will be able
to plant some seeds soon. The weather here is not very good. It is
quite cold and has been foggy for a few days.

The Falkland Islands are funny. There are no trees there at all
and only a few bushes called Diddle-Dee bushes. There are
thousands of sheep and wild cows, though, and lots of seals.

Look after everyone until I get home, including Tammy and
Hazey.

Lots of love
Daddy

The morning of 23 May dawned grey and overcast with regular heavy
showers sweeping across the bleak landscape of the Falkland Islands,
making the flight deck of HMS *Hermes* a colder and even more inhospitable place than normal. In the relative comfort of the briefing room,
I shoehorned myself into my 'goon suit', collected my favourite pistol,
loaded it with a magazine containing eleven rounds and placed it in the
leather shoulder holster which sat snug beneath the left side of my Mae
West. After a quick briefing from Gordie I followed him along the 2 Deck
passageway, mingling with the stream of people on their way to early

morning action stations, and up the steel ladders to the island. We checked the servicing records of our respective aircraft, signed for them and made our way through the dull red glow of the night lighting to the watertight door and out onto the flight deck. The cold steel of the deck was slick with rain and salt spray despite the layers of abrasive anti-skid paint, which was now beginning to peel off in places not able to survive the constant hammering from the foul weather and the red-hot blast of the Harrier engines. I inspected the outside of my aircraft carefully using the dim light of my hand-held torch.

I paid particular attention to the two Sidewinders sitting inert on their launchers on the outboard pylons. I checked the umbilical cord was connected to the front of each launcher and re-latched the cover. Underneath the protective noddy caps lay the smooth, translucent lens of the seeker head, for all the world like a large opal, some three inches in diameter. Inside, the highly sensitive rotating seeker lay dormant, awaiting the spark of electrical life from the aircraft to accelerate to its operational speed and allow it to search the skies for a target. Behind the seeker head was the laser fuse unit, with the pairs of small round windows arranged to form a circle of laser energy that would sense the first piece of target within its range and detonate the fearsome warhead, no matter from which direction the missile was approaching. The older versions of the missile used an infrared fusing system, which meant that the warhead detonation would only be successful if the weapon was fired from behind the target. We had been running desperately short of the newer Lima version of these missiles until a visit from a long-range Hercules transport a few days previously. From the back of this aircraft had dropped several boxes of missiles addressed to 'United States Air Force Europe – BITBURG'. This had been hurriedly crossed out in chinagraph pencil and replaced with 'HERMES – SOUTH ATLANTIC'. We were very grateful to the Americans and to those who had arranged the transfer of these state-of-the-art missiles as it gave us a true head-on capability against any target. Gordie Batt had briefed us on its capabilities on the way down to the Falklands and had informed us that the seeker head was so sensitive it would take out an Argie soup kitchen at two miles.

Years later I was on a training flight from Yeovilton, around the Welsh valleys and back to base. I was carrying a brand new AIM9-L training head on an inert missile and was letting it gently search in a circular pattern as I flew along at low level, admiring the late-summer evening. As I flew across the Bristol Channel the missile began to growl every time it passed the lowest part of its scan. Out of curiosity I pressed the lock button and the head immediately locked to a target in the haze ahead and started to chirp urgently, indicating that it had a valid launch solution. As I approached Newport I realised that the lock diamond was sitting solidly over a railway wagon, and as I overflew it I saw that it was full of newly rolled plates from the steel works. This was impressive enough but a few miles on the seeker locked onto a plume of smoke from someone's bonfire in a back garden. The most amazing lock came thirty minutes later as I ran across Exmoor at 250 feet. The missile locked to a patch of ground about a mile ahead of me and held until I flew right overhead. I was unable to see what had attracted the lock until I was right on top of the target. As I flashed over it, I realised that the missile had picked up a pile of manure. Quite a weapon that could lock onto a steaming dung heap!

Back on *Hermes*, at the rear of the weapon I checked that the coolant pressure was in the green band and that the gyroscopic rollers were all free to rotate in their respective stabilising surfaces, which were, in turn, held fast in the rear fins. This just left the safety pin with its large red 'REMOVE BEFORE FLIGHT' flag to be removed by the ground crew.

I crouched underneath the fuselage, my feet in the greasy puddles of water swilling around the main wheels, and checked that both Aden cannons were loaded, that the electrical connecters were secure and the access hatch closed. Finally, I pushed my finger through the small spring-loaded hatch at the rear of the gun, to locate the tiny metal pin which told me that there was a round in the breech ready to fire.

All seemed well with both airframe and weapons so I climbed cautiously up the slippery ladder and over the canopy rails into the cockpit. There, in the grey pre-dawn light, I settled myself into the comforting shape of the Martin-Baker seat and immersed myself in the well-practised routine of preparing for flight. First, I connected the lanyard which attached my Mae West to the seat pack dinghy, next I pushed home the large green connecter that dangled at my left-hand side and carried my oxygen supply, R/T connections and compressed air for the G suit. Once I had felt the reassuring click from the left side of the seat, I strapped myself in, lap straps first, followed by the negative G strap between my legs and finally the shoulder straps, which were handed to me by the maintainer standing on the ladder. When securely in, I took my helmet from the top of the ladder, eased it over my head, settling my ears snugly into the ear capsules, and connected my oxygen mask, letting it hang from the left-hand hook on my helmet.

As the ladder was removed and I started carrying out the familiar pre-start checks I was aware that all the external tensions were fading to be replaced by a single imperative, to be as efficient a killing machine as was humanly possible. The training I had received over the years had obviously worked and I melded into the aircraft as if we were one combined entity, a mechanical dragon with a human brain, ready for anything and supremely confident.

We started engines as the first streaks of dawn appeared in the eastern sky and I was soon following a few seconds behind Gordie as he accelerated up the ramp in a cloud of spray and clawed for airspeed in a ballistic curve that achieved normal flying speed just before he started to sink towards the sea. As I left the ramp he jinked to the right and reversed left to pick up formation as we headed off towards the islands in silence, both of us dousing our external lights and carrying out our airborne weapons checks in preparation for the unknown that awaited us beyond the horizon.

Our brief was to man a CAP to the south of Falkland Sound, and as we climbed up to 35,000 feet for the transit the shadows of our aircraft flitted across the layers of cloud in front of us. I was struck once again by the perfect circular rainbows which followed each shadow, an aura of peace and beauty around messengers of death and destruction.

It seemed that our luck had held so far and none of the amphibious ships had been hit in San Carlos Water, although several of the warships were *hors de combat* after the pasting they had received two days previously and the carriers were now standing off well to the east of the islands to reduce the likelihood of an Exocet attack by the Super Etendards. While I was very happy to keep my bunk out of range of the enemy, the positioning of the fleet did mean that our time on task was limited due to the increased transit. That morning it took us nearly twenty-five minutes to reach our destination and left us very little time on CAP.

That first sortie was entirely uneventful, although unnerving as we were forced once again to fly our patrol below the 500-foot cloud base in poor visibility and at low speed to economise on fuel. I knew that Gordie was as uncomfortable as I was about our vulnerability, with his eyes constantly straining and his senses ready for instant action should we see a bogey in the mist. We were both relieved when the time came to climb above the murk and head home into the early morning sun.

As the sun approached its zenith the weather changed dramatically, leaving the islands bathed in bright sunshine with only small amounts of cumulus cloud scattered here and there in east–west lines. My wingman for the second sortie of the day was John Leeming, fired up after his Skyhawk kill two days previously. This time we made sure we both knew who was leader of the formation so that we didn't repeat the embarrassment of our last trip together. We departed in radio silence and checked the functioning of our Sidewinders once we were well clear of the ships. John came up alongside and gave me a very definite thumbs-up to indicate that he had actually selected his missiles properly. I smiled quietly to myself; that was one mistake he would not repeat!

As we flew over Port Stanley on the way to our CAP station we were greeted by a barrage of anti-aircraft fire despite the fact that we were well above 30,000 feet. The Argentine 35-millimetre guns were not very accurate at this height and although the black mushrooms of their explosions looked rather frightening as they burst all around us, a gentle weave was all that was required to avoid them. In the distance we could see the silver specks of the ships in San Carlos Water and the toy-like outlines of Pucara attack aircraft on the grass strip at Goose Green. Once past the Goose Green defences, we let down to 8000 feet and set up our patrol on a north–south axis over the Hornby Mountains, which rose majestically up to over 2000 feet to the west of Falkland Sound. Our mission was to intercept any aircraft flying through the valleys to attack the landings. The Blue Fox radar was about as much use over land as a spare prick at a wedding, so we had to guess where the enemy would come from and put ourselves in a position to acquire them visually and engage them before they could reach their targets.

Flying a medium-level patrol is more relaxing than being at low level because it is easier to be sure that you and your wingman are not being threatened by a bogey. It also gives you the opportunity to accelerate rapidly as you dive onto the tail of a low-level raider and get a missile in the air before you are seen. What we did not realise as we cruised back and forth, searching the rolling scree and peat bog for telltale flashes of movement, was that the enemy were not aware of the change in the weather and would not be airborne for another couple of hours. The director controlling us asked us to confirm our position from time to time and it was obvious that he like us felt that things were too quiet to last. He could not use his ship's radar because of the surrounding hills and was relying on us to pick up and report any raids as they crossed the mountains. This would give our ships a maximum of three minutes' warning of attack. Sooner them than us! There was considerable empathy between us and we were very conscious of being the only ones standing between him and an enemy air raid.

Unknown to us, although the Argentine fighters were not airborne, there was indeed some air activity and it was heading in our direction. A formation of three Argentine Puma helicopters belonging to CAB601 had set off the previous evening to transport a vital cargo of Blowpipe anti-aircraft missiles and mortar ammunition from Stanley to Port Howard. They had turned back in Falkland Sound when they stumbled across an unidentified ship in poor weather and spent the night at Goose Green. This ship was in fact the hulk of the *Rio Carcarana*, now lying damaged and abandoned in Port King after the Sea Harrier attack a week earlier.

The following day, after the weather had improved, they set off once more for Port Howard. Because of the importance of their cargo the lead Puma had the company commander on board and they were escorted by an Augusta 109A gunship flown by the deputy commander. The Augusta 109A was a fast and very manoeuvrable helicopter which carried two pods of 2.75-inch rockets and a couple of forward-firing machine guns. This aircraft could have made life quite embarrassing for us in the right hands. Any fighter pilot shot down by a helicopter would never be able to hold his head up in a bar again. This formation crossed the Sound from Goose Green to Shag Cove and had just turned onto a northerly heading, with only about five minutes to go to its destination, when the Argentines' luck changed abruptly.

John and I had just completed a turn at the southern end of the CAP and were cruising slowly towards Port Howard when a movement caught my eye – a mechanical movement quite alien to the snipe-rich bogs and barren escarpments – the flash of sun on a helicopter rotor disc. There, a couple of miles south of me was a helicopter skimming over a small inlet a few feet above the glassy water! I yelled a warning to John, 'Helicopter over the lake below me! Going down!' and asked the controlling ship to confirm that there were no friendlies in the area.

I slammed the throttle open, rolled onto my back and pulled the aircraft into a steep dive towards the ground. The controller replied, 'Ah, stand by. I'll just check on friendlies.' But I realised that there was no time to wait. If this helicopter was Argentine and he knew how to evade a fighter, I would have to nail him fast before he managed to hide. He had already committed a cardinal sin. Something drummed into me when I was flying helicopters was never, *never* fly over water at low level. If you have to cross a water feature, then find another route. The shape of the fuselage and the movement of the blades stand out like nipples in a wet T-shirt. Even the downdraught from the rotors can leave a 'snail trail' across a calm lake which can be seen for miles. The camouflaged helicopter was now again almost impossible to see against the patchy green-brown of the valley floor and I knew that if I lost sight of him I might well not be able to find him again.

I dived down in a hard left-hand turn, head back, straining to keep my eyes on the target and grunting to counter the effects of the G force, which was trying to pull all the blood away from my brain. I had decided to dispense with the cumbersome G suit in the interests of comfort but now wondered whether that had been a hasty decision. I levelled out fifty feet above the ground and pegged the throttle to give me 450 knots. This was just about the best turning speed for the aircraft and gave a steady weapons platform. I instinctively positioned myself to the north of the target so that he would have to squint into the midday sun, and ran head on towards him in an attempt to identify the type of helicopter. I checked the gunsight depression was at fifteen mills for air-to-ground firing and made doubly sure that the master switches were on. Adrenalin pumped as the distance between us closed rapidly until at a range of about 500 yards I realised from the outline of the fuselage that it was a Puma and therefore had to be an Argentine.

I yelled, 'Hostile, hostile!' over the radio and John replied, 'Visual and I've got three more in line astern! Engaging the gunship!' Beyond my target I saw John's SHAR diving down towards the hills, a trail of black smoke streaming out behind him.

By this time I was too close to bring my weapons to bear on the Puma; it was inside minimum missile range and I could not depress my gunsight enough to strafe it without hitting the ground myself. Instead, I flew straight at it, passing as low as I dared over its rotor head. Just before I passed overhead I was aware of two white faces in the cockpit looking up at me. I passed about ten feet above the enemy and pulled the Harrier into a screaming five-G break, up and left, in order to fly a dumb-bell back towards it for a guns attack. I strained my head back and to the left under the crushing pressure of the G forces and saw the Puma emerge from behind my tail plane. It was flying in an extremely unstable fashion and after a couple of seconds crashed heavily into the side of the hill, shedding rotor blades and debris over a wide area, before rolling over and exploding in a pall of black smoke. I was absolutely amazed. We had previously discussed using wing-tip vortices as a method of downing helicopters and it obviously worked, although I had not particularly been aiming to try the method out at the time.

I reversed my turn to the right and dived back down towards the wreck of the Puma. It was lying on its side with the tail pylon separated from the fuselage, a fierce fire blazing and secondary explosions throwing debris into the air. Whatever it had been carrying was now in the process of cooking off and I hauled back on the stick in order to give the area a wide berth. I pulled the aircraft around to the west and saw John diving down towards a deep stream bed running up into the mountains. As he recovered from the dive the bottom of the ravine erupted in a storm of explosions from his cannon but I could not see his target. I tipped in right to dive down towards the area that John had strafed.

'Where is the target reference your fall of shot?' I shouted over the radio.

'One hundred yards to the east,' came the rather reluctant reply. Christ, I thought. How the hell did he miss by that much? The Aden was a pretty accurate weapon, although it had a limited rate of fire compared with more modern guns, and John should have been able to get closer than 100 yards.

I put John's problems out of my mind and concentrated on stabilising my speed and squinting through the green writing of the head-up display to find the target. I quickly picked up the flash of rotor blades and saw the helicopter, tail on to me running up a dry stream bed towards the hills. I had got my dive a little too shallow and the rising ground ahead of me was beginning to get worryingly close. I held the gunsight high for a few seconds, before lowering it smoothly onto the target and squeezing the trigger. The roar of the twin cannons instantly filled the cockpit, beating out a wonderful staccato tune as they fired forty rounds per second towards the enemy.

After a couple of seconds my healthy respect for the rising ground made me release the trigger and snatch the stick back into a high-G recovery to avoid the hilltops. As the nose began to rise I saw my first rounds strike the ground ahead of the helicopter. The subsequent rounds peppered the area within about thirty yards of it but the Argentine came through the hail of shrapnel without apparently being hit. I realised that I had opened fire at too great a range and wasted my first pass. I was bloody annoyed with myself as I knew that if the helicopter pilot flew his machine well I might not see him again and once in the hills he would easily lose us.

We had developed a method of hunting helicopters many years before which was referred to as the 'rat and terrier' system. The idea was that a pair of aircraft would attack in turn, so that one of the fighters could always maintain visual contact with the helicopter as it tried to evade the other's attack. John had automatically started to use this method, and as I called, 'Off. No hit!' he immediately replied, 'In visual!' After a short pause he called, 'What the hell is the sight setting for guns, Moggie?'

We had discovered another omission in his briefing on the differences between the Harrier and Sea Harrier weapons systems! The Sea Harrier was considerably heavier than the GR3 that John was used to and as a result the sight setting was further depressed. This accounted for the 100-yard miss on his first pass. I called out the correct setting to him as he started his dive towards the target again and made a mental note to give him a comprehensive brief when we got back, to make absolutely sure there were no more holes in his hastily acquired knowledge.

I watched John's little grey jet hurl itself towards the ground again and saw the storm of explosions erupt from the foothills of Shag Cove Mountain. As his aircraft crested the hills, turning hard left, he called, 'Off. No hit!'

Great, I thought. Another chance! I pulled my SHAR up into a high left wingover and dropped the nose towards the target. In the dive I recognised the unique tail pylon configuration of the Augusta 109A and realised that I was not attacking a helpless helicopter but a well-armed fighting machine. The aircraft was still pointing away from me, though, so I was fairly safe.

I held the sight high again, judged the rapidly closing range and gave the Augusta a solid two-second burst with both guns. As I recovered I saw the first explosions just short of the target, and when I looked back over my shoulder dust and smoke obliterated the whole area but the rotor blades were still turning. Somehow I had missed him again! I pulled my aircraft around onto an easterly heading again and flew for thirty seconds or so before tipping in again for another pass.

I pressed my third attack until the helicopter was filling the sight and I could clearly see the rocket pods attached to either side of its fuselage. I gave it a one-second burst, and as I pulled into a five-G recovery I saw the target disappear under a hail of sparkling explosions from my cannon shells, followed shortly afterwards by the massive orange bloom of a secondary explosion from the fuel tanks at the rear of the aircraft. Several of my rounds had hit him, and with nearly two ounces of explosive in each had done their deadly work well. The pilot had failed in his task of defending the formation and had paid the price for running away rather than trying to engage us with his rockets. Mind you, I felt that we should have been able to knock him down rather more quickly than we had done, as he really hadn't been a very difficult target. A point for the debrief.

As I turned away from the burning wreckage of the gunship John called that he had located a further helicopter, which had landed and shut down a few hundred yards west of the smoke which was still billowing from the wreckage of my first kill. He shouted in a very frustrated voice, 'I'm out of ammunition but I'll pull up right over the target.'

I watched him tip over into a dive and followed him with my eyes as he flew lower and lower over the rough terrain. He pulled up hard over a small dark patch of scrub with trails of vapour snaking away from his wing tips. I could not see anything that looked like a helicopter but rolled over onto my back and pointed the aircraft at the area that John had indicated.

I arranged my dive so that I was approaching from a slightly different direction but I was constrained by the lie of the ground as well as the position of John's aircraft. I did not want to risk hitting him with a ricochet. This would not be a good exchange for a Puma and would be guaranteed to hack him off. There had been several cases of aircraft being hit by their own rounds over the target on air-to-ground ranges and at least one of a plane being hit downwind a good mile away from the target. Admittedly, solid practice rounds usually caused these incidents but it was a hazard to be considered.

I planted my gunsight on the patch of heather that John had overflown but I could not make out a target. The airspeed increased and I throttled back to stabilise the attack, all the time searching the ground ahead for the slightest movement. I was aware of the horizon climbing in my peripheral vision and started to get a sense of the heather rushing up to meet me, a sure sign that I must pull up or risk hitting the ground. I was almost crying with frustration and on the point of pulling out when I realised that my gunsight was sitting directly over a Puma. It had shut down on the rough ground and was almost perfectly camouflaged against the boggy surface. I just had time to notice a number of highly excited Argentine soldiers evacuating rapidly in all directions. I pulled the trigger hard and heard a rapid *pop-pop* as my two remaining rounds fired and the guns fell silent. I hauled back on the stick and missed the ground by only twenty feet or so before soaring back into the sky and joining up with John.

We had both emptied our guns and were also low on fuel, so as soon as we had joined up into a defensive battle formation over the Sound we set heading for home and started our climb up to 36,000 feet. As we settled down and checked our fuel we heard our replacement CAP aircraft from *Invincible* come on frequency. I called up and passed them the position of the helicopters and I swear I heard the grin on Brave's face as they acknowledged it. I learned later that by a combination of good luck and good shooting one of my last two rounds had hit the tail pylon of the Puma, rendering it unflyable although repairable. The pair who relieved us found the damaged Puma and strafed it comprehensively, leaving it burning fiercely. By the time they arrived, however, the Argentine troops had set up a number of defensive weapons and the attacks were made in the face of heavy tracer fire interspersed with the odd shoulder-launched missile. I was glad that we hadn't had those problems; I am not sure I would have appreciated a target that fired back!

We returned to *Hermes* in silence and were greeted by grins and thumbs-up signs when we landed. News of our success had already been announced and everyone was aware of the importance of the engagement. We had managed to destroy 20 per cent of the enemy helicopter force at a time when they were desperately in need of such transport. Despite this, I was not particularly happy at the destruction of the first Puma. I believed that the crew must have perished in the crash; the destruction had been so rapid and so complete I could not imagine that anyone could have survived. The irony was that I had not meant to attack them on the initial pass, and as a former helicopter pilot I had a great deal of empathy with the crew. Still, I consoled myself, if they can't take a joke they shouldn't have joined.

After signing my aircraft over to the maintainers I went straight up to the bridge to brief the captain on our achievements while John headed off to order the coffees. The captain was delighted with our success but then told me something, which froze me to the spot.

'I'm sorry, Morgan,' he said. 'It is probably best that you hear it from me. I am afraid that we have intercepted a message saying that Jeff Glover was being transferred from Port Howard to Stanley by Puma at about the time of your engagement.'

I don't think that I had ever felt so desolate in my life. I managed to stammer, 'Oh shit,' before stumbling along the passageway and down to the briefing room.

My news was greeted by a stunned silence. The atmosphere of excitement and celebration evaporated instantly as everyone took in the awful implications. To lose a friend to enemy action was bad enough but to be directly and personally responsible for his death was something I was going to find very difficult to come to terms with. Everyone made the required comforting noises.

'Not your fault, Mog.'

'You weren't to know.'

'He knew the risks, mate.'

Even 'If he couldn't take a joke, he shouldn't have joined!'

As I went back aft I felt that I needed to have some time on my own and went down to my cabin and closed the door. I could only hope our information was incorrect – that he had not been aboard the aircraft – or had somehow survived the attack. I knew that if I was responsible for his death the boys of No. 1(F) would not blame me but I also knew that I would find it very difficult to look them in the eye from then on. I would also have to visit his family on my return and explain the circumstances of his death, not something I relished at all. Still, I might not survive myself, so the time to worry about that would be later when the job was done and the costs had to be finally counted.

I spent several days under this cloud before to my great relief we received intelligence that Jeff had been seen boarding a Hercules transport at Stanley airport. He was transferred to the Argentine mainland and received medical attention for his injuries before being repatriated after the end of the conflict. I never did have to explain to his family but I did let him know that he had given me nightmares for a while and he generously bought me a beer.

A visit to the site of the action after the conflict was over showed the importance of the cargo. There were several hundred rounds of 120-millimetre mortar in the wreckage of the first Puma. Some had exploded in the intense heat and some lay scattered around, still intact in the tussock grass. I was also very relieved when post-conflict research discovered that the crews of all the helicopters had survived the attack, despite the fact that I had found the charred remains of a flying boot in the wreckage. It was ironic that the aircraft I was flying on this sortie was the same one I had flown on the first raid of the war. Then, the Argentines had put a hole through the tail with a 20-millimetre anti-aircraft gun; this time the boot was on the other foot.

John and I were not the only ones to see action that day. Peter Squire's boys mounted attacks on the small landing strips at Dunnose Head and Pebble Island with a view to denying their use to the Argentines. They all returned without encountering any ground fire but unfortunately one civilian was injured at Dunnose Head when the late release of a bomb caused considerable damage to his house. Mark Hare visited him after the conflict to apologise for the incident and was told that if we wanted the strip made unusable we should have told him and he would have ploughed it up!

THE ARGENTINES NOW had a very good idea of where their priority targets were situated. Once the weather over the mainland cleared they started to launch raids with the intention of attacking the landings. However, their losses had reduced the number of available aircraft substantially and only sporadic attacks were made on the British forces. Of these, the first raid, by Grupo 5, was undoubtedly the most effective. This was planned as a six-ship attack but lost one pilot before they even started engines, when he slipped and fell from his Skyhawk, damaging his arm. A second A4 developed an unserviceability before take-off, leaving a flight of just four to continue with the mission. These aircraft refuelled successfully from a Hercules tanker to the west of the islands and pressed on towards the landings. They attacked from the north of San Carlos, from behind the Verde Mountains, and concentrated all their firepower on the Type 21 frigate *Antelope*, leaving her with two unexploded bombs lodged in her hull.

The attackers did not escape unharmed and the storm of anti-aircraft gun and missile fire from both the ships in the bay and the troops ashore resulted in the destruction of one A4 and the loss of its pilot. The leader's aircraft was badly hit by small arms fire and also damaged by the proximity blast from a missile. He managed to coax his damaged plane back to base, where he found that he had also hit *Antelope*'s mast as he recovered from his attack.

Antelope limped into the safety of the anchorage, her mast bent over several feet from its top. That evening, as the bombs were being defused, one exploded, tearing a huge hole in her starboard side and starting massive fires which spread to her magazines. The subsequent spectacular explosions tore out her heart and by morning there was little left of this proud warship but a blackened hulk, which slowly collapsed, her back broken as she slipped beneath the waves.

Two hours after the attack on *Antelope* 800 NAS were in action again. Andy Auld and Martin Hale were on CAP over West Falkland when Martin spotted a Dagger over Pebble Island, heading west at low level. He shouted a warning and slammed the throttle open, diving down towards the fleeing enemy. In a repeat of his engagement two days earlier the Dagger started to outrun the slower Sea Harrier and Martin was placed in the same frustrating position of being able to see the enemy but not attack him. As he desperately tried to get within firing range he realised that there was a second Dagger trailing the first one by a mile or so. He switched his attention to this one and managed to lock his missile and get it in the air before the enemy pilot was able to stretch the range sufficiently. The Sidewinder did its deadly work, homing straight up the target's jet pipe, and the Dagger exploded in a large fireball, smashing into the ground on the west side of Elephant Bay, killing its pilot instantly.

During the afternoon we received reports that the Argentines had installed arrester gear at Stanley. This was a worrying development as it would allow them to land jet aircraft there and might mean that the carriers would be in danger of attack. A decision was made to launch four SHARs, each carrying three 1000-pound VT fused (air burst) bombs, in order to persuade them that basing valuable attack assets at Stanley was not a good idea. I was one of the four pilots nominated to fly the mission and grabbed Gordie Batt to get a briefing on the weapon-aiming software, which I had not yet had the opportunity to try out. He started to talk me through the switches, sighting and delivery profile but after a few minutes paused and said, 'Actually, Mog, why don't I take this sortie? I've done loads of this stuff in the States and I'll finish the brief when I get back.'

I didn't need too much encouragement to hand the trip over to him. I was feeling pretty whacked and was quite happy to let him fly the mission. This decision was vindicated an hour or so later when the raid was delayed until after dark. This seemed a sensible plan, as it gave the SHARs the advantage of delivering their bombs when they would be immune to attack from visually aimed weapons. The loft delivery profile did put them into the engagement envelope of the radar-laid guns and Roland missiles but the combination of chaff and post-attack manoeuvring would reduce the threat to an acceptable level.

I must confess that I was somewhat relieved not to have to launch myself into the night without a thorough brief. I had heard horrific stories about night flying at sea and was not desperately keen to give it a try just yet. I was much happier going aft for a lovely hot shower before heading for the wardroom and a couple of stiff horses' necks to relax after a hectic day. I was glad to find that the GR3 pilots were still happy to drink with me and not one of them made any mention of the fact that I might have shot Jeff out of the sky. I noticed that the stewards had already added three helicopters and another Dagger silhouette to the black outlines behind the optics. The tally was still mounting. I imagined that 800 miles to the west silhouettes of ships were appearing on the walls of Argentine crewrooms. How many more, I wondered, before this was all over?

Soon after dark I heard the unmistakable sound of Pegasus engines whining into life. I knew that the four pilots would be psyching themselves up to launch their heavily laden machines into the total blackness and quietly wished them the best of luck. On a whim I decided to go up to watch the launch and made my way through the dimly lit passageways and ladders up to the bridge. I quietly slid the bridge door open and slipped silently into the almost tangible darkness. I stood by the port window overlooking the ramp and let my eyes become accustomed to the dark. The only light came from the compass binnacle and the dials of the control panels along the forward bulkhead. Quiet orders were issued and repeated to bring the ship onto the flying course and to increase revolutions to give sufficient wind over the deck for the launch.

Outside, under the eerie flight deck lighting, the maintainers and aircraft handlers busied themselves preparing the SHARs for launch. Chain lashings were removed and stowed and the deck cleared of all non-essential personnel; to be blown overboard at night would be a very unhealthy thing indeed. The SHARs' navigation lights flashed dimly in the gloom to announce that they were ready to taxi and the handlers started to marshal them forward onto the centreline. What a far cry this was from the first night flying I had done – on the Chipmunk fifteen long years before. Then there had been a bright moon dancing on the River Ouse and the lacy patchwork of villages spread out as far as the eye could see. Linton, Newton, Tollerton, Marton-cum-Grafton; it seemed odd that these Yorkshire names were so etched in my memory. They came from a time of innocence and youth, when life was a great adventure and success was measured by a good trip or a beautiful girl, or not throwing up after a hard night out at the Green Dragon. The runway had been a bright beacon of lights surrounded by a pattern of dim blue taxiway lighting, all sitting in the only piece of black countryside for miles around – the very opposite of this.

The four aircraft lined up in turn, their navigation lights changing from flashing to steady dim to show they were ready for launch. At the drop of the FDO's illuminated wand, they tore down the deck and leapt into the black veil of the night. I had carried out quite a few night ramp launches from the ski-jump at Yeovilton, with plenty of other lights around to give perspective and horizon. There it was almost a non-event, as long as the head-up display did not fail. At sea, as I had learnt on the way south, it was a different kettle of fish. The massive acceleration along the deck and up the ramp caused the brain to believe that you were rotating nose-up. This, combined with the sudden reduction of acceleration rate as you left the ramp and dropped the nozzles, could completely disorientate a pilot. The only way to complete the take-off safely was to concentrate 100 per cent on the instruments in the head-up display and make absolutely sure that the wings were level and that the aircraft continued to climb gently away from the cold sea below. The first ten seconds, while the aircraft was still below stalling speed, were critical, and HUD failure at this stage was scary in the extreme. I was told that a night catapult launch was even more terrifying and was very grateful that I was unlikely to have that dubious pleasure.

I watched until the last aircraft had left the ramp and been swallowed up by the darkness before turning aft to pass back through the bridge door. I had just found the handle and was about to slide the door open when a flash of light stabbed the darkness behind me. I turned to look forward and saw a huge oily fireball sinking into the sea a few miles ahead of the ship. The stunned silence lasted only a couple of seconds before questions and orders were being barked back and forth through the gloom. It was soon clear that one of the SHARs had exploded. A quick radio check revealed that the number four, Gordie Batt, was not answering, and it only took a few minutes to establish that the explosion had probably been his aircraft hitting the water. A helicopter was launched to conduct a search but nothing was ever found: no debris and no sign of life. Gordie Batt – pilot, raconteur, rugby player, husband, father, friend – was dead, killed instantly in a maelstrom of exploding bombs and fuel. We were never able to discover exactly what had happened – whether he had become disorientated and flown into the water or whether one of his bombs had detonated prematurely – but it was purely academic in any case. He was gone.

I walked aft in a daze to break the news to the rest of the guys and found that the bush telegraph had beaten me to it. Shock was written on everyone's face as they tried to come to terms with what had happened. There was little time for reflection, however, as Andy Auld's aircraft developed an unserviceability which forced him to jettison his weapons and return to the carrier. Shortly after his recovery the other two aircraft returned, having successfully completed their mission. There was no time to grieve; we had a war to win.

Death says live while you may, for I am coming

Gordie's death hit me particularly hard. He had seemed invulnerable and even over twenty years later I find it difficult to define my emotions. It was supposed to be me flying that sortie, not Gordie. I still carry a certain burden of guilt, despite the fact that it was postponed until after dark and that in turn meant that it was extremely unlikely that I would have been able to fly the mission. The human psyche is a complex and inscrutable thing and I still struggle to come to terms with those events.

That evening we held the traditional wake in the wardroom. This started off as a rather sombre affair but before long the jokes started and by the end of the evening normal service had been resumed. It was even suggested that the reason Gordie had crashed was that his aircraft had been overloaded with secret documents and clothing. This was a reference to an occasional practice used to solve discrepancies in paperwork – 'losing' documents in aircraft crashes – and the fact that pilots had been known to put in insurance claims for 'lost' kit after they had been pulled out of the sea. This had backfired on one pilot, who had claimed for a lost watch only to be shown a picture of himself getting out of the rescue helicopter. He had been photographed waving at the goofers and his watch could clearly be seen on his left wrist.

CHAPTER 9

ON TO GOOSE GREEN

THE NEXT MORNING it was business as usual. Shortly after dawn 800 NAS launched a raid in support of our RAF buddies. Once again the airfield at Stanley was the target and Neill Thomas and Mike Blissett delivered VT fused 1000-pound bombs to suppress the defences ahead of a low-level attack by four GR3s. The weather was clear, with just a smattering of cloud over the islands, as the two SHARs pulled up off Mengeary Point to deliver their weapons. It seemed they had managed to surprise the airfield defences and their bombs exploded with mushrooms of smoke and flames at fifty feet above the ground, sending a storm of white-hot metal shards spinning across the desolate grass.

Forty-five seconds later Green Formation was over the airfield. Bob Iveson and Tony Harper were first over the target, with Peter Squire and Mark Hare following in a thirty-second trail from a slightly different direction. All four GR3s dropped their retard 1000-pound bombs and ran out to sea as the defences woke up to their presence. The Sea Harrier escorts remained exposed after their attack, albeit at a reasonably safe range, and were locked up by both gun radars and the Roland missile system as the low-level section escaped.

A review of the gunsight film later in the day showed that the second pair had ended up a little too close to the leaders and several large pieces of debris could be seen in the air uncomfortably close to their aircraft. Several bombs hit the runway but because of the low-level delivery and fuse settings little damage was done. I think that this finally convinced the captain that the only way we might be able to damage the runway was with steep dive deliveries, something we had tried to impress upon him from the very start.

A mere thirty minutes after the return of the first raid Andy Auld and Dave Smith were airborne on the first CAP mission of the day. They headed for the northern end of Falkland Sound, where *Broadsword* and *Coventry* had positioned themselves as a missile trap in an attempt to intercept any aircraft attacking from north-west of the landings. The theory was that any medium- or high-level targets could be engaged by *Coventry*'s Seadart system and *Broadsword* could take out any low-level threats while acting as goalkeeper for her larger partner.

Almost immediately the SHARs arrived on station, there was a shout from the Controller in *Broadsword*. His radar had picked up a four-strong raid approaching from the west. It was a formation of Grupo 6 Daggers intent on attacking the ships in San Carlos Water. As the Argentine aircraft crossed Pebble Island and settled down at ultra low-level over the sea, the pair of dark grey SHARs fell upon them from 10,000 feet above. Andy fired one missile from directly behind one of the leading Daggers and took it out in a fireball. While his first missile was still in flight, he acquired the second target and fired again. Within a matter of seconds he had destroyed two enemy fighters and their wreckage fell into the unforgiving sea.

Behind and slightly to one side of his leader, Dave had spotted the second pair of Daggers. They broke to the south, jettisoned their bombs and drop tanks, and tried to escape. Dave locked a Sidewinder to the nearest target and sent it streaking on its way. A few seconds later the third aircraft exploded in a huge gout of flame as the missile found its target, the debris cartwheeling into the edge of Elephant Bay. Within five seconds they had destroyed three enemy fighters but there was a fourth around somewhere and neither of them could see it. Suddenly Dave spotted him, underneath Andy, heading west at high speed. He called the boss to cover his tail and broke hard after the fleeing Dagger, which was able to engage afterburner and outrun the frustrated SHAR pilots, who now found themselves short of fuel and had to head for home. Two of the three Argentine pilots managed to make successful ejections with their British-made seats but it was still a heavy loss for Grupo 6.

Back on *Hermes* John Locke was soon informed of the engagement and had already made an announcement to the ship's company before the two aircraft landed. As a result there was a welcoming committee waiting for the boss on the flight deck and three very enthusiastic squadron members chaired him shoulder high from his aircraft to the island. He looked rather apprehensive, perched five feet above a very hard deck on some pretty unsteady shoulders, but once returned to deck level, he relaxed. His face broke into a huge grin as he acknowledged the plaudits of his squadron. The strain of the last few weeks still lined his forehead and the black marks from his oxygen mask still surrounded his nose and mouth but he had a new air of confidence, a mixture of pride and relief. The boss had got his first kills and was obviously very proud. If you get a bottle of advocaat for a 'left and right' on snipe, what could we give him for Daggers? Dave was also as pleased as Punch to have notched up his first kill but confided later that he was saddened and horrified to witness the savage death of a fast jet hit by a Sidewinder.

That afternoon I flew two CAP missions to the north of Pebble Island, one with Andy McHarg and the second with Andy George. Despite the successes of the morning, we had no contact with the enemy and returned disappointed with our armament intact.

In the evening we learnt that only a dozen or so Argentine aircraft had made it through to the beachhead and five of them had been hit by the ships or Rapier missiles. There was much discussion, over the congratulatory beers and whiskies, as to whether we were wearing the Argentine forces down, or whether they were husbanding their resources for a big push the following day. We were acutely aware that 25 May was their national day and that they would dearly love to stage a spectacular attack to impress the audience at home.

THE 25TH STARTED much as normal with the strangely comforting routine that seemed to help ward off the crushing tiredness that we were all feeling by now. I woke a couple of hours before dawn, had a quick wash in the captain's bathroom, put on my flying suit, secured my bedding and strapped on my survival belt, before heading up to 2 Deck and forward through the dimly lit passageway to the ACRB. A mug of strong tea and a full fry-up completed the ritual and just left time for me to brief John Leeming for our first Alert 5 mission, before climbing the ladders up to the island and out onto the slick deck as the sky began to lighten. During our briefing we were told that *Coventry* had just destroyed a medium-level target to the west of Pebble Island. By now we had become used to inflated claims by both ships and ground defences and paid little attention. In fact the target had been a Skyhawk of Grupo 5, one of a flight specifically ordered to attack the missile trap of *Coventry* and *Broadsword*. Unknown to us the Argentines had meant to start the day with a bang but their plans for a dawn attack had been disrupted by a long-range shot from the much maligned Seadart system.

Morning action stations was piped as we were strapping in, and the first pair of Sea Harriers taxied onto the centreline and roared off into the darkness, leaving a huge cloud of spray. We all knew this day was going to be a particularly tricky one; we were aiming to keep as many aircraft on task as possible and No. 1 (F) were to attack Stanley airfield as there seemed little in the way of close air support tasking. It was rapidly becoming obvious that the tasking and reporting system was virtually non-existent. This was already a source of annoyance and frustration for our GR3 brethren and would prove to be a great hindrance to their efficient employment as the ground war developed.

After an hour or so on Alert 5 we were scrambled to take up CAP over West Falkland and ploughed our weary furrows back and forth, eyes peeled for any movement. Someone once said that war is 99 per cent boredom and 1 per cent stark terror. I seemed to be having my share of the 99 per cent! That was due to change however on my next sortie.

After returning to *Hermes* we both remained in the aircraft for a cockpit turnround. To enable us to maximise aircraft availability we were now flying up to three sorties without leaving the cockpit. This actually reduced fatigue quite considerably as it took an inordinate amount of our flagging energy to climb in and out of the cockpit and up and down the ship's ladders, as well as putting on and removing our survival gear. It also reduced time spent briefing and debriefing and allowed us to grab some very welcome sleep in the cockpit. So it was that John and I launched again as the sun climbed towards its zenith. This CAP was flown without any enemy sightings and as we set off towards *Hermes* for the second time that morning I allowed myself to think that perhaps we had broken the back of the Argentine fighter squadrons. Almost immediately I told myself that this was not a good attitude; I had to remain on the ball. I might be absolutely knackered but I must not become complacent. Complacency will kill you just as fast in wartime as it will in peacetime. But, God, I was tired.

Our return route took us directly over Stanley and I could make out the jumble of coloured roofs and the criss-cross of streets. There was the road leading down to the airfield and I could see the wrecks of several small aircraft littering the grass on either side of the runway. I ran my eyes along the waterfront and around the small natural harbour, with its wrecks of old wooden-walled sailing ships. I could see that there were no ships alongside the jetty but suddenly a movement caught my eye. Something glinted just off the jetty, over the grey water of the bay. It was a Pucara! I could make out the straight wing and twin engines of the little attack aircraft as it flew around in tight circles just a few hundred yards from the town itself. He had obviously been scrambled to hold in a safe area in case we were going to carry out some high-level bombing of the airfield.

I knew that the airfield defences were able to cover the whole of the harbour with both missiles and radar-laid guns but I decided that it would do the morale of the islanders a great deal of good if they could see this aircraft destroyed before their very eyes. It was also a few days since I had seen any action and I was damned if I was going to miss this opportunity.

'Red 2,' I called. 'One Pucara in a survival hold in the harbour. I'm going to try to splash him. You stay high and call me if you see any missile launches.'

'Roger,' John replied, always a man of few words.

I knew that the main threat to my continued existence was the Roland missile system. This could be aimed visually or controlled by radar and was capable of hitting an aircraft up to around 14,000 feet. In addition, I would be within range of the 35-millimetre Oerlikon guns, but their chances of hitting me were slim if I remained unpredictable. The maximum range of the Sidewinder was about three miles at 15,000 feet, and I reckoned that if I fired it in a steep dive it would have enough energy to hit the target. Certainly it would still be able to home onto the target, even if its motor had burnt out.

I tightened my lap straps, wriggled my fingers to relax myself and selected the missile to 'Boresight'. That fixed the missile seeker head so that it looked directly ahead of the aircraft. I then took a deep breath, called, 'Tipping in,' and pulled my aeroplane up in a lazy wingover to end up pointing at the ground.

From 25,000 feet the ground looks a long way away and the target was a very small cruciform shape against the steely water of the harbour. I dropped the nozzles to the braking stop in an attempt to limit my forward speed and placed both hands on the stick to steady my tracking. The target flew neatly underneath the missile cross and I flicked the safety flap off with my thumb. I then moved it across and held it poised over the lock button, waiting for the missile to growl, telling me it had seen the heat from the target's exhaust.

Man and machine fuse into one entity with a single purpose – to kill. I focus my mind on the tiny target some four miles below me as it grows slowly larger. My eyes flick from the missile cross to the altimeter. Passing 20,000 and still no growl. Passing 18,000 and he has turned towards me – not a good aspect for the missile but still possible. I doubt that he has even seen me, as I am high above him in the unbelievably blue heavens. He probably knows we are in the area but has no idea he is in the middle of my gunsight. Passing 16,000 and time to recover. Nozzles aft, full power, pull hard into a steep climb, back to the relative safety of the sky.

'No joy that time. Climbing up for another shot,' I called to John, who was weaving back and forth above me in a sky now pockmarked by exploding 35-millimetre shells.

Back to 25,000 again, weather nice and dry so no contrails to give us away to onlookers on the ground, just the occasional flash from the perspex canopies as we manoeuvre. Despite its rather stubby appearance, the Sea Harrier is quite difficult to spot head on, the only telltale being a thin trail of smoke left by its AVTAG fuel, which burns rather dirtier than the air force's AVTUR.

As I start my second dive from 25,000 feet the Pucara passes right over the jetty next to the cathedral on the waterfront. I hold my missile cross out over the water in the harbour and wait for him to clear the town. It would be a little counterproductive to shoot him down into the rows of corrugated-iron-roofed houses that line the southern side of the bay. Passing 20,000 and he clears the coast. Missile cross now squarely over the tiny target. He must be totally unaware that I am sighting my weapons on him as he continues to fly a lazy orbit without taking any evasive action at all. Passing 17,000 and he is turning back towards the town. Damn! If I fire now he will crash into the middle of the streets of Stanley. Full power, pull the nose up and claw for height again.

'Still no joy. I'll give it one more try,' I call to John. 'Roger, Joker,' he replies, telling me that he is now on the bones of his arse for fuel and needs to depart.

'Joker acknowledged,' I reply.

I climb back up to height, calm the breathing and recheck my weapons switches. It would be very silly to make a switch pigs at this stage. I just have enough fuel for one last try before we will really have to leave for home.

'Tipping in!' I call again as I enter the steep dive for the third time. Absolute concentration, breathing slowing to a stop as the target grows in the head-up display. Speed very nicely under control this time, with the nozzles in the braking stop and loads of power on. Probably making quite a lot of black smoke but that can't be helped. This will have to be the last try, so I need to make it a good one. Passing 20,000, no growl but he is turning tail on. Passing 18,000 – a growl! Just a fraction of a second but definitely a growl! I concentrate more than ever on keeping the sight on the target and a few seconds later I am rewarded with a good solid growl. I mash the lock button with my thumb but the missile doesn't lock; the growl has gone. Another couple of seconds and the growl is back. He is now completely tail on to me in a left-hand turn towards the open water. Things will not get any better than this. I mash the lock button again but the missile symbol staggers drunkenly down to the left hand-corner of the head-up display. Damn!

'Missile launch! Missile launch from the north side of the airport road!' John's urgent call cut through my concentration. I had omitted the altimeter from my scan for the last few seconds as I concentrated on tracking the target. I glanced across to the right of the head-up display and saw to my horror that it was decreasing rapidly through 14,000 feet.

Shit! I'm too low – right in the Roland envelope, I thought.

Full power, nozzles to twenty degrees, pull to eight units angle of attack and pray!

I looked back over my left shoulder as the nose came up, oh so slowly. Just to the north of the airport road I saw a small puff of dust and heard John call, 'Second missile launch!'

From the dust I now saw a small black pencil shape heading in my direction, leaving a thin grey smoke trail. A little way ahead of it was the first missile and both were smoothly tracking the point in space where I would be in a few seconds time. The altimeter was reading 13,000 feet and increasing terribly slowly. I slammed the nozzles fully aft, tripped the engine limiters, turned on the water and stood the aircraft on its tail to try to outrun the tiny black pencils. I can remember thinking quite clearly that they didn't look as if they were large enough to do much harm but I knew that they were both guiding properly and my only chance was to try to out-climb them. If I could just get to their maximum ceiling before they hit me, I might just make it. My mind was very clear and everything seemed to be happening in slow motion as I calculated the distance between us, the rate of closure and the remaining height to safety.

I had a feeling of resignation; I had done all I could and just had to wait for the outcome. I was not looking forward to losing an irreplaceable Sea Harrier for what was after all not a very important target and my idea of boosting local morale seemed to be going badly awry. Altogether a pretty bad decision it would seem.

As I passed 14,000 feet the little grey trails were getting desperately close and I called to John, 'I guess we are about to confirm the maximum ceiling of the Roland!' As I watched, with the height passing 14,500 feet, first one grey trail then the second ceased and the little black pencils slowed and finally tumbled earthwards. I let out a huge sigh of relief and realised that I hadn't taken a breath since I first saw the missiles coming up at me. It had only been a matter of some ten seconds but had seemed like a lifetime.

I rolled out in battle formation on John at 30,000 feet. 'Good call, 2. Let's go home!' He had undoubtedly saved my life.

A couple of years after the conflict was over I took a Sea Harrier to the Farnborough Air Show. After my display on the press day I was wandering around the stands looking at various weapons systems when I came across the Aerospatiale stand advertising the Roland as 'combat proven', with seven kills in the Falklands conflict. On further investigation I was able to identify every engagement and the French team were very upset to learn that their missile had actually only been successful on two occasions. They accepted this with good grace, however, and presented me with a very large 'combat proven' sticker to celebrate my escape.

As we decelerated to the hover alongside *Hermes'* pitching deck two GR3s loaded with 1000-pound bombs launched and turned towards the islands. This was the second bombing sortie of the day against the airfield and I hoped that we hadn't stirred things up for them too much. I spoke to Bomber Harris and Mark Hare later on and discovered that they had indeed been engaged by the Roland system but had remained well above the maximum effective height. Very wise! The high-level bombing attacks did very little in the way of damage but they certainly made the Argentine forces think twice about deploying fast jets to Stanley.

We had by now discovered that they had fitted a CHAG halfway down the runway. The chain arrester gear was a very primitive method of stopping a jet aircraft fitted with a hook, and consisted of several hundred yards of thick anchor chain attached to a cable stretched across the runway. Once the aircraft had hooked the cable, it would pick up progressively more weight of chain to slow it down. This certainly would have allowed both Skyhawks and Super Etendards to land at Stanley but there was great debate as to whether either could have taken off from the short runway with any useful weapon load.

As I settled down to eat my lunch it seemed that my excitement was over for the day. So far there had been little sign of the spectacular Argentine attack that we all thought was going to happen and I contented myself with climbing the ladders up to Flyco to watch the rest of the boys as they continued their cycles of launches and recoveries. The deck was working like a well-oiled machine: the yellow shirts choreographing the deadly ballet and the engineers milling purposefully around their charges with fuel lines, bombs and missiles. Pilots emerged from time to time to plod to their aircraft, helmets on against the continuous cacophony and visors lowered against the biting wind, each lost in his own world, preparing mentally for the fight which all knew might come with savage suddenness.

IT WAS MID-AFTERNOON before the next action took place. Neill Thomas and Dave Smith had launched to cover *Coventry* and *Broadsword*, to the north of the sound. At around 1400 local time *Broadsword* detected a raid approaching from the west and vectored them onto it. The Sea Harriers dived down towards the incoming Skyhawks and were within three miles of them, closing rapidly, when the ships called them off.

'Haul off, haul off. Bird targets,' came the call from the controller.

The Seawolf system had acquired two of the A4s and it had been decided to take them with missiles rather than let the SHARs continue the intercept. Neill was certain they would have been able to reach the attackers before they were anywhere near the ships but had no choice but to turn away. Not to do so would have risked being shot down in error by the ships and we could not risk losing aircraft to friendly fire. With a bitter sense of frustration they turned away to clear the field of fire.

Aboard *Broadsword*, the Seawolf locked and tracked the inbound fighters but as it was about to fire, the system failed and the lock was lost. As a result, Capitan Carballo and Teniente Rinke were able to press their attack unhindered and dropped four 1000-pound bombs on the ship from extremely low level. Three of them missed completely but the fourth skipped on the water and hit the stern of the warship. It passed upward through the hull without exploding and arced into the water some distance beyond. *Broadsword* had been very lucky, which was more than could be said for her Lynx helicopter, which was on the flight deck at the time and had its nose destroyed by the bomb as it tore its way through the ship's fabric.

As the first wave of aircraft cleared the area, a second pair of Skyhawks attacked from about ten miles to the west. The Sea Harrier CAP started towards the incoming raid but were once again hauled off by *Broadsword* and forced to watch helplessly as the attack developed. Both ships manoeuvred hard to bring their weapons to bear. *Coventry* launched a Seadart and then began firing her 4.5-inch gun at the rapidly approaching enemy. The missile never had a chance against the ultra low-level targets and passed harmlessly over their heads. *Broadsword* then brought her Seawolf system to bear and was locked on ready to fire when *Coventry* made an error which was to prove fatal. Instead of ensuring that the goalkeeper could do her job by remaining up-threat, *Coventry* became so caught up in her own attempts to shoot the attackers out of the sky that she sailed between *Broadsword* and the incoming raid. I later saw the film from the Seawolf system, showing the target cross tracking the lead Skyhawk perfectly until seconds before launch, when *Coventry* suddenly appears in the frame and the targets are lost behind the looming bulk of her superstructure.

From this moment her fate was sealed. The attackers were able to evade the 4.5-inch shells and the leader, Primer Teniente Velasco, planted all three of his bombs straight into the destroyer's port side. The destruction was horrific; machinery spaces were devastated and massive fires sucked the lifeblood out of the ship. Attempts at damage control met with no success and less than half an hour after the attack the order was given to abandon ship. Forty minutes later the once-proud warship rolled over.

Neill and Dave arrived back on board spitting nails. I watched from Flyco as they walked across the deck from their aircraft, helmets off, arms waving. When I saw them in the crewroom they were beside themselves with anger. Dave had a reputation for being quick to 'flash up' while Neill was always calm no matter the provocation, but they were both in a high state of agitation and cursing the stupidity of the surface navy in very specific terms. We had just lost a ship as the direct result of a couple of idiotic decisions in the ops rooms of the two warships. This sort of decision was lamentably common during peacetime exercises, where everyone assumed that missile systems functioned perfectly and always splashed the targets. Unfortunately ships' warfare officers seemed to believe their own propaganda and had come to trust their own defences more than the SHAR pilots. We hoped fervently that this event would change their attitude and I decided that if I were ordered to haul off when I was in a position to fire, I would press the attack and take my chances.

Luckily the *Coventry* was reasonably close to the landings and it was not long before helicopters were on the scene to pull the survivors from the icy grip of the South Atlantic. Loss of life was remarkably small considering the ferocity of the attack but the episode was a severe blow to the morale of the surface fleet and even the admiral must have been wondering how many more losses we could sustain.

There was little time to reflect on the loss of *Coventry* before the final attack of the day burst upon us. I was halfway down 2 Deck passageway, heading for the wardroom, when there was a huge bang followed by an incredibly loud whooshing noise. I had no idea what it was but turned about and rushed back to the briefing room. Seconds later the commander came on the ship's broadcast.

'Do you hear there? We are now Air Raid Warning Red. Close all doors and hatches! A Handbrake radar has been detected to the north of us and it is possible that we may be under Exocet attack.'

Handbrake was the code for the Super Etendard's search radar. We knew that the preferred Etendard attack method was to approach at low level before popping up to a few hundred feet and carrying out a couple of radar sweeps to pinpoint the target. The pilot would then close a few more miles before pulling up again to acquire the target and fire the missile. The noise that had scared the wits out of me was a chaff rocket being fired to seduce the radar.

As I arrived at the briefing room pilots were running up the ladders to man all available aircraft and the deck was shuddering as the ship came up to maximum speed to allow full manoeuvring. There was an eerie calm among those few of us left below. I became acutely aware that we were sitting at the precise centre of the ship's radar cross section, which meant that if the missile came in from the starboard side it would explode directly beneath my feet.

Christ, what a silly way to go, I thought.

A couple of minutes later John Locke calmly informed us that an Exocet radar transmission had been detected and that we were under attack.

'Estimated time to impact, three minutes.'

The next minute dragged into hours as I stood in the corner of the compartment, my feet spread and my hands on the bulkhead to steady myself. I imagined the nose of the missile coming inboard. What would it be like? Would I be aware of the impact before the 380-pound warhead exploded? Would the overpressure kill me outright or would the fireball suck the life out of me? Perhaps it would hit the stern and we would survive. The old girl was built to solid Second World War standards after all, not like *Invincible*, whose plates had been bowed by rough seas. If the missile exploded in the hangar there would be one hell of a conflagration but at least the blast would be dissipated. We might lose a lift though.

'Estimated time to impact, two minutes.'

I wish he would shut up! You can take the dissemination of information a little too far.

'Estimated impact in one minute. Brace! Brace! Brace!'

Feet spread, knees slightly bent, leaning towards the bulkhead, anti-flash pulled right down over the eyes so that only the minutest part of my face is exposed. Waiting, waiting. My dread of dying in a fire is palpable; the smell of burnt flesh hangs in my nostrils.

One minute – nothing. Two minutes – still nothing. My thoughts began to slow down. Perhaps we had been successful and deflected the missile. Perhaps the chaff rockets and decoy helicopters had done their job. For a few minutes everything was calm and then suddenly there was a tremendous roar, followed by another and then another. Missiles roared overhead as *Invincible* engaged a low-level target to the north. Chaos reigned and it was some time before the phones began to ring again and we started to get some information.

We suspected that a ship had been hit but no one seemed sure which one. I experienced mixed feelings: on the one hand I was incredibly relieved that the *Hermes* was still in one piece, on the other I was desperately concerned to know what had happened. I began to feel the onset of survivor's guilt without even knowing whether anyone had been hit. Looking around the compartment I could tell that others were thinking the same. We all felt the desperate helplessness, the inability to have any influence over events taking place somewhere close to us but removed, almost in a different dimension.

Before long it became clear that the *Atlantic Conveyor* had been hit by an Exocet. They had no countermeasures and no defences capable of downing the surface-skimming missile.

A pair of Super Etendards had launched from Rio Grande in the late afternoon; each carried one of the deadly missiles, balanced on the other wing by a drop tank. They rendezvoused with a Hercules tanker and, once refuelled, routed well north of the islands and approached the fleet on a southerly heading. They carried out their attack very profession-ally, firing both missiles at a group of large targets and then making good their escape to the north-west. Whether *Invincible*'s Seadart salvo had been fired at an incoming missile, a retreating Super Etendard or merely a will o' the wisp we would never know but both pilots were able to carry out a further refuelling from the C-130 and return to their base. This sortie lasted a total of three hours and fifty minutes, the longest Super Etendard sortie of the war.

The two missiles accelerated to over 600 knots and descended to a few metres above the waves for their final approach. After a few miles they popped up to switch on their radars and pick out the biggest return. From then on, they homed actively onto that target.

One missile disappeared without trace but the other struck the *Atlantic Conveyor* squarely on the port side, slamming through her hull just above the waterline, the warhead exploding deep inside her. The initial explosion was powerful enough to distort bulkheads throughout the area of the stern and very soon massive fires had taken hold among the cargo of trucks laden with tentage, ammunition and aviation fuel. A huge hole had been blown in the side of the ship, opening her up from just above the waterline almost up to the weather deck. The ship's engineers managed to start the emergency generators and provide pressure to the fire mains but it soon became clear that it was a lost cause. The damage control teams were faced with a rapidly deteriorating situation, poor communications and the very real possibility that the ammunition stored below might start to cook off in the heat. As night closed in on the stricken vessel, they attempted to use the carbon dioxide drenching system but the breach in the hull allowed the inert gas to escape to atmosphere before it could starve the flames of oxygen. With the decks now too hot to walk on and the ship dead in the water, the order was given to abandon her.

I went up on deck and watched from the island as the drama unfolded. A pall of black smoke billowed out of her and flames roared through doors and hatches. Along the sides of her deck had been placed walls of shipping containers, three deep, which had served to protect the cargo of Harriers and helicopters from the elements on the journey south. These containers could not protect the remaining aircraft from the conflagration and one by one they caught fire and were destroyed. All around the blackened hull were Sea King helicopters combing the water for survivors, swinging their landing lights back and forth over the darkening sea. There too was the Type 21 frigate *Alacrity*, attempting to nose alongside to take off survivors and then shepherding the life rafts away from the burning ship before dropping scrambling nets over her side to allow those in the rafts to climb to safety. As the fire spread through the packed cargo decks, the sides of the doomed ship began to glow cherry-red. The fire became so intense and the deck so hot that the fire party on the forward section became trapped. They were saved by the crew of a Sea King which braved the heat and choking smoke to hover over the bow and winch them to safety.

The death of a ship was a thoroughly depressing sight. I knew that not only were men dying out there but also we were losing huge amounts of vital supplies which could not readily be replaced. On the rear deck I could see the skeleton of a giant Chinook helicopter, its blades forming a bizarre cruciform against the burning superstructure. *Conveyor* carried a large store of cluster bombs, a number of much-needed helicopters and large quantities of prefabricated surface-aluminium (PSA) planking earmarked for a Harrier landing strip in the San Carlos area. We desperately needed this forward operating base in order to give us more time on CAP over the islands. There had been times over the previous couple of days when we had arrived on station with only enough fuel for a couple of minutes flying before we headed home.

We were very aware that we had to offer the ships more protection if we were to avoid further losses and Fred Frederiksen was sent ashore by helicopter to liaise with the ships in the Sound. His brief was to find out what we could do to improve the situation and on his return the captain had asked him what the ships had asked for.

'They asked us to send more CAP, sir,' answered Fred.

To which the captain mumbled platitudes about needing to keep aircraft available to attack the Argentine carrier and the necessity of keeping *Hermes* out of range of attack from the mainland. He then asked Fred if he had by any chance seen his son, who was a Lynx pilot on *Broadsword*. Fred had indeed had a chance to talk to him briefly and the captain asked if his son had sent him any message.

'Yes, sir,' replied Fred. 'He said send more fucking CAP!'

The mood was very subdued that evening. The tally of kills behind the bar was increasing but our losses were also mounting. A further two Skyhawks had been downed during the afternoon, one by the San Carlos defences and a second by a Seadart from *Coventry*, in the Sound. The pilot of the first aircraft, Teniente Ricardo Lucero, had managed to eject from his disintegrating machine at extremely low level and was rescued by the crew of *Fearless* suffering from an excruciatingly painful dislocated knee. The second pilot, Capitan Garcia, was not so lucky. He survived his low-level ejection but neither side was aware of this and he was found over a year later having perished in the cold waters of Falkland Sound.

On the other side of the coin, *Conveyor* was probably the third most important ship in the fleet, purely because of the stores she carried. She was now a total loss, together with some two hundred cluster bombs, our 'tin strip', six Wessex and three Chinook helicopters. She had been about to go into San Carlos to unload her stores when she was hit. Her captain had declared that he was prepared to run her up the beach stern first so that they could unload the stores directly ashore using the stern ramp. Now she was a just fiery hulk, lighting up the sea for miles around.

The only saving grace was that if the *Conveyor* had not soaked up the missile, it would have almost certainly have hit *Hermes*. This would have made it impossible for us to win the conflict. Without our aircraft 801 NAS on *Invincible* would not have had a snowball's chance in hell of warding off the Argentine attacks long enough for the troops to retake the islands and the enterprise would have been over. In addition to that, I might be one of those poor souls bobbing about in a dinghy in the gathering gloom.

Twelve people died on *Conveyor* including the master, Captain Ian North, a seventeen-year-old Royal Naval Writer and two Chinese laundrymen. It was not possible to mourn the loss of these men properly – there was too much work to do for that – but black humour saved the day as usual. Some wag pointed out that both Exocet attacks so far had resulted in the death of laundrymen and wondered whether the homing radar in the nose of the missile had been changed to a device that sought out Chinese.

25 May

Two CAP sorties without trade over West Falkland. Tried to take a Pucara over Stanley but they were too low and I wasn't going down for them. Airport defences fired two Rolands at me but I was too high. Interesting though!!

Atlantic Conveyor hit by Exocet at teatime. Aimed for us but seduced by chaff. *Conveyor* now burning and going down.
Coventry hit by low-level raid north of Falklands and sunk.

Three aircraft downed by ships/shore fire.

The Super Etendard pilots had no idea whether their attack had been successful until a BBC news bulletin some three hours later when the

MOD spokesman merely stated: 'During the last hours we have heard of further attacks on our ships. One of our ships of the task force has been badly damaged and early reports are that she is in difficulty. Rescue operations are in progress. I have no further details at present.'

THAT EVENING WE were joined by the crew of the only Chinook to survive the strike on *Conveyor*. They had been airborne when the missile hit their ship and operated from *Hermes* the following day before flying ashore to carry out vital work moving the troops and their equipment forward. One of the pilots was an old rotary buddy of mine, Dick Langworthy. Dick was a great character, with a very expressive face and huge eyebrows. He had an identical twin brother who was a Jaguar pilot and the two were constantly being confused.

By the evening of the 25th the fleet had landed over 5,500 troops in the San Carlos area with almost no losses but we were aware that they now needed to break out of the beachhead or risk getting bogged down. It seemed that the Argentine forces on the islands were either unable or unwilling to bring the fight to us, so we would have to take the fight to them. The naval screen had taken a battering which could not be sustained for long and we were numb with tiredness. No one now talked of a quick war. We all privately thought that it would be long and bloody unless we could convince the Argentine forces that they had no chance. Their pilots had proved they were willing to press their attacks with bravery and vigour despite mounting losses, and they still had the advantage of numbers, not to mention the security of their own beds at night.

The following morning, on my way up to the briefing room, I came across a group of Chinese squatting in the passageway waiting to be taken by helicopter to one of the RFAs heading north, away from the fighting. They had obviously come to the same conclusion as us about the Exocet homing head and decided that they were going home, despite the orders from Hong Kong. The cobbler was there with his pathetically small bag of possessions, trying to sell the last of his shoes before he went. There were several pairs of mess boots laid out in front of him, all beautifully crafted in fine leather. These normally sold for around thirty to forty pounds and I found one pair that fitted me perfectly.

'I give you ten pound,' I said in my best pidgin English.

'Ah, no!' he cried. 'Cos' firty poun' to make!'

'Take it or leave it,' I said, knowing he would not be allowed to carry any extra weight onto the helicopter.

'Twen'y poun',' he pleaded. 'I got family to support.'

'Oh OK. Fifteen, last offer,' I said, feeling a bit of a heel, but he agreed with much grimacing and I went on my way, the proud owner of a superbly made pair of soft calf-leather boots.

Ten years later those boots were still going strong despite almost daily wear. They had been resoled many times and filled with beer on more than one occasion but still fitted like a glove. The time then came for what I suspected might be their last resoling, as the uppers were starting to show their age. I therefore took advantage of one of my spells aboard *Illustrious* to visit the cobbler in his tiny compartment in the bowels of the ship. The wizened old Chinese looked over the boots carefully, making sucking noises through his few remaining teeth. I was waiting for him to declare them unworthy of repair but after a couple of minutes he turned his rheumy eyes up to me and asked, 'Where you get? – Hermee?'

'Yes, *Hermes* ten years ago,' I replied.

His face cracked into a wide toothless grin. 'I make! They my boot!' he declared.

I was struck with remorse for my haggling all those years before and immediately ordered two new pairs of boots, one black and the other brown. Hopefully this helped rebalance my karma. I still wear the brown ones today, fifteen years on.

THE FOLLOWING TWO days were unremarkable from the air threat point of view. It seemed that we might have fought the Argentine Air Force to a standstill and our CAPs proceeded routinely, without any sign of the enemy. The weather was definitely starting to become colder and the deck was occasionally slick with ice as we shuffled out to our aircraft for the dawn launch.

No. 1(F) was kept busy with attacks on Stanley as well as raids on identified Argentine positions. On the afternoon of the 26th Jerry Pook and Mark Hare were tasked to carry out an armed recce mission in the area from Teal Inlet to Stanley. The tiny hamlet of Teal Inlet was remarkable only for its small clump of trees, a rare feature in the otherwise desolate landscape of the islands. What made it more important was that it lay on the northerly route between San Carlos and Stanley. The roads that connected the settlements were never more than dirt tracks, driveable with care in the summer but impassable to all but the toughest of four-wheel-drive vehicles in the winter months. In places the tracks deteriorated into rows of ruts up to 100 yards wide, as subsequent attempts to pass soft patches forced ever wider detours into the wilderness. It was over these tracks that our troops would have to advance. The alternative route, via Goose Green, approached Stanley from the south. The conditions here were no less taxing and this route had the disadvantage of a large Argentine garrison based at the airfield at Goose Green.

Jerry and Mark saw nothing on their initial run to the north of the central mountain range and turned back some three miles from Stanley after being illuminated by a Super Fledermaus anti-aircraft radar. As they turned to the west, to run back through the area, Jerry spotted a Puma helicopter on the ground, on the slopes of Mount Kent. Initially they assumed it to be one of the aircraft they had attacked five days earlier but as Jerry flew past to take some recce photographs Mark saw small arms fire directed at his leader. Jerry then decided to carry out a further pass to see if the helicopter was serviceable and had a Blowpipe missile fired at him, which exploded above his aircraft. A lesser man would have taken the hint and left the area but Jerry had the bit between his teeth and returned for a final pass, planting three cluster bombs squarely over the Puma which caused several secondary explosions. The pair then returned to *Hermes* and a bullet hole was found in Jerry's starboard drop tank. He had been very lucky to survive that many re-attacks with minimal damage and the hole was repaired overnight by an imaginative engineer with two alloy discs, a small bolt and Araldite. I gave Jerry top marks for aggression but expressed some concern over the re-attacks. They had been, after all, the downfall of Jeff Glover on his first mission. It transpired from post-war analysis that the Puma was in fact the one which had been damaged by Mark Hare on the 21st.

Later in the afternoon we heard that the breakout from the beachhead was about to begin and that evening, to our horror, it was announced on the BBC World Service. This was the second huge breach of security in the past few days. It seemed that the MOD was releasing sensitive information from London without any reference to the front line. A couple of days earlier there had been a report in which it was stated that most of the Argentine bombs had not been exploding when they hit our ships. To the ordinary listener this meant that fewer of our people were being killed but it told weapons experts that the fusing of the bombs was incorrect for the height at which they were being dropped. Little wonder that the Argentines had cottoned on and most of their weapons now seemed to be functioning correctly. Ashore, Lieutenant Colonel 'H' Jones, commanding 2 Para, was incandescent about the breakout report, threatening to sue both the BBC and MOD for manslaughter. In the event it transpired that the report was probably the result of conjecture rather than a deliberate leak of intentions.

Dave Braithwaite cheered us all up that evening as details of one of his missions trickled down the grapevine. He had apparently been briefed while airborne to 'Strafe turtle' at a position to the north of Falkland Sound. When he arrived there was nothing to be seen on the surface. He updated his NAVHARS on the nearest point of land and checked the position again. Still nothing to be seen. Not allowing himself to be defeated by logic, he set up a ten-degree dive pattern and emptied his cannon into the sea. On his return to *Invincible* he was informed that his task had been to sink the upturned hull of *Coventry* in order to stop it falling into Argentine hands. However, in the meantime, the wreck had sunk of its own volition. We toasted his health that evening with many a chortle. It made us feel a lot better, having something to laugh about, and it is always easier to laugh at someone else's expense.

After a couple of beers I made my way up to the briefing room to check the programme for the following morning. In the dim red lights I noticed a body stretched out on the bench at the rear of the compartment; it was Fred Frederiksen, fully kitted-up and ready to spring into action. That is what I call keen, I thought as I tiptoed out and closed the door after me.

27 May

Quiet day for us generally. Bit of CAP and a probe for the *25th May*. Bob Iveson was shot down in a GR3 over Goose Green but we think he ejected.

Laser-guided bomb kits arrived and we hope to use them later this week. Just watch this space, Argies!

Thursday 27 May got off to a slow start; early-morning fog delayed flying until mid-morning and I flew just two missions. The first was the now inevitable CAP over West Falkland without the slightest sniff of the enemy and the second was a surface search to the south of the islands, looking for the Argentine carrier and her escorts. I have no idea where the intelligence came from to suggest that the *25 de Mayo* was in the area but we found absolutely nothing. Still, negative results can be just as important as positive ones. While the SHARs were mounting continuous CAP to the west, the GR3s were tasked with close air support of the troops breaking out of the beachhead. The weather over the islands was pretty dire, with most of the high ground being in cloud. This made CAS very difficult to begin with and the chaos in the tasking system and poor communications added to that difficulty. Despite this, No. 1 (F) carried out three missions in support of 2 Para as they advanced towards Goose Green, with mixed success. The targets were very difficult to acquire as they were mainly well-camouflaged defensive positions and a number of re-attacks were made in order to release weapons.

On the third mission Bob Iveson and Mark Hare were unable to find their first target and made a second run to attack a company position with cluster bombs. They were then asked to carry out a further attack with cannon very close to the settlement. As they pulled off the target Bob felt two large thumps. Almost immediately, his controls seized solid and his warning panel lit up like a Christmas tree. The nose of his Harrier started to drop towards the ground, which was now getting very close, so he dropped a handful of nozzle in an attempt to coax the aircraft into a climb. This did little good and he realised he was going to have to eject. He was not very keen on ejecting close to the Argentine troops he had just attacked, and when the controls suddenly became free his immediate thought was that he could make it a little further to the west before ejecting. It rapidly became obvious, however, that although the controls were now moving, they were not affecting the flight path of the aircraft. He then became aware that flames were starting to come into the cockpit and made the decision to get out. He grabbed the seat handle, closed his eyes tightly and pulled the handle hard into his ample stomach.

Instantly there was a massive thump as the seat fired, followed by a half-second of rapid acceleration as its twelve rockets fired under his backside. He was aware of a violent tumbling sensation and when he opened his eyes he was travelling horizontally at high speed just above the rough terrain. He narrowly missed the fireball made by his disintegrating aircraft before his main chute opened and he started to fall towards the ground. There was no time to assume the correct landing position or even to brace for the coming impact and he landed hard on the uneven ground, winding himself badly.

Mark returned to *Hermes* alone. He was not sure whether Bob had managed to eject or had ridden the aircraft in. In an attempt to discover the flight commander's fate, Jerry Pook launched on a singleton recce mission at medium level to try to contact him. Jerry carried out photographic runs over Stanley and Goose Green at 18,000 feet, before letting down to 15,000 feet for a further run over Goose Green. Nothing was seen or heard of Bob and dusk fell with us still uncertain.

As Jerry headed for *Hermes* a flight of Skyhawks was approaching from the west. This was the only raid to reach the landings on this particular day and two pairs of these nimble little fighters attacked from the south-west, over the Sussex Mountains. Their target was the old meat packing plant at Ajax Bay. This was the only building of any size in the area and had been commandeered by the British forces as a cookhouse and general equipment store. It was here that Surgeon Commander Rick Jolly had established a casualty clearing station and field hospital, soon to become known as the Red and Green Life Machine. Because of the general use of the area it was not legal under the Geneva Convention to mark the buildings with the red cross. The raiders were greeted by a hail of anti-aircraft fire despite the minimal warning of their approach but pressed their attack, hitting the buildings with two bombs which detonated near a meal queue, causing several deaths and a large number of injuries. A fire was also started in an ammunition store, and as the chaos was being sorted out four more unexploded bombs were found, two of them lodged in the roof of the building.

The two bombs in the open were soon disposed off by the resident RAF bomb disposal team but those in the roof posed a more serious problem. Flight Lieutenant Alan Swan examined them and realised that they were 400-kilo retard bombs of French manufacture. He had no knowledge of the fuses used in these weapons, both of which had landed very close to the operating theatre where wounded from both sides were undergoing surgery. To attempt the hazardous task of defusing unknown weapons would have taken several hours, during which time many of those waiting for surgery might have died. The decision was taken that it was less hazardous to leave the bombs in place and hope that they were not fitted with delayed-action fuses, and the medical teams continued to operate. To give the rest of the troops confidence, the bomb disposal team packed sandbags around the bombs and bedded down in the part of the building closest to them.

The decision turned out to be the right one – the bombs never did detonate – but Alan admitted later that he was rather less certain of the correctness of his decision than he allowed others to realise at the time.

The attackers did not escape unscathed however. Primer Teniente Mariano Valesco's aircraft was hit in the port wing root, lost hydraulic power and caught fire. With no way to extinguish the fire, he was forced to eject over West Falkland and after five days managed to meet up with the Argentine garrison in Port Howard. He had suffered no more than a sprained ankle.

Shortly before teatime on the afternoon of the 27th I was contacted by one of our armourers, who had a problem. A number of large drums had been delivered on board, reputedly from a long-range Hercules drop. The top had been removed from one of these drums to reveal a jumble of fins and bolts, and the armourers were trying to work out what they were. I took a look at the opened container and realised that it contained a guidance system of some sort but I couldn't identify exactly what it was. After a little digging and careful unpacking, we found a leaflet explaining that it was a kit for converting a 1000-pounder into a laser-guided bomb. I had seen LGBs but never worked with them. Their accuracy was legendary and they could be the answer to our prayers for a weapon to crater the runway at Stanley. It didn't take very long before a swarm of 'bomb heads' armed with spanners and screwdrivers had transformed one of our 'dumb' 1940-vintage bombs into a piece of cutting-edge technology. Now perhaps we could start getting some good results from our high-level bombing.

IN THE EARLY HOURS of the following morning, while I was still tucked up in my sleeping bag, 2 Para crossed their start line and advanced on Goose Green. Unknown to them, the Argentine garrison had been reinforced after the BBC broadcasts two days previously and instead of the expected advantage in numbers they faced a disadvantage of more than two to one. The fighting was hard and dirty. *Antrim* was positioned to the north-west to give naval gunfire support but her 4.5-inch gun jammed after only a few rounds and the Paras were forced to rely on their own artillery.

For the first time in a generation British soldiers found themselves fighting a full-scale night action on foot, over appalling ground and against a tenacious, well-prepared enemy. Artillery, anti-tank rockets, machine-gun fire and grenades flew back and forth, turning the night into an inferno. The first tentative fingers of dawn found both A and B Companies short of their objectives and very exposed to the enemy. Accurate artillery fire began to hammer them and their advance slowed. Out at sea the ships were wreathed in fog, making flying an impossibility. All we could do was wait for a clearance and hope the troops could hold out.

The first GR3s were airborne at 0930 and found the weather over the target area completely unsuitable, with a cloud base of between fifty and 100 feet in rain. Despite this, Peter Squire and Bomber Harris managed to release their weapons in the target area and some secondary explosions were seen.

The Argentines were also trying to support their ground troops and several missions were flown by Pucaras and MB339 light attack aircraft from Stanley. The second Pucara mission arrived in the Camilla Creek area around 1100 and found two Scout helicopters. These were evacuating casualties back to Ajax Bay but were not marked with red crosses and therefore regarded as fair game. Both Pucaras attacked and Teniente Miguel Gimenez was able to shoot down the helicopter flown by Lieutenant Richard Nunn, killing him outright and seriously injuring his observer. His success was short-lived however, as the two Pucaras became separated in bad weather and Gimenez was never seen again. It seems likely that he flew into high ground in the foul weather; the wreckage of his aircraft was never found.

Later that afternoon a pair of MB339s arrived and rocketed our troops in the Darwin School area, only to lose one of their number to a Blowpipe fired by Marine Strange of 3 Brigade Air Squadron. The little jet dived straight into the ground, killing the pilot. This was the last operational mission flown by the MB339s. A few minutes after this expensive attack two Pucaras arrived. They dropped napalm, narrowly missing some of the

Paras, and were rewarded by a hail of small arms and missile fire which forced one of the pilots to eject. He was immediately captured.

After lunch I flew two CAP sorties to the west of Goose Green and could only watch impotently as the battle progressed. Through gaps in the cloud I could see the explosions of artillery and naval gunfire support to the north of Goose Green. Several areas of peat were well alight, with clouds of smoke drifting on the wind. My only excitement of the afternoon was when I spotted a crashed Pucara some ten miles to the south-west of the battle. I asked Fred Frederiksen to watch my tail as I dropped down to low level to photograph it. The airframe was remarkably intact and the six feet of tubing projecting up from the front cockpit told of an ejection. I later learnt that this was the wreck of Mayor Tomba's aircraft, which had been shot down by Sharkey Ward and his two wingmen a week previously.

As I returned from my final sortie of the day I heard Bomber Harris on his way in to help the Paras again. That GR3 mission was particularly successful. The weather had cleared dramatically during the afternoon and as the troops fought their way ever closer to Goose Green they had come under devastating fire from the 35-millimetre Oerlikon anti-aircraft gun based on the small peninsula to the east of the village. This was the gun which we believed had shot down both Nick Taylor and Bob Iveson.

Bomber and Tony Harper both planted cluster bombs over the small promontory and Jerry Pook fired two pods of 2-inch rockets directly into the gun emplacement. Despite the age of these rockets, seventy-two of them concentrated into a small area made a very satisfying bang. There was a large secondary explosion from the gun pit and the weapon fell silent. After this, the battle began to turn in our favour.

The Argentine resistance faltered after No. 1 (F) Squadron's demonstration of firepower and early the next morning the Argentines negotiated their surrender. Lieutenant Colonel Jones, the Paras' CO, had been killed in the fighting, leading from the front as was his wont. For his action he was awarded the Victoria Cross. His deputy, Major Chris Keeble, took the surrender and was amazed as the column of troops marched from the village towards the airfield for the ceremony. He had expected a few hundred soldiers, but when they were all counted, including the air force detachment, the total was nearly 1500. It had been an epic victory even though casualties had been high.

The evening before we heard news of the surrender we had had some good news of our own. Two separate aircraft had heard a transmission on the Guard frequency using the call sign allocated to Bob Iveson two days previously. We were fairly sure that this meant that he was alive and on the run, but the captain would not give permission for us to launch a recce mission to try to find him. The conditions were not good for flying and by late evening we were experiencing gales and low cloud which would have taxed the best of pilots.

CHAPTER 10

TIGHTENING THE NOOSE

THE LOW CLOUD CLEARED through overnight but come the morning of the 29th the wind was still very strong with frequent gusts, leaving the large Atlantic swell confused and unpredictable. These conditions would have made the operation of conventional aircraft impossible but the Harriers were able to continue to fly, albeit with a certain amount of caution. The SHARs were tasked with nuisance bombing of Stanley airfield again, as well as the standard CAPs over West Falkland. The carrier group was now standing off well to the east of the islands, giving us very long transit times to our designated stations. We were regularly flying missions of ninety minutes duration, with only five or ten minutes being spent on patrol. We knew that if we had to engage an enemy formation we were unlikely to have enough fuel to return to the ship. On both my sorties that day I turned on my Blue Fox radar as we started our descent from high level with the sole intention of frightening away any inbound raids. The Skyhawks had the advantage of air-to-air refuelling both outbound and on their return flights.

Returning from the first mission of that day I passed over Stanley at a very comfortable height, surrounded by the ever-present puffs of exploding 35-millimetre shells. It was obvious that we had stirred up the defences but nothing should have been able to threaten me at 25,000 feet. I idly ran my eyes over the airfield to see if there was any movement but nothing seemed to have changed. Then a cloud of white smoke caught my eye on the south side of the runway. A missile launch! I immediately checked my height in the head-up display and, reassured, looked back down in time to see a brilliant orange fireball enveloping the launcher and throwing long white streamers across the grass. The Tigercat had obviously malfunctioned and exploded as it was fired. I chuckled into my oxygen mask and muttered a thank you to the Irishman who had assembled that particular missile. I doubted that we would have any more trouble from that fire unit.

There was very little air activity over the islands by the Argentine forces during this period but further to the north a bizarre attack took place on the 15,000-ton tanker *British Wye*. She was carrying fuel for the task force and passing some 800 miles east of Buenos Aires when an Argentine Hercules flew overhead and eight 1000-pound bombs were rolled out of its door. Seven of these missed but one hit her, bouncing off into the water without exploding.

In the afternoon another Sea Harrier was lost but not to enemy action. Mike Broadwater was unlashed and about to launch from *Invincible* when the ship rolled heavily in the rough seas, causing his aircraft to slide across the deck and over the side. Mike ejected as his doomed machine teetered on the brink and was picked up by helicopter. He damaged his back quite severely and did not fly again during the conflict. That evening Captain J. J. Black was invited down to the wardroom for a drink, where he was accosted by Brave in one of his less subtle moments.

'That'll teach you to treat this ship like a fucking speedboat, sir,' he boomed, before being hurriedly led away.

This was not the only misfortune to affect 801 that day. Earlier one of our junior pilots had come into the crewroom with a smile on his face having heard a radio exchange between Sharkey Ward and his phlegmatic wingman Steve Thomas. They were nuisance bombing from high level on their way to their CAP station and as they flew in formation over Stanley Sharkey had called for the bomb release. A few seconds later Steve had called, 'Ah, boss, you just fired a Sidewinder.'

'I can fucking see that, thanks, Steve!' came the terse reply. Sharkey had made a major switch pigs and wasted an irreplaceable missile on some sheep on a far hillside. We all had a great laugh at his expense and hoped that it didn't turn out to be Steve's fault somehow in the subsequent debrief!

29 May

GOOD NEWS! Bob has been recovered alive and well by 2 Para! They took Goose Green finally and captured 1400 Argies! There were 15 killed (including CO) but they did it. Rapiers shot down another A4 (50 per cent of raid). We put 30-odd bombs on Stanley and they fired a Tigercat at me, which seemed to explode on the rails. What a shame!

The atmosphere in the bar that evening was one of huge relief. We had won the first set-piece battle against vastly superior odds and Fatty Ives was on his way back to us apparently unharmed. It also appeared that the Argentine air attacks had petered out. Maybe they could not take the attrition, or maybe they were husbanding their recourses for one last push. Peter Squire's boys had discovered how difficult it was to acquire troops against the uneven landscape of rock and bog that made up 90 per cent of the Falklands. Now we had to try to keep any Argies away from our troops as they advanced towards Stanley.

HMS *Hermes*
30 May

Hello, love,

Got your letter today, written on 16th. I wish I could be with you moving into our cottage. Still it will give you a chance to sort out the garden before I get back! The war is progressing well. As you will have heard, Bob Iveson was shot down three days ago but was picked up by 2 Para when they took Goose Green. He is perfectly

OK apparently and should be back with us today. It has all been rather quiet since the couple of busy days after D-Day and we haven't shot anyone down for a couple of days. I don't think they have a lot left, to be honest.

I had a few missiles launched at me the other day (from Stanley) but was well out of range. Yesterday they launched another one at me but it blew up on the launcher! Very satisfying.

Now we have got Goose Green, it won't take very long to get through to Stanley. In fact it could all be over bar the shouting by the time you get this letter. This doesn't mean we will be back straight away, though, as I am sure that we will keep a presence here for some time. Still, think of all that lovely separation allowance!

Please thank your Ma for the book of mother-in-law jokes; I take back all I said about her sense of humour.

Well, I hope you had a good move into our little house. Look after it till I get back. I promise to agree with anything you decide. How's that for an offer! I think we are going to be very happy there and I am really looking forward to getting back. I love you very much.

Give the kids a hug for me.

Love D

PS Your mother's letter was addressed to <u>NORTH</u> Atlantic!

The penultimate day of May was to be a memorable one for Jerry Pook. The No. 1 Squadron tasking for the day was split between armed recce to the west of Stanley and attempting to drop laser-guided bombs on the airfield. The first attempts at LGBs proved a failure. The laser rangefinder of one GR3 was used to guide the bombs from another but due to a logic mismatch no guidance was achieved. Nor were any detonations seen, which made us think there may have been a fusing problem as well.

On Jerry's second mission of the day he was tasked to search for helicopters to the west of Stanley and inadvertently flew over a column of soldiers on the road leading to the town. As he passed over them the Argentines fired up at him and he was aware of a distinct thump as he was hit. His wingman John Rochford immediately noticed that Jerry's aircraft was venting fuel. In the cockpit nothing else seemed wrong, so Jerry hauled his aircraft to the left and attacked an artillery position he had just spotted, against the side of the hill. To his great satisfaction he saw his rockets exploding among the gun pits before he pulled the nose skyward to gain height and hightail it back to *Hermes*. He soon became aware that his radio had failed and at 10,000 feet, still in cloud, he suddenly realised that most of the lights on his radar warning receiver were on. He had wandered straight into the coverage of the Roland system at Stanley and was a sitting duck. His guardian angel had not forsaken him yet, however, and he managed to get above the system's ceiling before it could engage him. He climbed straight up to 30,000 feet and realised that his fuel was disappearing at an alarming rate. He jettisoned his fuel tanks and empty rocket pods to reduce drag and pointed himself in the direction of home. After a few minutes John pulled up alongside and stayed with him as he headed east. He had already informed *Hermes* of his leader's plight and a Sea King had been dispatched towards them. Jerry signalled frantically that he was running out of fuel and with still over forty miles to run the gauges fell to zero. He then made the signal that he intended to eject and prepared himself for a cold bath. With more than thirty miles still to run the engine wound slowly down and he waved goodbye to John as he settled into a glide. At 10,000 feet and 250 knots he tightened his straps, braced his head back against the head box, closed his eyes and pulled the handle.

Despite his perfect preparation, the ejection was incredibly violent. His head was forced down between his knees by the 3000 pounds of thrust from the seat and he momentarily lost consciousness. When he came round, he was struck by how peaceful everything was as he hung beneath his parachute in the winter sunlight. His first action was to activate his PLB so that it could be heard at maximum range. Next he lowered his personal survival pack containing the single-seat dinghy and survival aids. This caused violent oscillations and he had to pull it back in again and hang on to it.

As he descended into the top of a small cloud he heard the noise of helicopter rotor blades, which made his spirits soar. The navy was here already! Unknown to Jerry he had ejected almost exactly over the Lynx positioned forty miles up-threat to pick up the radars of any incoming Super Etendard raids.

The peace of his serene descent was rudely shattered as he smashed into the freezing waters below the cloud. The wind was still gusting up to forty knots and he was immediately dragged downwind, skipping from wave top to wave top. The tension on the parachute rigging and his rapidly freezing fingers made it impossible for him to release his canopy. At last the parachute caught in the water and collapsed. Jerry realised that he had to get rid of the canopy before it dragged him under the water. He located the inflation handle of his dinghy, pulled it hard and with the last of his failing strength pulled himself on top of the tiny rubber raft as it began to inflate. There he lay for several minutes, not daring to move in case he fell back into the waves.

After a short while a Sea King joined the circling Lynx and lowered a rescue strop which Jerry managed to loop under his arms. He was winched up into the hovering helicopter and finally pulled back into the door and safety. The winchman was a little surprised to be given a huge hug by the elated Harrier pilot. Fifteen minutes later I was on the deck of *Hermes* waiting for Jerry to arrive. He reached the island with a very bemused expression and blood all over his face from the miniature detonating cord, which blows a hole in the canopy on ejection.

'Welcome home, Jerry,' I said, shaking him by the hand. 'Are you OK?'

'Yeah, yeah, I'm fine,' he replied. 'I'm just a little bit confused, that's all.'

'I'm not surprised,' I said. 'It's not every day you get shot down and have to eject.'

'No, no it's not that, Mog. I've just kissed my first bloke!'

While Jerry's drama was unfolding, Bob Iveson had arrived back in another helicopter. At least the RAF had their two pilots back, even though they now had only three serviceable aircraft. I must admit that I was happy not to be involved in 'mud moving' any more. Being shot down by a guy with a rifle was not very glamorous.

Within a few minutes of the two survivors landing back on *Hermes* the klaxons were blaring to announce another air raid. A suspicious radar return had been fleetingly observed to the south of the task force. Within minutes we were closed up at action stations waiting anxiously for news. Almost forty-five minutes passed and we were beginning to feel that it might have been another spurious warning when the ship began to vibrate as engine revs increased to maximum and the ship manoeuvred rapidly to starboard. The roar of chaff rockets firing left us in no doubt that we were under attack and John Locke's broadcast that it was a Super Etendard seemed rather superfluous.

We waited silently, each with his own private thoughts as the minutes ticked by. Then came reports that *Avenger* and *Exeter* had splashed a number of low-level targets some forty miles to the south. For some time chaotic reports came in but after a while it became obvious that the raid had been unsuccessful and any surviving aircraft had left the area.

Analysis after the conflict showed that two Super Etendards had attacked in concert with four Skyhawks. The final Argentine Exocet had been launched at around twenty miles and the Skyhawks had followed it into the target area to attack with bombs. Two of these aircraft were destroyed, probably by Seadarts from *Exeter*, and *Avenger* claimed to have destroyed the Exocet at a range of eight miles. Whatever the details of the attack, it left Argentina with no further Exocets and Grupo 4 de Caza with two less pilots. The surviving pilots were convinced that they had attacked and damaged *Invincible*. This misapprehension survives to this day and one of the first questions I was asked by a French Navy Super E pilot when we invited him on board in Marseille in 1988 was, 'What damage did the Exocet do to the ship?'

HMS *Hermes*

30 May

Dear Elizabeth,

Hello, Boggit, how are you? I hope the move to our new house
went well. I expect you have got your room sorted out by now.
You should have more room for your things than you had at
Esmonde Drive.

How are all the animals? I imagine that Tammy and Beauchamp
will find it a bit funny to start with but I am sure they will like it
when they get used to the house.

I expect that the weather is quite warm there now. Down here
it is getting towards winter and it snowed on the islands yesterday.
It is nice and warm on the ship, though, and we have got heating
in the aircraft.

Give everyone a big kiss from me and give the animals a hug.

Lots of love
Dad

HMS *Hermes*

30 May

Dear Charles,

Hello my lad, how are you? I expect you are in our new house now.
I hope your new bedroom is nice. Have you got somewhere to put
your fish? When I get home we will have to make a proper
fishpond in the garden and get some big goldfish for it and
perhaps some frogs as well.

The weather is getting a bit colder down here and there was
some snow on the Falkland Islands yesterday. It is nice and warm
on the ship, though.

Take care of everyone and look after the new house for me.

Lots of love
Dad

That evening we received news that Jeff Glover was in Stanley hospital with a broken arm and jaw. There was a huge feeling of relief throughout the Harrier community and I was personally extremely relieved that we now had positive evidence that I had not killed him in my helicopter attack. If I had believed in a supreme deity, I would certainly have thanked him that night. After sundown we all gathered in the wardroom bar and downed a considerable volume of CSB and dubious whisky. Songs were sung with gusto and survival stories told by both Bob and Jerry.

It transpired that Bob had had an amazingly cushy time. Having hit the ground hard, his sight had been affected and when he noticed a series of blurred dots running towards him he assumed that they were Argentine soldiers coming to capture him. He dropped his survival gear and ran as far as he could in the opposite direction before dropping exhausted into a ditch. As he lay there getting his breath back he realised that the force of the ejection had torn the pockets off his immersion suit. Unfortunately one of those pockets had contained his pistol and he was now completely unarmed apart from his dinghy knife. After some minutes his sight returned to normal and he slowly raised his head to check on the progress of his pursuers. To his chagrin he found that he had been running away from a flock of inquisitive sheep. He continued to walk west, away from Goose Green, until shortly before dark, when he spotted the vanes of a wind generator over the crest of small rise. He approached the isolated farm, called Paragon House, with caution and was forced to hide in a patch of heather as a helicopter approached from the direction of the airfield using its landing light to search for him.

Once the helicopter had given up the search, he let himself into the empty house to find that the beds were made up, a fire was laid in the grate and the larder was full of food. Not many survivors had it that good! From the upstairs windows he had a grandstand view of the desperate battle for the airfield to the east before tucking himself up in one of the beds and falling asleep.

The next morning Bob woke early and left the house to take cover in some undergrowth. Here he lay for a long time in case the Argentines decided to search the house. He could hear the distinctive sound of the Harrier engine from time to time and attempted to contact us using his emergency radio. Finally, as darkness approached, cold and tired, he slipped back into Paragon House to raid their larder again and fall asleep. On the second morning he awoke with sunlight streaming through the windows and the unmistakable noise of rotor blades on the morning air. He had slept too long and now feared he would be captured. From the window he could see the blades of a helicopter, its fuselage partially hidden by a rise in the ground. For some time he tried to decide whether it was friendly or not. He recognised the aircraft as a Gazelle but did not recognise the six-tube rocket pods mounted on the side of the fuselage. Finally a tentative wave from the cockpit made up his mind. He left the house and discovered it was a Gazelle from 3 Brigade Air Squadron which had been tasked to find him. The rocket pods had been a hasty addition before they left the UK. Within seconds he was strapped into a seat and whisked away to safety. He owed his recovery to some civilians in Goose Green who had witnessed his ejection and told British troops where he might be.

The story of his survival and return was greeted with many a hoot of laughter and we now realised why he didn't seem to have lost any of his considerable bulk. He had probably eaten better than we had over the last three days. It was great to see him and Jerry propping up the bar with pints of beer in their hands, comparing miniature detonating cord scars on their faces.

30 May
Bob Iveson picked up by 2 Para last night and returned to us today. Jerry Pook took small arms near Mount Kent and had a large fuel leak therefore ejected 40 miles short of Hermes but was picked up by Sea King. Good piss-up!!

While we were gathered around the piano in the dimly lit bar, running through our repertoire of songs, other action continued in the air. Several helicopters were engaged in moving troops and weapons forward towards Mount Kent. Dick Langworthy was flying the last surviving Chinook back towards San Carlos, having delivered three 105-millimetre guns and a stick of troops under enemy fire, when disaster struck. He was flying at ultra low level, using light-intensifying night vision goggles, when he ran into a snowstorm. This instantly reduced his visibility to zero and immediately there was a huge bang, the engines began to wind down and the hydraulics dropped off line. They had hit the surface of a creek at something above ninety knots and the spray had flooded into the engine intakes. The co-pilot jettisoned his door and both pilots hauled up on their respective collective leavers, managing to stagger the aircraft back into the air after a considerable period of time in contact with the water. In the rear cabin one of the crewmen had lost his helmet on impact and was now about to jump out of what he assumed was a doomed aircraft. He was only stopped by the frantic gesticulations of the other crewman and was horrified to discover that he had been about to leap out of a helicopter which was by now at 1500 feet and climbing.

Thousands of miles to the north a further Vulcan raid was beginning. This was the third of the Black Buck missions and its aim was to attack the surveillance radars at the airport. The previous raid had failed because the bombs were not properly fused and not one had exploded. This raid fared little better and resulted in only slight damage to the radar, which was operating again within twenty-four hours. We were beginning to seriously doubt whether the Vulcans were contributing much to our efforts other than being a strategic threat to mainland Argentina. Our initial admiration after the first raid on Stanley was fading fast and we all thought it would be better to give us the bombs and the fuel and let us do the job.

The last day of May was very nearly disastrous for the GR3s. A returning 801 NAS patrol reported possible swept-wing aircraft parked at the eastern end of the runway at Stanley. The photos were forwarded to *Hermes*, and the captain decided they could be Super Etendards and ordered an immediate attack. Peter Squire and Mark Hare were launched from alert to attack with 2-inch rockets and Mike Blissett and Bill Covington were tasked to provide cover using lofted 1000-pound bombs.

I was returning from CAP only a couple of miles to the south of Stanley when they reached the target and had a grandstand view of the attack – first the two sets of air-burst bombs shattering the sky with massive fireballs just above the ground, then the tracery of fire directed at the GR3s. I saw the explosions on the eastern end of the runway and followed the little camouflaged aircraft as they egressed, flat out, to the east. When I landed back on *Hermes* I found Peter Squire fuming mad. They had not seen any swept-wing aircraft and they had both taken damage from the intense ground fire. It transpired later that the sightings had been of previously damaged MB339s and the raid had been a desperate overreaction.

No Argentine air raids were intercepted that day and a further attempt by Spag to drop LGBs on a GR3 designation failed. It was decided that we would have to wait for a ground-based laser designator before any further drops were attempted.

By the end of the day No. 1 (F) had only one serviceable aircraft remaining. One needed an engine change, which is difficult at sea at the best of times. To change the engine, the wing has first to be removed. Before the wing can be removed, the airframe has to be securely attached to a solid framework lashed to the hangar deck. The actual process of removing and replacing the massive engine requires the ship to remain as stable as possible for long periods of time. This is not really compatible with the requirements of a warship in time of conflict. Another problem was that Sea Harrier engines were not interchangeable with those in the GR3. Their spare engine had gone down with the *Atlantic Conveyor* and it took several days to obtain a second one from *Intrepid*. Peter Squire was now desperate for replacement aircraft and finally persuaded the admiral to allow direct flights from Ascension using Victor tankers to refuel them. The captain was very much against the operation and regarded it as a risky RAF publicity stunt.

31 May

801 misidentified A4 decoys as Super Etendards at Stanley and Peter Squire and Mark Hare launched to hit them. Both aircraft damaged by ground fire; one engine change. 801 need a kick up the arse! Tried a third LGB. No joy! Vulcan fired 2 Shrike overnight.

The first day of June began early. Shortly after 0300 I awoke to the rattling of chain lashings somewhere forward on the flight deck. Soon afterwards there was the unmistakable sound of a Pegasus winding up followed a mere three minutes later by a couple of engine acceleration checks and a mighty roar as a SHAR launched into the darkness. I lay on my camp bed, eyes open in the velvet darkness, wondering who was now heading towards the enemy, hunched over the controls, face bathed in the eerie green glow of the radar scope as he searched for the target. We did not launch without good reason at night so there was either very good intelligence of a raid or one had been picked up by one of the ships. It was even possible there was an Exocet raid inbound, as we were not sure at that time whether the Argentines had any more in their inventory. As the minutes passed that possibility faded but I was unable to get back to sleep until an hour later, when the loud whistling roar overhead told me that the aircraft had returned safely.

Andy McHarg had been scrambled to intercept a number of high-flying contacts to the north of Mount Kent. These were Canberras of Grupo 2 which had been carrying out extremely hazardous but ineffective low-level attacks against our forward troops. Andy got within four miles of the targets before shortage of fuel forced him to return to *Hermes*, bitterly disappointed. He was a victim of the policy of keeping the carriers as far to the east as possible. We desperately needed to get closer to the action if we were to be able to cover our troops effectively. Our average flight time was now in the region of one hour and twenty minutes, with only five to ten minutes being spent actually on CAP. This was a terrible waste of resources and meant that not only were there large holes in our defensive screen but also a distinct possibility we would not make it home if we got into a fight. In addition, we still had two aircraft on standby loaded with bombs in case the *25 de Mayo* came within range. This was at the captain's insistence, despite the fact that we had intelligence that the Argentine Navy's air group had been disembarked and the carrier was heading for port. These aircraft were hidden in Fly 3, tucked around behind the island, so that Admiral Woodward could not see them. It was suggested that if we went any further east, we would have to clear it with Cape Town air traffic control before we launched any aircraft.

For the rest of the day most of the action fell to our sister squadron on *Invincible*. Shortly before ten o'clock Sharkey and Steve Thomas were climbing out on their way back from CAP when HMS *Minerva*'s controller saw a fleeting radar contact to the north of Falkland Sound. He immediately told the returning SHARs and started giving them vectors for an intercept. Despite being low on fuel they followed the ship's instructions and soon had radar contact with the target. After a chase lasting several precious minutes Sharkey visually identified the target as a Hercules and closed for the attack. He fired his first missile at too great a range and saw it drop away to explode in the sea behind the fleeing transport. There was no mistake with the second Sidewinder; it impacted the starboard wing starting a serious fire in both engines. Sharkey then closed to guns range and put one long burst into the rear of the fuselage before breaking off and telling Steve to attack.

'Don't think I'll bother, boss. I think it's crashing,' replied his laconic wingman.

Sure enough, as they watched, the right wing started to drop and the huge machine plunged into the South Atlantic. It was totally destroyed, killing the entire crew. Sharkey and Steve were rightly elated at downing one of the elusive Hercules but I could not help feeling sorry for the guys on board. Their final moments must have been horrific, as the high-explosive rounds tore the back of their aircraft to shreds. It was a good hit, however, and reduced Argentine airlift and recce capability considerably. I am sure it also had a marked effect on the morale of their transport force.

The squadron's luck changed later in the afternoon, when they lost one of their own aircraft. Ian Mortimer, another of my ex-Germany buddies, was launched on a CAP mission shortly after 1300. His wingman discovered that his missile system was unserviceable and decided to return to *Invincible*, leaving Morts to carry on alone. This earned him a rebuke from Sharkey for leaving his leader without vital cross-cover, although to be fair it would not have affected the outcome.

The CAP station to the south of Stanley was positioned to catch any Hercules which might try to sneak into the airfield and Morts was combining his patrol with a recce of the road between Darwin and Stanley. This was the route that our troops were intending to take and any intelligence of enemy movements or defences would have been very welcome. He was flying an east–west racetrack at about 13,000 feet and was turning some five miles to the south of Stanley. Although he had been locked up by the Roland system a couple of times this did not worry him unduly as he knew its maximum range was 6.5 kilometres and he had heard my running commentary when the same unit fired at me a week earlier. He was about to start his third run when a movement on the airfield caught his eye. Turning towards the runway to get a better look he descended to about 10,000 feet. Almost immediately he saw the flash of a missile launch.

The missile and its trail were exactly as I had described them and Morts correctly identified it as a Roland. He turned away from the airfield, put his aircraft into a climb and watched the progress of the missile, happy that he would be well out of range. After a few seconds the thin grey trail seemed to fall away underneath his aircraft and he dropped his port wing in an attempt to catch sight of the missile as it dropped into the sea beneath him.

The next thing he knew was a huge explosion from the rear of his fuselage; the Roland had hit him! His aircraft started tumbling violently, completely disorientating him. It was obvious that he had to eject and he pulled the handle between his legs within a half-second of being hit. He was probably inverted when the seat left the aircraft and the ride was so violent that he was not initially sure whether he had actually left the cockpit. The seat functioned perfectly, however, and he soon found himself floating under a large billowing parachute. The descent was without incident and he splashed into the sea some three miles south-east of the airfield.

Despite the violence of his ejection Morts was unharmed but had great difficulty releasing his parachute harness and climbing aboard his dinghy. Once aboard the tiny life raft, he put out a quick Mayday call on his PLB and heard someone reply in English before he turned it off to deny the Argentines the chance to home onto his beacon. The airfield garrison had obviously seen his ejection and within a few minutes a helicopter was searching the area in which his aircraft had crashed. This was eventually joined by a twin-engined aircraft, which carried out a wider and more thorough search. After a few minutes it flew directly overhead; it had obviously seen him, and soon a Chinook was heading towards him from Stanley.

Morts switched on his PLB again and called, 'Anyone in the area, strafe the helicopter south of Stanley, but make it quick because it is about to pick me up!'

He then sat on the Day-Glo dinghy canopy to make himself harder to see and waited for the inevitable. The Chinook flew over him and set itself up into wind with the winch rigged to pick him up. A series of thoughts ran through Morts' head. Could he possibly get the drop on the crew once he had been picked up and force them to fly him back to *Invincible* at the point of his pistol? Should he try to shoot the helicopter down before it rescued him? Neither of these options stood much chance of success and he realised that he was probably destined to become a prisoner. That being the case, it was probably better not to aggravate his rescuers. The helicopter got to within yards of his dinghy and he was able to see the crewman quite clearly as he readied the winch, but then suddenly it sheered away and headed for the airfield at high speed.

At this very moment I was heading for the islands with Fred

Frederiksen. Our task was to locate some helicopters in the Pebble Island area where intelligence had suggested there might be Sea Kings armed with Exocets. If this was the case then they would be very high-priority targets and we could not afford to spend much time looking for Morts. We flew over at medium level and could see neither a dinghy nor any air activity. It was our presence which had caused the Argentines to abandon their rescue and leave Morts alone in his tiny life raft in the near-freezing water.

After a couple of hours darkness fell and Morts began to regret not being picked up. He made the odd transmission on his PLB but got no replies. Unknown to him the aerial lead had broken and none of his transmissions were going out, despite the radio showing every sign of being serviceable.

As all this was happening the eagerly awaited GR3 reinforcements arrived direct from Ascension. Flight Lieutenants Mike Beech and Murdo MacLeod had flown for eight hours and twenty-five minutes, refuelling several times from a Victor tanker, before jettisoning their ferry tanks and carrying out their first-ever vertical deck landings. Murdo was a dour Scot with a fiery temper who had previously done an exchange tour with the navy on Phantoms, so he was used to naval life. To Mike however it was a very new experience.

Both of the new pilots were weapons instructors and a great asset to the force. They also each brought with them radar jammers mounted in one of their gun pods. We hoped these would help reduce the effectiveness of the Argentine gun and missile radars. In true naval tradition this cobbled-together system was given a code name beginning with 'Blue' – for instance the SHAR radar Blue Fox. The jammer was named the Blue Eric, in tribute to the Monty Python team.

1 June
Sharkey got a C-130 this morning off the north coast of West Falkland. First AIM9-L missed, he then hit the starboard wing with the second and finally gunned it into the sea. Morts was lost P.M.

but heard on PLB; trying to find him tonight. Murdo MacLeod and
Mike Beech arrived in GR3s (with I-band jammer) after 8^1/$_2$-hour
flight from Ascension (with in-flight refuelling).

That evening we welcomed the new boys to the wardroom but the
celebrations were muted by the fact that one of our number was missing.
Morts was known by everyone and highly regarded both as a friend and
a colleague. My personal assessment was that he had probably been
captured; this would account for the lack of radio calls after he had said
he was about to be picked up. I hoped we would receive some intelligence from Stanley; a number of islanders were getting messages through
using their long-wave radios.

On *Invincible* 820 NAS mounted a rescue operation and searched the
area to the east of Stanley. Nothing was found and after some seven
hours the admiral suggested that the search should be abandoned as
nothing more had been heard from the survivor. This was a reasonable
decision but Lieutenant Commander Keith Dudley decided that he
would spend a few extra minutes and look just a little further inshore. To
his delight and amazement he spotted the tiny water-activated six-volt
bulb on the canopy of Morts' dinghy, and after more than eight hours in
the water he was finally rescued, cold but in one piece.

The following morning I flew one CAP mission and returned after
an hour and a half for a cockpit turnround before being scrambled for
another sortie. I had just started to taxi onto the centreline for my second
launch when the ship suddenly rolled violently to port. I jammed on
my brakes but the wheels just skidded on the slick deck and I continued
to slide majestically towards the port catwalk. I realised that if I didn't do
something drastic I would be over the side of the ship in a matter of a
couple of seconds, just like Mike Broadwater on *Invincible*.

I grabbed the nozzle lever, slammed it into the braking stop and put
on a handful of power. The reverse thrust did the trick and I slid
to a halt with the deck edge disappearing beneath the nose. Once I
had calmed down and the marshaller had picked himself up I put the

nozzles aft again and cautiously lined up on the centreline. I quickly ran through the pre-take-off checks and checked that the bottom-end acceleration was within limits. I then attempted to lower the nozzles to fifty degrees for a final check of the duct pressure. Nothing happened. The nozzles were stuck in the fully aft position and would not move. The FDO had his green flag above his head ready to launch me but when he saw the urgent shaking of my head and the thumbs-down signal he quickly taxied me into Fly 1 to clear the deck for the rest of the launch.

I shut down and climbed out of the aircraft mystified. When the engineers checked the system out, they found that the air motor servo unit exhaust had sheered and jammed the nozzle controls. Had I not taken the braking stop to avoid going over the side I would have got airborne safely enough but then been unable to hover when I returned. This would have meant an ejection and the loss of an otherwise serviceable Sea Harrier. A conventional landing, with the nozzles fully aft, would have required some 6000 feet of runway, about 5500 feet more than we had available.

The next couple of days were a complete washout. The whole area was blanketed in thick fog and even the sheathbills were grounded. At least it gave us the time to write some letters home. Meanwhile, the yellow shirts used the lull to scrub some of the greasy deposits off the flight deck. I think that my little episode had made everyone realise that the surface was becoming a hazard to operations. We certainly could not afford to lose another aircraft over the side. The weather was also a boon for the 1 (F) squadron engineers, who now had much better conditions for completing their engine change.

HMS *Hermes*
2 June

My dearest disciple,
The touches of spring were beautiful; they really brought a little colour into my otherwise dreary and unexciting life! It is nearly winter down here and we had snow over the islands a couple of

days ago. The scenery is really bleak and godforsaken. As bare as a baboon's bum in fact, with only one small clump of trees on the whole island and they are in someone's back garden. Our routine consists of flying, sleeping, thinking of home and the odd drink but the bar is only open for $2^1/2$ hours a day. We do get a few films, which help to remind us what the female form looks like, so I hope to be able to recognise it when I get back to the UK!

We are all settling down to life here now and although we have lost a few people, morale is very high. We have destroyed about half of the Argie Air Force over the Falklands, with some people getting two kills in one sortie, and the ground forces are doing very well. In fact the fighting will probably be over by the time this reaches you. I am looking forward to getting back to my 500-year-old cottage and being able to potter in the garden and walk to the pub and all the normal pleasures of life.

When I get back, you must both come down and help with the garden, which is a tip at the moment. You really must not worry about me, you know, but then I expect you have stopped by now because I have. Just keep the positive thoughts coming down this way and we will win through. We have some super little birds down here called sheathbills. They look like doves, are brilliant white in colour and incredibly friendly. They land on the ship and even on the aeroplanes on deck (which is disconcerting when you are about to take off) and sit there, a couple of feet away. I am sure that they are friends of Jonathan Livingston Seagull.

I hear that we have been on television and in the papers at home. I will have to start a fan club when I get back. Did you see the film reports of the Stanley airfield raid on 1 May? We have just got them here and I am very satisfied with the damage I did. (One Islander aircraft with the tail blown off and the airport buildings alight.) There seemed to be a bit more anti-aircraft fire on the day!

Well, my love, I must go and strap on my little jet again. Keep the good thoughts coming (and the naughty ones!) and don't be frightened of the yellow snake. It is not time for him yet. Give my best wishes to David.

Take care, little one, be good!

Love

David

HMS *Hermes*
3 June

Hello, love,

It's me again. I hope that your move (our move?) went without too many problems. I expect the kids are thrilled even if you are a bit harassed by it all. I guess the pets will like it once they have got used to it. (Except the goldfish, who might not notice too much difference.) Murdo MacLeod and Mike Beech arrived two days ago after tanking down from Ascension and they are both in good spirits. Chris Gowers is coming soon, it would seem. The war in the air has slackened off a bit over the last few days and the only kill we have had was Sharkey's Hercules. I have not been able to improve on my ship and two helicopters.

The land battle is progressing apace now that Goose Green has fallen and I expect it will be over by the time you get this letter. We have got confirmed kills on nearly half the Argie Air Force so far, so I don't think that they will give us too much trouble now. I have just seen the Argie pictures of the 1 May airfield attack. I was the last one over the target (just behind the missile) and hit the red and white Islander (with its tail knocked off) and the airport buildings. There was a very satisfactory amount of damage.

Today it is foggy and we are not doing a lot of flying but most of us got about 50 hours last month, so it's not bad for the logbook. The Sea King boys have been getting twice as much, so they are a bit knackered. The enclosed grass is from the Falkland Islands, by the way. Don't ask me how I got it; I thought the

kids might like it. I will try to get some heather and send it to you
if I can. That is about all that grows on this godforsaken place.
There are no trees (apart from one clump in a chap's garden),
hardly any fences but lots of penguins, albatrosses, sheep and
wild cattle. The latter can present a bit of a problem to low-flying
Harriers!

I hope that no one has bashed you with a rounders bat again
and that the kids are not giving you too much of a hard time. Give
my regards to your parents when you next talk to them and give
the Boggits a big hug from me. I wish I were back home again to
help you with the move. I expect I'll have to take you out for a
meal for being so clever when I get back! Still, I'm saving lots of
money <u>and</u> getting paid extra, so it can't be all bad.

Take care, my love. I think of you all the time and can't wait
to get back.

I love you.

D

On 3 June we were passed the text of an intercepted Argentine signal
which stated that British forces were preparing a landing strip in San
Carlos. We had a good laugh at this as we knew the PSA planking had
gone down with *Atlantic Conveyor*. However, the following day we were
amazed to receive a message telling us that a strip had indeed been
prepared and was now ready for use. I cobbled together a quick brief for
the Sea Harrier pilots and as soon as the weather cleared led Dave Smith
ashore to christen the tin runway.

The strip was an absolute boon. The 850 feet of planking enabled
us to get airborne with sufficient fuel for an hour in the air. It also meant
that we were only a few minutes' flying time from our CAP stations.
On the afternoon of 5 June Dave and I carried out three sorties, refuelling twice at the strip. Here I was delighted to be met by another old
buddy of mine, Squadron Leader Syd Morris, who was in charge of the
strip, which I had named HMS *Sheathbill*. Syd had commanded the

Belize detachment when I first went out there and I well remember his initial briefing, which went along the lines of, 'OK, there's lots of good low flying to be had out here, but if anyone gets a bird strike, they had better make sure it was not on its nest at the time.' It used to be fair game to buzz army trucks on the straight road in the jungle between Belmopan and Belize City and on one occasion a truck driver was so surprised by seeing a Harrier at head height that he ran off the road. Happy days!

It felt very odd walking on solid ground for the first time in two months and I was aware of certain unsteadiness in my step as I wandered over to the nearest clump of gorse to relieve myself. I was trying to undo the pee tube in the front of my immersion suit when a rather annoyed voice from the undergrowth called out, 'Oi, mate, what the hell do you think you're doing?' I mumbled an apology and found another bush not occupied by someone in a slit trench.

On that first day Dave and I were on station for one hour and forty minutes for a transit time of less than an hour. The missions were without incident but I did bring back a couple of dead geese. Upland geese are indigenous to the islands and in common with all the local wildlife not at all frightened of humans. They very soon realised that the metal strip was warmer than the surrounding grass and took to sitting in the middle of it. Syd and his men had tried shooing the birds away but they merely waddled straight back. Eventually they had to be shot and several were brought back to *Hermes* over the next few days and put in the freezer. It was rather bizarre to have one of the strip-based ground crew climb up the side of the aircraft and say, 'There you are, sir. Five thousand pounds of fuel and two geese up the back hatch.'

5 June

Foggy in the morning. *Invincible* went south of Falklands last night but just missed a high-level overflight, which was probably escorting a low-level drop somewhere. Flew into San Carlos FOB [forward operating base] for a couple of refuels and did my first night landing. No probs really but no trade either. Our troops are now within eight miles of Stanley and have secured the Mount Low area but the political damper appears to have been put on the advance.

NO HEROES

There were no heroes here
Amongst the men who tramped through
Rutted quaking moor
Or crawled, cat-silent,
Over skittering scree
To prove the way.

No heroes fought the blazing fires
Which sucked the very blood from
Ship and man alike.
Or braved knife cold
Without a thought to save a life.

No heroes they, but ones who loved
Sweet life and children's laugh,
And dreamt of home
When war allowed.
They were but men.

The next two days passed without major incident. On the 6th the weather was awful, with a massive area of low pressure bringing low cloud and gales. Very little flying was done, although Peter Squire led Mike Beech on an armed recce mission immediately to the south of Stanley. Peter dropped his cluster bombs only 500 metres from the town and they did not see any return fire for the first time ever. The SHARs flew a few CAP missions but no contact was made with the enemy. Tuesday 7 June was a glorious day but once again there was very little action in the air, although *Exeter* did manage to shoot down a high-level target to the west of San Carlos. This was originally thought to be a Canberra but turned out to be a Learjet.

On the ground British forces were gradually converging on Stanley, with a series of fierce battles developing for the high ground to the west of the town. The advance was seriously hindered by the appalling terrain and all available helicopters were pressed into service bringing forward artillery, ammunition and stores to support the Paras and Royal Marines as they struggled towards their final objective. It was clear that the Argentine pilots were having as much trouble as we were finding suitable targets to attack. While the deadly game was played out among the rocks and bogs of the islands we could only try to stay alert and ready to react to any threat which might appear.

CHAPTER 11

THE FINAL ENGAGEMENT

THE MORNING OF 8 June started much the same as any other: the ritual of a shower, putting on clean underwear and lucky flying suit (by now rather high), and a good breakfast in the wardroom before climbing the ladders to 2 Deck to check the briefing room for the day's commitments as dawn was breaking. It transpired that I was unlikely to be needed before midday as I was due to carry out the final part of my night deck landing qualification that evening. Night flying from the ship was fraught with difficulty. In peacetime an extended work-up was carried out with plenty of fuel and a good shore diversion close by in case you couldn't get the aircraft safely back on the deck. Now, however, it was to be one dawn launch, followed by a dusk landing and finally a dark landing. My dusk landing had been achieved with minimum hassle three days previously and tonight was my dark landing. I wasn't looking forward to it at all.

In the crewroom I met Lieutenant Ian Bryant, who was about to get airborne in his Wessex. He had been flown ragged since his arrival a couple of days earlier and looked absolutely bushed. I therefore volunteered to fly with him and help out. It had been nearly ten years since I had flown the Wessex full time but I found it soon came back and I spent a happy couple of hours delivering mail and supplies around the fleet. A relaxing change from the usual SHAR missions and it brought back happy memories of my time on No. 72 Squadron in Northern Ireland. There, despite the ever-present threat of terrorist attack, we had the freedom to fly as low as we deemed prudent to achieve the aim of the sortie. On a number of occasions I can remember the great fat main wheels of the Wessex hitting the ground at high speed, a very good reason for leaving the brakes off in flight. Once we even chased a fox across the top of the Sperrin Mountains, with one pilot flying and the other blazing away at the hapless beast with his 9-millimetre pistol. I am glad to say that the fox managed to outmanoeuvre us and headed home with a bizarre tale to tell her cubs.

The Wessex was a very sturdy machine with few vices and was loved by all who flew it. It was versatile and reliable and ideally suited to operations in rough terrain such as Ireland or indeed the Falklands. It was used to carry out all sorts of tasks. One of my strangest rescues occurred one evening as I was returning to Aldergrove along the north coast of County Londonderry. As we flew low along the beautiful sandy beaches west of Portstewart we came across a car stuck in the sand. A couple of young lovers had driven down to the water's edge to watch the sunset and been caught by the rising tide. My crewman quickly attached one end of a rope to the rear of the car and the other to the underslung load hook on the aircraft. I lifted the aircraft into the hover and gently towed the vehicle up to solid ground. I think we made a couple of friends that evening.

Another pilot came across a team of Post Office engineers attempting to erect a telegraph pole miles away from the nearest road and asked if he could help. They were most grateful and he attached the pole to his winch and started to lift. Unfortunately things did not go to plan and the pole swung up into his rotor disc, taking great chunks off the ends of all four blades. He managed to coax his vibrating aircraft as far as Armagh and landed safely in the barracks but was immediately grounded pending court martial for recklessly endangering his aircraft. When the investigators finally arrived at the site of the alleged incident they could find no sign of a damaged pole and the Post Office engineers denied seeing a helicopter all day. The case was dropped through lack of evidence and we subsequently discovered that the engineers had rolled the damaged pole into a ditch half a mile away and covered it with bracken.

Having enjoyed my morning's helicopter flying, I flew an afternoon mission, patrolling to the north of Falkland Sound. The weather had cleared beautifully with very little cloud over the islands and just the odd thunderstorm over the sea. The coast of West Falkland, to the south of us, looked like Scotland, its purple-clad mountains rolling down in easy terraces to the ocean. It was difficult to imagine that it was less than three months since I had been at home and that our families were now enjoying the beginning of summer some 6000 miles to the north.

It was now standard practice to use the metal landing strip at San Carlos to refuel between sorties. Unfortunately, Peter Squire had experienced an engine problem while landing there that morning and had spread his aircraft all over the strip, coming to rest on top of a slit trench. Luckily, neither Peter nor the troops in the slit trench were hurt and the aircraft rapidly became a useful source of spares for both GR3 and SHAR fleets. On closer inspection of the wreck, it became apparent that the airframe had been dangerously distorted during its roller-coaster ride over the uneven planking and the cockpit was very close to detaching itself from the rest of the fuselage. This would probably have had fatal consequences for Peter and deprived the RAF of a very fine officer and future chief of the air staff.

My sortie was completely uneventful but very soon after we set off back to *Hermes* HMS *Plymouth* was attacked by a formation of Daggers. Coming off CAP just before a raid was a frustrating but not unusual occurrence and we were glad to hear that her damage had not been serious. That evening, Lieutenant Dave Smith and I strapped into our aircraft to come to five-minute alert with our minds focused more on the night landing to come than the possibility of combat. Shortly before we were planned to launch we were jolted back to reality by the broadcast, 'Stand clear of intakes and jet pipes. Scramble the Alert 5 Sea Harriers!' We had a job to do.

Adrenalin pumping, I selected the start switch and hit the button. Ten seconds later, I opened the HP cock and the engine began winding up. As soon as the jet pipe temperature and RPM stabilised, I flicked the electrics on, checked the hydraulics and exercised the controls to check for full and free movement. Most of the switches had been left in the appropriate positions to facilitate a rapid start, so within ninety seconds I was ready to taxi. As *Hermes* steadied on the flying course my tie-down chains and outrigger locks were removed and held up for my acknowledgement by the ground crew. I taxied rapidly onto the centreline and carried out final checks. Tony Hodgson's green flag fluttered above his head, his body braced against the jet blast, as I slammed the Pegasus to full power, releasing the toe brakes as the tyres began to drag across the deck and feeling the huge push in the back as the aircraft surged towards the ramp.

Once away from the ship I jinked right for a couple of seconds before turning back to pick up Dave's SHAR leaving the ramp. We were airborne within three minutes and streaking towards the sun, which was now low on the western horizon. In the climb we contacted the *Hermes* controller, who was unable to give us any information, save that there had been an air raid over the islands. For the next quarter of an hour we flew in silence wondering what we would find when we got there. We took it in turns to check our Sidewinders by locking them onto each other, something which requires complete mutual trust. If you get it wrong, you might just have time to say sorry before your wingman became a fireball.

Finally the hazy outline of the islands began to appear in the distance, purple and indistinct in the gathering dusk. As we approached our nominated CAP station north of Lively Island I radioed the pair of Sea Harriers we were relieving. I wanted to get a picture of what was happening but all they would tell us was that they were 'over the action' to the north of our briefed patrol location. When I asked them for more precise information they told me that it would soon become obvious.

As we got closer I saw a huge column of oily black smoke rising from a bay to the south-west of Stanley. I was gripped by an awful sense of foreboding and as we arrived overhead the grim reality unfolded. Two Royal Fleet Auxiliary landing ships were at anchor in the bay, wreathed in a nightmare of smoke and explosions. From our perch high in the halls of the sky we could only watch with concern and frustration as the living beetles of lifeboats crawled back and forth between ships and shore with their desperate human cargoes. Overnight *Sir Tristram* and *Sir Galahad* had moved the Welsh Guards forward from Goose Green to Port Pleasant south of Fitzroy and that morning had been waiting for landing craft to take the troops ashore. Unfortunately for them the weather was crystal clear and their light grey hulls stood out like the proverbial dog's bollocks against the mottled grey-green of the coastline. An Argentine spotter on Mount Kent had seen them and the rest was inevitable.

As the guards waited to disembark, the ships had been caught by a formation of five Argentine Skyhawks from Grupo 5 based at Rio Gallegos. The damage was obviously severe and we both realised that we were watching a disastrous incident with considerable loss of life. I felt particularly angry that no one had given us any idea that the ships were about to move so far forward. Had we known, we could have easily provided continuous air cover and this awful loss of life might have been avoided.

As it was there was little we could do but search the lengthening shadows for further attackers as we ploughed our parallel furrows back and forth, a couple of miles overhead. It was a peculiarly impotent feeling to be sitting in the relatively comfortable, benign and familiar surroundings of the cockpit while the troops and helicopter pilots below us were engaged in a dreadful dance with death. To fly lower would have denied us radio contact with our controller in San Carlos and risked spooking the troops on the ground into thinking we were the enemy returning to cause further chaos. In addition, we had been informed that the troops were setting up a Rapier missile battery below us and I had no wish to end my day with a Mach 3 rocket up my arse. As I have mentioned before, unfortunately the Blue Fox radar was useless looking down over land and not much better against low-level targets out at sea. We were therefore committed to using the Mark 1 eyeball to search for any possible threats.

A visual search in such conditions is a particularly taxing routine. If you just let your eyes simply sweep around the horizon, they will eventually focus a few yards in front of you and you will never see a bogey. This phenomenon is known as empty field myopia and has been the cause of many a missed opportunity and could prove fatal should an enemy fighter be in the neighbourhood. It is therefore essential to intersperse your visual search pattern with a few seconds focusing on something at some distance from your cockpit. In our case we could include each other in our scans, as well as the coastline below. Thus both of us were scanning ahead with our radars, checking each other's tails and also searching the gathering dark below us for targets.

Some five miles to the south of our racetrack in the sky I noticed a small landing craft leaving Choiseul Sound and making its way up the coast towards Fitzroy. On checking with the controller, this was identified as friendly and I made a particular point of monitoring its progress each time I turned back onto a westerly heading. I imagined the crew cold and tired in their tiny boat and I wondered if they had any idea that we were watching over them. This was in fact one of *Fearless'* landing craft, transporting some troops and a Land Rover towards Bluff Cove.

The next forty minutes crept by as we circled, using the minimum possible amount of fuel, neither of us talking and both very much aware of the tragedy being enacted below us and feeling a burgeoning impotence. What we had no way of knowing was that ten minutes after we had launched, one of our submarines had reported a flight of aircraft leaving Rio Gallegos and heading east. I made a routine check of the fuel gauges as I rolled into another turn to reverse track and realised that I now had only four minutes' flying before I had to turn east into the rapidly darkening evening sky for *Hermes* and my night landing. I flicked my eyes out of the cockpit and searched the gathering dusk below me for the small landing craft. I soon picked it out, butting its way through the South Atlantic rollers towards Port Pleasant with white water breaking over its bows.

It was in that instant that I spotted something which triggered the explosive action lying like a tightly coiled spring beneath the outwardly calm carapace of the fighter pilot. My worst fears and fondest dreams had, in a moment, been realised. A mere mile to the east of the tiny vessel was the camouflaged outline of a Skyhawk fighter, hugging the sea and heading directly for the landing craft which had become a very personal part of my existence for the last forty minutes. This was the very thing that we had both been anticipating and dreading. Normally it was imperative to attack a low-level target in such a way as to ensure that your tail was safe from any counter-attack but in this scenario there was no choice. We had already briefed that anyone who spotted a low-level target would just throw caution to the wind and go 'balls out' for it. There was no time to be careful. Lives were at stake.

I jammed the throttle fully open, shouted over the radio, 'A4s attacking the boat. Follow me down!' and peeled off into a sixty-degree dive towards the attacker. As my airspeed rattled up through 400 knots I retracted my flaps and pushed to zero G to achieve the best possible rate of acceleration. Dave Smith wrenched his Sea Harrier around after me but lost sight of my machine as we plunged down with our airspeeds rocketing from the economical 240 on CAP to well over 600 knots, as we strained to catch the enemy before he could reach his target.

I watched impotently, urging my aircraft onward and downward, as the A4 opened fire with his 20-millimetre cannon, bracketing the tiny craft. My heart soared as his bomb exploded a good 100 feet beyond the landing craft but then sank as I realised that a further A4 was running in behind him. The second pilot did not miss and I bore mute and frustrated witness to the violent fire-bright petals of the explosion which obliterated the stern, killing the crew and mortally wounding the landing craft. All-consuming anger welled in my throat and I determined in that instant that this pilot was going to die!

The world suddenly became very quiet. I was completely focused and acutely aware that this was the moment for which all my training had prepared me. I had flown many hours of mock combat against all manner of fighters but this was the defining moment. As I closed rapidly on his tail I noticed in my peripheral vision a further A4 skimming the spume-flecked water, paralleling his track to my left. I hauled my aircraft to the left and rolled out less than half a mile behind the third fighter, closing like a runaway train. I had both missiles and guns selected and within seconds I heard the growl in my earphones which told me that my Sidewinder could see the heat from his engine. My right thumb pressed the lock button on the stick and instantly the small green missile cross in the head-up display transformed itself into a diamond sitting squarely over the back end of the Skyhawk. At the same time the growl of the missile became an urgent high-pitched chirp, telling me that the infrared homing head of the weapon was locked on and ready to fire.

I raised the safety catch and mashed the recessed red firing button with all the strength I could muster. There was a short delay as the missile's thermal battery ignited and its voltage increased to that required to launch the weapon. In less than half a second the Sidewinder was transformed from an inert eleven-foot drainpipe into a fire-breathing monster as it accelerated to nearly three times the speed of sound and streaked towards the nearest enemy aircraft. As it left the rails the rocket efflux and supersonic shock wave over the left wing rolled my charging Sea Harrier rapidly to the right, throwing me onto my right wing tip at less than 100 feet above the sea. As I rolled erect the missile started to guide towards the Skyhawk's jet pipe, trailing a white corkscrew of smoke against the slate-grey sea. Within two seconds the missile had disappeared directly up his jet pipe and what had been a vibrant flying machine was completely obliterated as the missile tore it apart. The pilot had no chance of survival and within a further two seconds the ocean had swallowed all trace of him and his aeroplane as if they had never been.

There was no time for elation. As I was righting my machine after the first missile launch I realised that I was pointing directly at another Argentine aircraft at a range of about one mile – the one I had seen hit the landing craft.

I had heard it said many times by armchair warriors that war in the air was a cold, sterile, almost esoteric form of combat, where you fought against machines without feelings or personal involvement. How wrong they were! This was not a computer game; I was not destroying machines; I was determined to kill these pilots. They had dared to attack my colleagues *on my watch*! Those same pilots that I would probably have been very happy to share a drink with in different circumstances now had to die.

Unknown to me, on my entry into the fight I had mistaken the third Skyhawk for the rearmost man, a mistake that should have cost me my life. As I was about to line up my sights on the second A4 the rear man was manoeuvring in an attempt to spoil my whole day with a stream of high-explosive rounds. I had made the classic mistake of barrelling into the fight without total situational awareness. As a result I had nearly collided with the fourth Skyhawk and was now directly in front of him. However, purely by chance Primer Teniente Hector Sanchez had taken some ground fire a few minutes earlier which had damaged his gun and it would not fire. He had to watch helplessly as his formation fell prey to my deadly missiles.

I mashed the lock button again with a strength born of righteous anger and my second missile immediately locked onto the jet efflux of the next A4 as he started a panic break towards me on Hector's call. As I was about to fire the homing head lost lock and the missile cross wandered drunkenly onto the sea some fifty feet below him. Cursing, I rejected the false lock, mashed the lock button again, obtained the chirp and fired, the missile whipping across my nose to the left to head him off.

He obviously saw the Sidewinder launch because he immediately reversed his break and pulled his aircraft into a screaming turn away from it. This was without doubt the best possible evasive action he could have tried as it made the missile expend a huge amount of energy and control power to reverse its course. His best efforts were to no avail, however, and the thin grey missile flashed back across my nose and, seemingly in slow motion, pulled to the right and impacted his machine directly behind the cockpit. The complete rear half of the airframe simply disintegrated as if a shotgun had been fired at a plastic model from close range.

The warhead of the AIM9-L is a fearsome piece of engineering. It has a blast fragmentation action which produces a large pattern of high-speed fragments that make mincemeat of airframe and engine components alike. A few nanoseconds later a disc of zirconium is detonated which sends a circular fan of white-hot metal scorching through the debris. This normally results in a catastrophic and instantaneous explosion. Very few fighter aircraft have survived an AIM9-L hit.

The air was filled with the aluminium confetti of destruction fluttering seaward. I watched fascinated as the remains of the aircraft yawed rapidly starboard through ninety degrees and splashed violently into the freezing water. I can vividly remember the detail of the cockpit, with the stubs of the wings still attached, as it impacted the waves.

I felt a terrific surge of elation at the demise of the second A4 and started to scan the murk ahead for the others. I had just picked out the next one, fleeing west, his belly only feet from the water, when a parachute snapped open almost in front of my face. The pilot had somehow managed to eject from the gyrating cockpit in the half-second before it hit the water and he flashed over my left wing so close that I saw every detail of the rag-doll figure, its arms and legs thrown out in a grotesque star shape by the deceleration of the silk canopy. My feelings of anger and elation instantly changed to relief and empathy as I realised that a fellow pilot had survived. An instant later immense anger returned as I started to run down the next victim before he could make good his escape in the gloom.

I learnt later that Teniente Arraras had not survived. I suspect that he was a victim of the Escapac ejection seat fitted to his aircraft. This seat has a ballistic spreader which opens the parachute immediately regardless of the speed of the aircraft. This can result in massive injuries during a high-speed ejection and would have almost certainly rendered him unconscious before his entry into the water.

Now that I had launched both missiles I had only guns with which to dispatch the remaining Skyhawk and as I lifted the safety slide on the trigger I realised that my head-up display had disappeared and I had no gunsight. This was a well-known glitch in the HUD software and could be cured easily by selecting the HUD off and then on again. This I duly did, but in the ten seconds it took for the sight to reappear it was all over.

The A4 broke rapidly towards me as I screamed up behind him with a good 150 knots overtake. I pulled his blurred outline to the bottom of the blank windscreen and opened fire. The roar of the 30-millimetre rounds leaving the guns filled the cockpit. I kept my finger on the trigger and relaxed then reapplied the G in order to walk the rounds through him as best I could. Air-to-air gunnery at fifty feet is not easy at the best of times and without a gunsight in the semi-darkness it was verging on the impossible.

Suddenly over the radio came an urgent shout from Dave Smith: 'Pull up, pull up, you're being fired at!' All he had seen of the fight until now, because of the failing light, had been two missile launches followed by two explosions. He then saw an aircraft only feet above the water flying through a hail of explosions and assumed it to be me. By now I had run out of ammunition and at Dave's cry I pulled up into the vertical through the setting sun and, in a big lazy looping manoeuvre, rolled out at 12,000 feet heading north-east for *Hermes* with my heart racing.

In the vertical climb I looked back down over Choiseul Sound and saw a white trail accelerating towards the fleeing A4. The trail was so low to the water that my first crazy thought was that it was a torpedo. I soon realised however that it was a missile and watched transfixed as it headed for the enemy fighter. About halfway to the target the rocket motor burnt out and for a few maddening seconds I thought it had been fired out of range and would drop into the water. Dave had not misjudged it, though, and after some seven seconds of flight there was a brilliant white flash as the zirconium disc in the warhead ignited. The Skyhawk target was so low that the flash of the warhead merged with its reflection in the water of the Sound. A fraction of a second later the aircraft disappeared in a yellow-orange fireball as it spread its burning remains over the sand dunes on the north coast of Lafonia near Hammond Point.

Climbing rapidly through 20,000 feet I checked my engine and fuel gauges and saw that we were going to be very tight for gas. We used a figure of 2000 pounds of fuel over Port Stanley as a good rule of thumb for returning to the ship and my gauges were reading less than 1400 pounds. As I overflew the battered runway, climbing through 25,000 feet between the odd mushroom of anti-aircraft fire, my low-level fuel lights came on, indicating 1300 pounds remaining. At 40,000 feet I called the carrier and told them that I was returning short of fuel and they obliged by coming up to thirty-two knots and heading towards us to close the distance.

The next twenty minutes was a period of enforced idleness. All I could do was watch the fuel gauges decrease and think about my night recovery. Every time I calculated the fuel remaining in the tanks against that required to get home I came up with a negative answer. This was really not good!

I mentally rehearsed an ejection into the cold, dark water below me. Ideally it should be initiated just below 10,000 feet so that the parachute deploys immediately and gives the maximum time in the air to prepare for impact. In the dark it would be very difficult to judge height and it was likely that I would not see the surface before it came up to meet me. I would have to lower my tiny dinghy and be prepared to release my chute immediately after impact. The problem then would be to inflate and board the single-seat life raft in a fairly high sea. Without the life raft survival would be a matter of an hour or two as the sea temperature was only a few degrees above zero. I would then have to hope that there was a convenient Sea King to find me and winch me up, as had happened with Jerry Pook.

If I did make it back to the carrier I would have to carry out my first really dark deck landing. A full carrier-controlled approach, the only approved recovery method, would have used an extra 500 or 600 pounds of fuel. This was clearly out of the question. If I had any chance of getting back on board I would have to squeeze the last drop of fuel out of my faithful aircraft. This meant staying as high as possible for as long as possible before gliding down to the snappiest landing of my life.

I also started thinking about the recent engagement. It had been an incredibly rapid and violent fight lasting . . . how long? Ten minutes? One minute? I eventually came to the conclusion that the whole action had lasted less than three minutes, probably closer to two. In that time half a dozen men had probably died. I thought that I was probably directly responsible for the deaths of two Argentine pilots. That was something I managed to push to the back of my mind at the time but which was to have a huge impact on the next twenty years of my life.

After a while I decided there was little to be gained by calculating the fuel every couple of minutes so I covered the fuel gauges with two patches of masking tape. At least I was not then quite so distracted. Thus, when I closed the throttle to start a cruise descent from ninety miles out I was still uncertain that I was going to make it before I flamed out and took an unwanted bath in the freezing waters of the South Atlantic Ocean.

At 40,000 feet the sun was still a blaze of orange on the western horizon but as I descended the light became progressively worse. By the time I had descended to 10,000 feet my world had become an extremely dark and lonely place. The adrenalin levels, which had been sinking back to normal during the twenty minutes after the engagement, now started to increase again in anticipation of the landing. To compound the problem and to give final proof of the existence of Sod's law, *Hermes* had managed to find one of the massive thunderstorms in the area and

was in heavy rain and gusting wind. I knew that I did not have sufficient fuel to carry out a proper radar approach and asked the controller
to just talk me onto the centreline while I adjusted my glide so that I
would not have to touch the throttle until the last minute.

With three miles to run, descending through 1500 feet, I was still in
thick turbulent cloud when my fuel warning lights began to flash
urgently, telling me I had 500 pounds of fuel remaining. At two miles
I saw a glimmer of light emerging through the rain and at 800 feet
the lights fused into the recognisable outline of the carrier. I slammed
the nozzle lever into the hover stop, selected full flap and punched the
undercarriage button to lower the wheels. I picked up the mirror sight,
which confirmed that I was well above the ideal glide path but dropping
rapidly towards the invisible sea. With about half a mile to run I added
a handful of power and felt the Pegasus engine's instant response,
stopping my descent at about 300 feet. The wheels locked down as I
applied full braking stop to position myself off the port side of the deck
and seconds later I was transitioning sideways to hover over the centreline of the deck, level with the aft end of the superstructure. I knew
that I had very little fuel remaining so finesse went out of the window as
I closed the throttle and banged the machine down on the rain-streaked
deck. Once safely taxied forward into the graveyard and lashed in place,
I shut down the engine and heard Dave's jet landing on behind me. My
fuel gauges were showing 300 pounds, sufficient for a further two
minutes' flying! On checking the Pilot's Notes later, I discovered the
sentence: 'For unusable fuel, allow 150 lbs per side.' It had indeed been
very close.

We met in the line office, both of us with eyes bright with adrenalin,
hands and knees shaking. The results of our mission had preceded us
and everyone crowded around to congratulate us. The plane captains
of the two aircraft were over the moon as their aircraft had achieved
kills. There was great rivalry between crews and it was made very clear to
all of us that pilots only borrowed the aircraft for the duration of the
mission before returning them to their rightful owners!

There was no time for an immediate debrief as we were asked to report to Flyco to brief Wings on our success. Robin Shercliff congratulated us on not only achieving our kills but also becoming night deck qualified. I must admit, however, I never wanted to night fly again after that approach, a feeling which didn't ever really change. There is an old saying that only birds and fools fly but you have to be bats to fly at night.

After spending a few minutes with Wings we were taken to see the captain in his cabin for a further debrief. Here it transpired that Sharkey Ward had reported seeing four explosions during our engagement as they were running in to help. This led to a supposition that we had splashed all four Skyhawks. I was always sceptical about this claim and neither of us ever claimed the fourth kill, although the myth was perpetuated in the daily signal sent back to C in C fleet in the UK that evening. It is worthy of note that while many of the kills claimed by the ships and ground forces were discredited after the conflict every single SHAR claim was substantiated by independent research. Indeed, Clive Morrell was credited with one Skyhawk that he did not claim at the time.

From the captain's cabin we were escorted by John Locke to see the admiral. He was fulsome in his praise and as we left him I looked at my watch to find, to my horror, that the bar had just closed. This was a disaster. Denying two tired and very hyped-up fighter pilots a drink was the worst possible torture! The commander saw the look of despair on my mask-lined face and said, 'Don't worry, Moggie; we have kept the bar open for you.' True to his word, when we arrived, still in our goon suits, at the wardroom bar there were three pints of beer each, lined up ready for us. Never had drinks been so welcome. As we supped our Courage Special Brew the barman was already stencilling another three aircraft onto the scoreboard behind the optics.

Dave and I did not require much of a debrief. We had done a good job in very difficult circumstances and recovered two very valuable aircraft to the ship despite a desperate shortage of fuel and adverse weather conditions. I was then and remain terribly sad that I hadn't seen the Skyhawks a minute earlier. That might have enabled us to foil their attack run and save the lives of the landing craft crew. At the time, because of the extremely poor light conditions we were unsure whether the enemy aircraft had been Skyhawks or Mirages, and the final mission report stated they were the latter. This misidentification was only corrected after the conflict.

In reply to the daily signal, which had stated that we were on a training mission, C-in-C fleet sent: 'Congratulations your evening sortie. If this is what you do on a training mission, I can't wait to see what you do when you are operational!'

That evening I made my way back up to the briefing room through the eerie red glow of the night-lit passageways and sat on my own for a while. My feelings of satisfaction and pride were tempered by melancholy. I was aware that somehow my life had changed but I could not identify how or why that should be. I took out my copy of *For Johnny* and copied onto the briefing board the words of John Pudney's famous poem 'Combat Report':

Just then I saw this one come out.
You heard my shout? You, light and easy,
Carving the daylight. *I was breezy*
When I saw that one. O wonder,
Pattern of stress, of nerve poise, flyer,
Overtaking time. *He came out under*
Nine-tenths cloud, but I was higher.
Did Michael Angelo aspire,
Painting the laughing cumulus, to ride
The majesty of air. *He was a trier,*
I'll give this Jerry that. So you convert
Ultimate sky to air speed, drift and cover:
Sure with the tools of God and lover.
I let him have a sharp four-second squirt,

Closing to fifty yards. He went on fire.
Your deadly petals painted, you exert
A simple stature. Man-high, without pride,
You pick your way through heaven and the dirt.
He burnt out in the air: that's how the poor sod died.

This done, I sat on the hard, leather-covered bench at the front of the room and became aware that there was moisture running down both my cheeks. This could not be tears. Fighter pilots don't cry; they eat glass and bite the heads off babies and die young no matter how long they live. But somehow it felt cathartic. Best not to tell the rest of the boys, though. Best keep it quiet, like my poetry.

I discovered some years later that the fourth pilot, Hector Sanchez, had in fact escaped after jettisoning his bombs and fuel tanks. His flight had taken off from Rio Gallegos with six aircraft but had lost two to unserviceabilities during the outbound transit. After refuelling to the west of the islands they had tried to attack the landing craft in Port Pleasant but had been greeted with withering fire from the troops on the ground. Hector had been hit and their formation integrity lost in the heat of the battle. Only minutes later we had bounced them. After the engagement he had headed south over Lafonia before climbing out to the west and trying desperately to find the C-130 tanker. He made it with a teaspoon of fuel remaining. He had also lost his pressurisation as a result of ground fire from the Fitzroy area and had to continually scrape the ice off the inside of the cockpit, which made refuelling very difficult indeed. Hector survived the war and went on to command an Argentine Airforce Skyhawk wing. In the summer of 1993, through the good auspices of Maxi Gainza, a mutual friend, we met in London and spent the afternoon flying aerobatics in Maxi's Zlin 526 at White Waltham airfield. A few days later Hector and his wife came to stay with us in our Somerset cottage and after several pints of scrumpy we discovered what had really happened that evening over a decade before.

I found out that I had ended up in front of Hector in the heat of the engagement and, had it not been for the fact that his gun had jammed, he might have been the only Argentine pilot to shoot down a Sea Harrier. Clearly I might not have survived.

THE NEXT DAY was 'as quiet as a Mirage crewroom', as Gordie Batt had once said. Poor old Gordie; I missed his ugly face around the place. He had the knack of being able to lift the mood with a few well-chosen, usually irreverent quips. Everyone was going about their business wondering if the lack of air activity meant that we had worn the enemy down. They had certainly received a bit of a bloody nose over the previous two weeks and maybe, just maybe, they were having second thoughts. But then we had thought this before.

That evening I flew a dusk sortie in the area of Lively Island. It seemed almost surreal that only twenty-four hours earlier I had been right there, engaged in a desperate battle. Neither the sky nor sea showed any evidence of those hectic few minutes but on the northern horizon still stood a tall column of now hazy smoke, evidence of the death of two ships and the funeral pyre of some fifty men. The previous day's action had taken its toll of my spirit. I hardly dared think that we had won but the Argentines were no longer challenging us. Was this a mere lull before the storm or was the end actually in sight?

The daily intelligence summaries continued to tell us that the ground troops were advancing towards Stanley but no one seemed to be fighting much. I was very happy to be able to relax in the bar for an hour or two in the evening and then crash out in a dry, reasonably comfortable camp bed for the night. I was aware that the land battle was nearing its endgame but there was very little air activity and most of our patrols were uneventful. All we could do was maintain a presence and try to put ourselves in position to intercept any possible raids on our troops as they prepared for the final push on Stanley.

On the morning of the 10th I flew as wingman to Neill Thomas, patrolling once again in the mouth of Choiseul Sound. We had only been on station for ten minutes or so when I picked up an intermittent contact to the south-west of us. Immediately, we turned towards the target and tried to sort out the radar picture. Neill also found the fleeting return on his scope and I dropped back into trail as it became obvious that the target was in a line of rain showers over the north of Lively Island. As my leader disappeared into the first of the clouds I was aware that it would be extremely hazardous to plunge in after him. My radar-handling skills were basic at best, not having had time to complete my training before rushing off to the South Atlantic, and I had always found that instrument flying required my full attention.

Rather than fly on instruments while attempting to remain in radar trail on my leader and simultaneously carry out a radar search for the enemy, all at fairly low level, I decided that it would be more sensible to remain clear of the cloud. For the next ten or fifteen minutes we stalked up and down on either side of the squall line, both of us trying to sort out the fleeting radar return from the large areas of bright green clutter caused by the rain clouds. The initial elation of finding the contact began to be replaced by frustration. We were certain there was something hiding in there, probably a Hercules transport, as the return was very large when we actually saw it. The pilot did his job well, however, and stayed in the clouds until we ran out of fuel and had to return to the ship. In the subsequent debrief I apologised for my failure to hunt down the target by claiming, in a paraphrase of the old margarine advert, that I couldn't tell Arge from clutter. This major shortcoming of the SHAR radar was only remedied in the mid-1990s with the introduction of the Blue Vixen multi-mode radar, which could not only see low-level targets over land but was also reputed to be able to see frogs and rabbits jumping around in the grass!

The GR3s of No. 1 Sqn were considerably busier than us over this period, flying close air support missions in support of the ground forces. I was very happy to let them carry on with this task after my traumatic introduction to ground fire on 1 May. Most of their sorties provoked intense ground fire, consisting mainly of small arms but interspersed with the odd Russian SAM 7 shoulder-launched missile. On the 10th Murdo Macleod took a hit from a 7.62-millimetre round on the base of his windscreen. Had this not been constructed of bulletproof glass he would probably have been killed. As it was, he returned safely if somewhat shaken and the aircraft flew for the rest of the conflict with a metal plate glued over the bottom two inches of the windscreen. That same day a GR3 flown by Mark Hare returned from a seemingly uneventful reconnaissance mission to the west of Stanley with a nasty surprise in the camera. On developing the film we discovered images of an Argentine soldier tracking him with a Blowpipe missile at very close range and behind him, in the rocks on the summit of Two Sisters, a further soldier trying to bring a SAM 7 to bear. Luckily Mark was travelling like an express train at a height that only adrenalin will allow and was blissfully unaware of either threat. He did, however, turn rather pale when we presented him with a glossy print of the incident. This just reinforced my view that air defence missions were certainly the best bet from the survival point of view.

HMS *Hermes*

10 June

Hello again, my love,

Just a quick note as mail leaves in 30 minutes. Hope the move went OK. I thought of you. In fact the 8th was a good day; I got $2^1/_2$ hours Wessex flying, $2^1/_2$ hours Sea Harrier flying and two Mirages! Dave Smith and I found four Mirages attacking one of our landing craft, so we had them. I shot the first two down with missiles within about fifteen seconds of each other and then attacked the others with guns. Unfortunately I lost my gunsight but I sprayed them anyway and caused one to break left, where Dave shot him at about ten feet above the water. The fourth one was seen to crash into the sea (not sure why but I might have hit him with guns) about two minutes later. So I am now leading the score with two Mirages, two helicopters and a ship.

Also yesterday I listened to the tape, which was super. It is so good to hear your voices again. Mike Beech and Murdo MacLeod arrived the other day and I hear that Chris Gowers is on the way as well. Life here is fairly comfortable if predictable and we are getting a lot of flying in. There isn't really a great deal of danger, as long as you are not silly and I am always very careful because I have every intention of:

a coming back to live in our cottage.
b drinking some of my home-made beer and
c growing old with you gracefully!

Perhaps I could get a job at the Fleet Air Arm Museum.

I gather that the weather is absolutely super in UK at the moment. That makes up for the times I have been in Belize over the winter and you have been snowed in! I hope to get back before the end of the summer so I can start on the back of the house.

Well, I must go otherwise I will miss the post. Take care of yourself and the menagerie, love. I miss you very much and I'm always thinking of you.

Love
   D

PS Can you tell my dad about my kills, please?

HMS *Hermes*
10 June

Dear Elizabeth and Charles,
Thank you very much for the tape recording, I listened to it yesterday. You both sounded very grown up. Did Beauchamp really knock Hazey's cage over? I bet Hazey was not amused. I have managed to pick you some more grass from the Falkland Islands so you can show other children at school if you want to. We were right about their aircraft not being very good. I saw four of them two days ago and I shot two down and the pilot with me got another one.

Take care of Mummy and the pets.

Lots of love
   Daddy

On the morning of the 11th I was tasked to fly CAP off the north coast of East Falkland. The launch and transit into the area went without a hitch but there was fairly thick cloud over the islands, layered from a couple of thousand all the way up to over 20,000 feet. Before we started our descent to low level I called a 'shackle' so that we could have a good check behind us. As we started the turn I saw an anomaly in the cloud tops about five miles behind us and suddenly realised that it was two vapour trails descending into the overcast. I called, 'Bogeys six o'clock!' and hauled the aircraft round to point at the end of the trails.

Frantically I searched with the radar. Within a few seconds I picked up two contacts some 5000 feet below us in a gentle turn onto an easterly heading. I called the contact to my wingman and called the controller in San Carlos to see if there were any friendlies in the area to the north of Stanley. After a few seconds he replied, 'Negative, Red leader. No friendlies known in your area.'

Heart racing, mouth dry, I accelerated to 400 knots and started to descend after the contacts. My wingman, Martin Hale, rolled out a couple of miles to my right and locked his radar onto the southerly target. We were now in a very good position to take one bogey each but I was concerned that we should not react too quickly in case these were in reality SHARs from *Invincible* or even GR3s. As we descended, getting ever closer, the cloud started to break up into thinner layers and at around 10,000 feet I got a visual tally on my contact. It was small and not leaving a smoke trail but I could not be sure it was not a Harrier. It had been several days since the last air raid and I didn't want to generate a blue on blue incident. To knock one of my pals out of the sky would have been very difficult to live with and we needed every airframe we had. Rather than risk the loss of one of our own, it would have been preferable to let an enemy escape.

I called to Martin to hold fire until he had a positive ident on his target and started closing to within missile range. At about a mile and a half, with the Sidewinder locked and chirping, I realised that the bogeys were in fact Harriers and called, 'Knock it off, knock it off. Friendlies!'

A couple of seconds later there was a frantic call on the Guard frequency: 'SHARs north of Stanley, behind two GR3s, knock it off, knock it off!' The No. 1 Squadron guys had just seen us storming up behind them and had feared the worst. They had been working the forward air controller's frequency, having been scrambled from *Hermes* shortly after we launched. There was never a possibility of us firing without a positive ident but they took a bit of convincing in the bar that evening.

Peter Squire was hit by small arms fire that afternoon. A 7.62-millimetre round entered the cockpit below his right foot and exited above his left foot, managing to miss the soft fleshy parts on the way. It did, however, cause substantial damage as it destroyed a large electrical loom carrying vital weapon-aiming circuits. The aircraft nose resembled a hedgehog for several days as the maintainers tried to mate up dozens of unmarked wires.

On the 12th Murdo was hit again. He and Bomber Harris had taken off during the afternoon to attack targets on Sapper Hill. Bomber landed back without incident but Murdo was not so lucky. He had taken shrapnel damage to the rear of the aircraft, including damage to the reaction-control ducting. This ducting is redundant in normal flight but as soon as the nozzles are lowered past the twenty-degree point is pressurised with high-pressure air direct from the engine at a temperature of nearly 400 degrees Celsius. Thus when Murdo approached the hover alongside the ship he had jets of very hot air playing straight into the electronics bay.

From the ship he appeared to be making a lot of smoke, and then bits of debris started falling away from his aircraft. Flyco told him he was on fire and suggested he eject but Murdo thought, bugger that, and did an extremely rapid deceleration to a very swift vertical landing. He was instantly surrounded by the fire crew and covered in foam. The airframe suffered considerable damage and had he taken longer to land he might well have had to deal with a catastrophic failure. As it was, the aircraft played no further part in the conflict. Murdo, with his dour sense of humour, decided that being hit three times in as many days was past a joke and let it be known that he would be happy to re-role to air defence at any time.

For the next couple of days the SHARs had to remain very much in the wings as the ground assault was played out. Some ferocious fighting was taking place in the mountains to the west of Stanley but we could do nothing but set up CAP stations to prevent the Argentine Air Force from interfering. The GR3 boys were busy with rockets and cluster bombs and were still taking a lot of small arms fire.

We had also received intelligence that the Argentines had transported some Exocet missiles out to the islands. These were quickly dubbed the 'wheelbarrow-launched Exocets' and were the object of a number of reconnaissance sorties to the south of Stanley. Nothing was found but in the early hours of the 12th HMS *Glamorgan* made a fatal decision. She had been on the gun line to the south-west of Stanley, pumping 4.5-inch rounds into the area all night, and decided to cut a corner on the way home. They had also stood down from action stations and a number of people were already queuing up for breakfast. At a range of about eighteen miles the Exocet had a flight time of only a couple of minutes and there was little chance of escape. The missile hit above the waterline just below the helicopter hangar. It destroyed the Wessex in the hangar and started some serious fires. By the time these were eventually brought under control the toll was thirteen killed and seventeen injured. It seemed to us a terrible and totally avoidable loss of life, another example of what we regarded at the time as the 'cocktail party' mentality demonstrated by a large proportion of the surface navy. I discovered many years later that this judgement was unduly harsh. The decisions made by HMS *Glamorgan* that night were based on flawless intelligence and the requirement to be back with the rest of the task force by dawn. It was a tragic accident of war.

We had been told by our intelligence officer on a number of occasions that the Argentine troops in Stanley were running short of ammunition and food. Obviously no one had thought of telling them this as on my way back from a sortie that afternoon I was surrounded by dozens of black–orange puffs of 35-millimetre anti-aircraft fire. These look quite benign, even pretty, until you realise that every small puff is dispensing a large cloud of white-hot metal fragments designed specifically to ruin your day. A gentle weave was usually enough to put them off their aim but the odd gunner would second-guess you and get the pulses racing a little.

The following day was another quiet one from the air defence point of view but did yield a few interesting moments. Neill Thomas and Simon Hargreaves carried out a CAP sortie in Falkland Sound and were about to land at San Carlos to refuel when a Chinook blew the strip away. The downdraught from this huge helicopter lifted a large portion of the planking about ten feet into the air and turned it over. This made it unusable for Harrier operations for several hours and must have made Syd Morris feel that someone had it in for him. Neill and Simon did not have enough fuel to get back to the fleet and made the instant decision to land on two of the ships in the bay. Luckily, both *Fearless* and *Intrepid* had reasonable-sized flight decks, which they quickly cleared to receive one SHAR each.

No sooner had they landed than the ships' flight deck teams pumped in enough fuel to get them over to the strip when it was repaired. After only a short time, however, there was an air raid warning and both aircraft were ordered to scramble. With not much fuel on board the pair were fairly poorly placed, but as luck would have it the air raid warning was cancelled as soon as they launched and they were able to land at the FOB to refuel and return to *Hermes*. As a token of their appreciation of our efforts the wardroom of *Intrepid* managed to stow a case of wine in the back hatch of Simon's aircraft.

That afternoon the GR3 boys finally managed to sort out delivery of the laser-guided 1000-pound bombs. Peter Squire took out a position on the side of Mount Longdon and Gerry Pook turned a 155-millimetre gun into a swimming pool in a couple of nanoseconds. Peter's bombs were delivered using the loft profile and the attacks were planned so that his aircraft was hidden from view behind the hills surrounding

Stanley until the last minute. Unfortunately, the Royal Marines and Paras had been continually harassed by Argentine aircraft for the last three weeks and did not take kindly to aircraft pulling up over them and releasing bombs. Their aircraft recognition was a bit blurred by lack of sleep and a surfeit of hard fighting and a number of them did their best to shoot the Harriers down.

Idleness is the worst possible thing in wartime. It saps the spirit and deadens the senses. Our morale was starting to slip, watching the GR3s doing all the work while we flew up and down with no trade. We even heard that a Wessex had made a rocket attack on the police station in Stanley! What was the world coming to? The command would not allow us to re-role to ground attack as we had no idea whether the Argentines were conserving their assets for a last big push against the troops on the ground or even against the ships out at sea. It was essential that we conserved our air defence assets against all possibilities. So we waited.

I collared the squadron air engineering officer that evening and asked him where the bits of tail plane from my first raid were. His reply was a vague, 'Oh, I think we probably ditched them over the side.' I was horrified and told him so in no uncertain terms. Didn't he realise how precious that memento would have been to me?

Ashore, the troops took Tumbledown and Wireless Ridge with some vicious hand-to-hand fighting. This put them within one mile of Stanley itself but the weather was turning wintry with a light covering of snow on the islands and strong winds. In addition, there was a desperate shortage of ammunition with infantrymen down to twenty rounds and artillery pieces to a handful of shells. Out at sea we could only wait and hope that the Argentine troops would surrender. They had done so to a much smaller force at Goose Green but we feared that their machismo would not let them do so again.

On the morning of the 14th Bomber and Nick Gilchrist left to attack positions on Sapper Hill. One hour later they returned still carrying their bombs. I met Bomber in the crewroom and he broke the amazing news that there were white flags flying over Stanley. There was a mixture of elation and disbelief. The rumour was around the ship within minutes and the mess decks were alight with conjecture. Was it true? Had they really given up or was this all a cruel mistake? A few hours later it was confirmed: there was a ceasefire in force and negotiations were taking place for a surrender of all Argentine forces on the islands.

We still did not know whether their air force had stopped playing, however, and were afraid that they might try a final attack on the fleet. That evening was very quiet and we were all rather nervous. Would we be called upon to fight one last battle or could we actually relax?

14 June
Cardiff got a medium level Canberra last night and there were no air raids today. Troops took Tumbledown, Wireless Ridge and Sapper Hill and it looks as if the Argies have surrendered. Thank God! Tomorrow will be an interesting day!

The following day we learned that all 13,000 Argentines on the islands had indeed surrendered to our 3500 troops. As if the gods agreed, the weather was awful for the next two days, with thirty-knot gales and lashing rain. I spent some time up in Flyco watching the white water breaking over the bows and coursing down the deck. It did seem that the war was over and I had survived. Things would be very different now. I had no idea how I was going to settle back into my old life.

CHAPTER 12

THE JOURNEY HOME

IT WAS NOT QUITE over however. On the morning of the 17th I was tasked to lead Dave Smith on a long-range probe to within 130 miles of the Argentine port of Santa Cruz. This would put us within range of four major Argentine airbases and well within the coverage of their long-range radars. I could not believe that someone in the command structure was willing to risk two aircraft and their pilots at this stage; the war was won. The task was to confirm that a contact was a hospital ship. *A hospital ship!* I could not believe my ears. Was I supposed to risk the wrath of the whole Argentine Air Force in an attempt to identify a bloody hospital ship?

It had not taken long for the navy to revert to type and totally disregard the safety of their assets in order to 'verify the surface plot'. I could not think of a single reason why we should carry out such a hazardous mission. I looked at the position of the contact we were to identify and calculated that we would only have enough fuel to get to within forty miles of it before turning back and landing at *Sheathbill*. Even though I stressed to ops that we would not be able to identify the vessel and the best we could offer was a radar plot, they still insisted that the mission be flown.

It was with heavy hearts that Dave Smith and I launched that morning and turned our Sea Harriers due west. We flew in total silence with our radars and dopplers turned off. For the first time in many weeks I was afraid of what awaited us out there. I could visualise the shore-based radars picking us up and scrambling their fighters to intercept. I could imagine the glee of the Mirage pilots as they headed towards us at the speed of heat to avenge the death of their many colleagues. I convinced myself that this might be the mission that I would not survive and I cursed the captain for his stupidity.

At fifty miles short of the position we had been given I switched on my radar and allowed it to carry out one sweep. There, right on cue, was the surface contact, bright green in the centre of the screen. Mission accomplished. Time to go!

I pulled my machine around in a tight turn towards Dave, checked that he was also turning and pushed the speed up as high as I dared without running myself out of fuel. With each mile we covered away from the Argentine coast I felt happier. I scanned behind Dave continuously and I knew that he was doing the same for me. I knew that we would not make it back to the islands if we were bounced, even if we successfully fought the attackers off; we just didn't have sufficient fuel. It seemed a very long time before the coast of West Falkland came into view and it was with great relief that I eventually slowed to 200 knots, lowered the gear and flaps and turned on all my lights, before entering San Carlos Water and landing on Syd's pad to refuel. The mission had taken a full ninety minutes and was one of the longest undertaken during the whole conflict. It was also the last operational mission I was to fly in the South Atlantic.

Friday the 18th saw the bullshit really set in. The ships lined up in review formation to allow the 'Fisheads' (seamen officers) to practise what they did best: peacetime manoeuvres. It was stressed at morning briefing that 'Charlie' (landing) times were now mandatory and would be strictly enforced. I couldn't believe that having operated flexible timings for the last six weeks without any problems, the ship had now reverted to fixed sortie lengths. My faith in the naval system of flying evaporated. That morning we were briefed for an intercept training mission. This was mainly for the benefit of the controllers, who had done very little intercept controlling since we started fighting. We were also briefed to take photos of the ships and of each other as a permanent record of the end of the conflict.

After starting my engine I discovered that the inertial platform would not align. Normally this only took three and a half minutes but that morning the kit would just not play the game. No platform meant no head-up display and no radar stabilisation, which meant that I would be unable to use my weapons system in any meaningful fashion. I switched the NAVHARS off and back on again without success. The kit was obviously sulking so I made a thumbs-down to the plane captain and prepared to shut down. But before the ground crew had time to put the chain lashings back on a yellow shirt rushed over and started marshalling me forward. I shook my head and repeated the thumbs-down signal by this time feeling rather aggrieved that no one seemed to be taking any notice.

'Red leader, what's the problem?' asked Flyco on the radio.

'NAVHARS u/s. Closing down,' I replied.

'Negative. Follow the marshaller,' came the reply.

I did as I was bidden, assuming I was going to be put in the graveyard to clear the deck, and found myself being lined up on the centreline ready for launch.

'Flyco, Red lead,' I called. 'Just confirm I am not serviceable, repeat, not serviceable.'

There was a short pause before Robin Shercliff's voice came over the ether: 'You may find this hard to believe, Red lead, but we are going to launch you anyway.'

The captain was determined to be the first to launch his aircraft, serviceable or not, and Wings had been ordered to make it happen. Leave has been cancelled until morale improves!

HMS *Hermes*
21 June

My dearest disciple,

We did it! Just you and I, we stopped the war. I must admit that I had to keep going just a day or so longer so that I could shoot down some Mirages.

I came across four of them attacking one of our landing craft off Bluff Cove, so the two of us dropped onto them and were in behind them doing 600 knots before they saw us. I shot two down within 20 seconds and then my gunsight went unserviceable so I sprayed bullets around the other two without a sight. This caused one of them to break left at about 10 feet above the sea and my wingman splashed him with a missile and shortly afterwards the fourth one crashed into the sea trying to avoid me. Who owns this place anyway? That will teach them to mess with a Messiah. I feel no remorse; after all, you cannot hurt anyone who does not wish to be hurt.

I am now much more relaxed about things. I have washed my 'lucky' flying suit, which I have been wearing since 1 May, and I didn't crash!

Your touches of spring really make me want to come home. I miss my friends and family very much and I want to find out whether I have changed subtly. I don't think I will be worried about trivia anymore and I will certainly make the most of all my opportunities (so watch out!). Since my interview on television I have received quite a few letters both from old friends and complete strangers. I even got a letter from an Australian university student who fancied me! Must try to get to Sydney! Apart from that, things have now got very boring. The weather has turned bad and we are not doing much flying, so I must try to get ashore and take some pictures of Stanley and find some pieces of the Mirages and helicopters that I have shot down.

I don't know how long this letter will take to get to you but have a happy birthday if it gets to you in time. (In fact have a happy birthday anyway!) Do you know, I still don't know exactly when your birthday is! Isn't it silly.

Actually I had a very vivid dream about you a few nights ago. I can remember lots of detail. We were in a large room without much furniture but a large ornate fireplace. Perhaps I have achieved an out-of-body experience at last. I must try it again. I hope soon I will be returning to my friends and I cannot wait to see you. We will have a long talk when I get home and crack a few bottles of wine. In fact, I'm going to get legless and totally uncontrollable, so watch out!

In the meantime, my dearest pupil and teacher, look after yourself and be good to David.

All my love
David

The dream I had experienced was the most vivid I had ever known. Antje was standing in front of a large ornate Victorian fireplace, which was edged with coloured tiles. The room was large and airy, with a window in the wall to the right of the fire and a large mirror above it. She was standing in the middle of the room on polished floorboards, wearing a long evening dress. Another person was busying herself around the hem, apparently making final adjustments. I had been struck by the detail in the dream and the feeling of reality – as if I was actually in the room but unable for some reason to communicate my presence. Years later I visited Antje's flat in Stanhope Road and was dumbfounded to find that her living room was the one in my dream. The fireplace, the floorboards, the window were all identical. And she still has the evening dress.

The following few days were spent showing the flag. We sent aircraft to fly around all the settlements and were greeted at every location by madly waving groups of people. It gave me a great feeling of pride and achievement to see such unrestrained joy. We also started to work up No.1 (F) pilots in intercept work so that they would be able to take over the air defence commitment from us when we left for the UK. The captain became more and more keen to get rid of the GR3s ashore and instigated an inquiry into an attack on Dunnose Head on 23 May, where a late drop by Mark Hare had caused some damage and injuries. There was a general perception that this was part of a plot to blacken the name of the RAF contingent aboard. John Locke confirmed this many years later when he was the commander at Yeovilton. 'The captain was fighting four wars,' he said. 'The first was against the crabs, the second against *Invincible,* the third against the admiral and the final one was against the Argentines!'

During this period we also tried out some new chaff and flare panels, which had arrived from Ascension. The chaff appeared to work well against I-band radars and the flares were very effective against infrared homing heads, especially when combined with manoeuvre. It was a pity they were not available earlier in the conflict, as they might well have saved a couple of aircraft and at least one pilot.

On Friday 25th I wandered up to Flyco to watch stores being winched across from one of the RFAs. I noticed that the crates were not ones I had seen before and on asking what they were I was treated to a series of sideways looks but no straight answers. It was several minutes before someone told me in a low voice that they were '600-pounders'. It took me a few moments to work out the significance of this nomenclature; they were the ship's stock of nuclear weapons!

'Christ,' I said, 'I hope they don't drop them!'

Captain Middleton stormed through from the bridge and demanded to know why we hadn't got a Sea King airborne in case one of the weapons dropped in the water. Wings explained that the transfer was nearly complete and that it would take at least twenty minutes to launch a helicopter but the captain would not be placated. Red-faced and blustering he ordered Wings to launch a Sea King and stormed back to the bridge. I decided it was better to let the navy sort their problems out in private and slunk away to my cabin.

That evening I had a phone call from one of our squadron petty officers. He was a little evasive but told me that he had found something of mine and I could have it back if I brought some beer to the forward maintenance office. Buying beer for the troops was a heinous offence, as their daily consumption was strictly limited. I assumed, however, that I had dropped a chinagraph pencil in the cockpit, or something equally blameworthy, so quietly signed for a case of 'tinnies', put them in a plastic sack and set off towards the front of the hangar looking like a shifty Father Christmas.

On arrival I was greeted by half a dozen grinning maintainers, who presented me with a trophy which I cherish to this day. They had taken the section of tail fin damaged on my first raid and mounted it on a piece of varnished marine ply. Under the hole they had mounted a picture of the airfield taken after the raid and below this they had affixed a brass plaque on which were the words:

Flt Lt D. MORGAN
1st MAY 1982
FALKLAND ISLANDS
Gt BRITAIN vs ARGENTINA
TAIL FIN SEA HARRIER ZA192
800 SQDN HMS HERMES

The part had not been ditched at all and I had been well and truly had. It was difficult to fully express my thanks for this wonderful gesture and I felt that a few tins of beer were a poor exchange for such a great trophy. More than that, I felt that I had now been fully accepted, even if I was a crab.

HMS *Hermes*
25 June

Hello my love,

How are you? I hope you have got over the trauma of the move. This letter should get to you pretty quickly because we are expecting the first Hercules flight out of Stanley tomorrow. Everything has gone very quiet here now and we were told today that we might be home by the end of next month (July). Some of us will probably have to stay down here to bolster the *Invincible*'s numbers but we don't know who yet. I'll repeat a few bits of news because this will probably overtake a couple of letters.

My score now is: 1 boat (*Narwal*), 1 Puma, 1 Augusta 109 (helicopter), 2 Mirages (+another crashed into the sea). The ground crew have mounted the hole in my tail and presented it to me, so you will have to think of a place for that. (Not in the loo!) We have just been told that all trophies must be handed in so I don't know if I'll be able to get any 'ashtrays'. We haven't flown for several days now because of fog etc. so I'm going to try to get ashore by helicopter and take some pictures. Apparently Stanley is a hell of a mess, with Argies having shat everywhere, in the streets, gardens, rooms, baths; really quite nasty. The place is also stacked with all sorts of ammo and mines etc. with quite a few boobytraps.

I am really looking forward to getting home. I expect you have got lots of things for me to do. (I've got some things for you to do as well!!) You'll have to be nice to me because of the war neurosis. I'm glad I was down here but I'm bloody pleased it's over. I've not got any eczema, by the way. Funny that. I've had letters from all sorts of people including a bird in Aussie, two in England, Sue Smith, John Blanch and lots of others.

I don't think I'll get a chance to get any presents for the kids on the way back, so you'd better brief them or there will be ructions. If I go ashore, I might be able to pick something up but I doubt it. You'd better get a crate of brandy and lots off beer in for when I get back because I might need to just 'relax' a bit!

How is the house coming along? Have you managed to get the curtains and carpets you wanted? I can't wait to see it. I hope the menagerie hasn't eaten too much furniture or crapped on too many carpets. Hopefully I'll get three weeks leave or so when I get back, which will be nice because it will hopefully be during the hols.

Well, take care and give the kids a hug for me.

Lots of love

D

The next few days passed slowly, with little flying and increasing amounts of bullshit as the ship began to slip back into peacetime routine. One positive development was that we were allowed back to sleep in our own cabins. I think this decision might have been hastened by the fact that John Locke discovered that Bomber Harris had been doing his laundry in the captain's bathroom.

'He has no idea that anyone is sleeping in his cabin,' he remonstrated with Bomber. 'If he knew you were using his bathroom he would have my balls!'

Now that the fighting had died down we started to receive mail on a more regular basis. My next letter from home was a tale of woe. I was glad it had not arrived earlier as it probably would not have helped my state of mind. The move to the cottage had been marred by three major problems. First, the electrics had been condemned and the whole house had had to be rewired before a cooker could be installed. Second, after a heavy downpour Carol had discovered water had run off the fields at the rear of the garden, in through the kitchen door, through the kitchen and dining room and out of the front door onto the road. Finally, the plasterwork on some of the walls had started to fall off and the whole place had had to be Artexed to stabilise the surfaces.

HMS *Hermes*
28 June

You poor love,
I have just got your letters detailing the problems with the cottage. I reckon you have had a worse time than I have. As I said before, I will go along with any decision you make and I won't shout. After what I've been through down here, I don't give stuff about the money, so you can spend as much as you like as long as you leave me a bit for beer! I've only written cheques for about £100, so don't worry about me spending all our money. Has there been any sign of the land at the back being sold?

Actually, don't bother to answer that because we expect to leave here within a week and steam balls out for UK, arriving probably 28 July (ish). This hasn't been confirmed yet but I expect you will know as soon as I do.

Life has become very boring and rather depressing over the last week and I'm getting fed up with the whole set-up. I certainly won't transfer to the navy but I might go to Airwork! By the way, Stanley airport is now HMS *Penguin* and our other Harrier site is HMS *Sheathbill*. Syd Morris is OC *Sheathbill*.

Try to keep some sun for me cos I have not seen warm sun for ages and I want to do a barbecue and have a few Pimms on the patio. I'm also going to treat you to a slap-up meal for being so clever and good. I might even bring you breakfast in bed. (Or even supper, come to that!) You can't believe how much I'm looking forward to getting back to you and the Boggits. I hope the dog has stopped crapping on the mat and the goldfish have stopped drowning themselves and you have stopped going grey. I don't care if you have scratched the car; I still love you very much. And anyway it's not worth worrying about.

Yes, I did give Antje the address, she said she wanted to write to you and she wrote me several letters asking how you were and sending her regards. Anyway, I'll need a secretary for my fan club. So far I've got letters from girls in Scotland, America and Australia! Perhaps I should come home the long way round!

Take care my love, it won't be long now. Give the kids a kiss for me when you tuck them in.

Love,

D

By the 29th we were all feeling a little fed up but morale was raised dramatically by a Harrier squadron piss-up. We sat down to a fine dinner, navy and air force pilots alike, and afterwards consumed copious amounts of alcohol. The piano was broken out and rousing choruses of naval and air force songs echoed around the wardroom. It was a glorious, irresponsible cathartic few hours and we turned in feeling rather drunk but much more at peace with the world. The following morning, as if to show that there was still another world out there, we received news that Wing Commander Keith Holland had been killed in Germany. Keith was a wonderful, charismatic, kind man, a highly regarded Harrier pilot and squadron CO. In a moment of inattention he had tried to get airborne on a short strip with too much fuel on board and no flap. He hit the trees at the end of the strip and was killed instantly, a sad reminder that service flying is a dangerous business, even in peacetime.

The pressure on No.1 (F) to disembark was now growing daily and John Locke offered Peter Squire a case of cost-price whisky to be gone by the 4th. Peter managed to negotiate the offer up to three free cases, an indication of the strength of the ship's desire to get them ashore.

On the 3rd *Hermes* steamed into Port William, just outside Stanley harbour. The catwalks were lined with members of the ship's company staring silently at the islands. At long last they were able to see the land we had been fighting over for the last six weeks. From the deck the dunes on the northern edge of Stanley airfield looked remarkably like those I had known in Sandwich Bay when I was at school. I had spent many happy hours exploring the area around the Royal St George's golf course. The bay had been used for manoeuvres in the weeks leading up to the D-Day landings in June 1944 and the ditches and dykes still contained the detritus of war. Live ammunition, from .303 bullets to mortar bombs, was regularly found and squirrelled away for nefarious and highly dangerous purposes. It was not unusual to hear the crack and whistle of a live round over your head on a CCF field day as you fired your blanks at the opposing forces. Good training, I suppose, for later life!

Here the dunes held a far richer explosive crop. The golden sand and scrubby hillocks were peppered with abandoned weapons and ammunition. The beaches and dunes had been liberally seeded with mines, some of which were moved by every high tide and would take months to clear. There were also many booby traps left behind for the unwary souvenir hunter. None of this was however visible from *Hermes* and the scene was peculiarly tranquil with only the odd skyward-pointing tail to bear witness to the fury of the recent battle. In the distance the red corrugated roofs of Stanley looked more like a sleepy village on the Western Isles than the headquarters of a defeated army. As I walked down the flight deck to man my aircraft I overheard one of our young maintainers say to his oppo, 'Bloody hell, is that it?' It did indeed all seem very anticlimactic – a very odd place for a war to be fought and so many young men to lose their lives.

As I strapped in, the ship sailed slowly past the Tussac Islands and Kelly Rocks, which had been on my attack route on 1 May. It was inconceivable that I had actually been below the level of these small outcrops surrounded by surf. Amazing what adrenalin can do.

There was quite a feeling of finality as we launched the whole *Hermes* Air Wing. The helicopters flew low past Stanley and the SHARs and GR3s flew overhead them in a very professional fifteen-ship formation, with me in the number eleven slot.

The following morning we said farewell to our RAF brethren, who disembarked for Stanley, and *Hermes* turned onto a north-easterly heading towards Ascension Island and home.

A COUPLE OF DAYS out I got airborne and was carrying out some practice intercepts when we were suddenly vectored for a target.

'Red, snap 350. Possible Hercules north, twenty-two miles!' came the call.

Instantly the world changed. I dropped into battle formation on the leader's starboard side and started frantically scanning with the radar.

'355, fifteen miles, heading 220,' called the controller.

Still no radar contact. Heavy weather ahead as we flew through a series of cumulonimbus clouds. Range down to ten miles and still no contact. I dropped into trail behind the other SHAR, keeping him centred on my radar scope. The one thing I did not want to do was collide with him. For several minutes we stumbled around in thick cloud, becoming more and more frustrated as the target got ever closer to the ship. I was very concerned that we were about to be attacked in the same way as

British Wye had been five weeks earlier. I was also very keen to get my fifth kill if at all possible, to make me an official 'ace'.

Eventually we got the call from a seemingly very composed controller: 'Red, knock if off. Bogey is clearing to the south.'

Andy Auld was as disappointed as I was and asked for confirmation. He was told, 'Affirm, Red. Target is clearing to the south. Ah . . . he's friendly.'

It was an RAF Hercules flying from Ascension down to Stanley, not an Argentine interloper at all. We both heaved a sigh of relief that we hadn't found him in cloud and splashed him by mistake.

THE TRIP HOME GAVE time for reflection. There was little flying and I spent a lot of time with my own thoughts in my cabin. I began to be aware of periods of melancholy which came on with little warning and with no obvious trigger. These were normally dispelled quite easily by the application of copious amounts of alcohol and the air group certainly had some excellent parties.

On the 9th we had a Sea Harrier dinner. We met at 1930 for predinner drinks, everyone resplendent in their squadron cummerbunds, starched short-sleeved shirts and epaulettes. I wore a shirt borrowed from Simon Hargreaves with RAF shoulder flashes attached with staples. Not having a squadron cummerbund, I wore the light blue RAF one around my waist and had on my feet my newly purchased mess boots.

Shortly after 2000 we were called through to the dining room and sat ourselves in a large horseshoe around the polished mahogany tables set with mess silver. Wine flowed freely as we ate our way through a meal fit for conquering heroes. The main course was Goose Galtieri, a wonderful roast prepared using the upland geese which had been shot on the strip at San Carlos and shipped back to *Hermes* in various Sea Harriers. The loyal toast was drunk seated, in traditional naval fashion and the youngest member present was invited to propose the day's toast. Luckily he remembered it correctly and we all raised our glasses to 'A willing foe and sea room.'

The port was passed round a number of times before we made our way up to continue the party in Wardroom 2. This compartment was right aft, over the quarterdeck and out of the way of the rest of the wardroom. Here small groups could be self-contained and let their hair down without upsetting others who might be rather less uninhibited.

A few days earlier I had received a letter from a member of the public in Manchester. She explained that she had already made a contribution to the South Atlantic Fund but felt she wanted to do something more personal. By this time newsreels of the attack on Stanley had been shown on television and my name had become fairly well known. She had sent me a crisp twenty-pound note and had asked me to buy the boys some beers. I used the money to purchase several liqueurs from the bar and had placed the bottles, with the appropriate glasses, in Wardroom 2.

As the evening developed, so we all became louder and more frenetic. Bill Covington suddenly arrived through the door with a blazing newspaper held between the cheeks of his naked backside. This caused a roar of incredulity before it was deemed wise to extinguish him with a couple of beers. Dave Smith had been suffering from piles and it was suggested that port might be a good remedy. Neill Thomas therefore administered large quantities of rather fine port to the appropriate area and this seemed to do the trick as Dave announced the next day that he was cured. As the evening stretched into the early hours of the next day and judgement became increasingly impaired, it was suggested that someone should try to stop the ceiling fan. Simon Hargreaves was hoisted shoulder-high and his head thrust firmly into the path of the rotating blades. There was a series of sickening thuds and a lump of his hair flew across the room before he decided that this was probably not a good idea.

High on the starboard bulkhead of the compartment was a small brass scuttle. This could be opened just wide enough to squeeze a small body through. As usual where there is a challenge you will find a fighter pilot, and this was no exception. Some months earlier Mike Blissett had declared his intention of climbing out of the scuttle and up to the flight deck. But he had not given sufficient thought to the overhang of the deck above and although he managed to get out and grab hold of some bars used to secure painting stages, he could not pull himself up. This left him unable to go forward and no way to get back. It was looking as if he would end up in the ocean before someone had the bright idea of hooking his legs back into the scuttle with a broom. Luckily, no one was stupid enough to try to repeat this, although there was some discussion about it as the night drew to a close. As a thank you, I sent some pictures of these antics to our kind benefactor. It certainly showed her the other side of Britain's finest fighter pilots.

The following day it was the turn of 826 NAS to have their post-conflict thrash and when we arrived off Ascension the following morning it was they who could not bear to look at the sun and we who were feeling fine. I became the proud owner of a 105-millimetre shell case as a result of that evening. One of the Sea King boys had picked up several on Mount Kent and was glad to swap one for a leather shoulder holster which I had brought down with me. A fair bargain and it now stands next to my open fire as a mute reminder of those desperate days.

HMS *Hermes*
10 July

Hello, love,

You probably have heard by now that we are on our way home. ETA Portsmouth 210930 ish and docking on the Northwest Wall at about 1315. I will almost certainly have to stay on board to fly an aircraft off the next day, however, and will be arriving at Yeovilton around lunchtime (22nd). Neill Thomas is flying back from Ascension tomorrow and he or Sabrina will have the last-minute details. Families will be allowed on board one hour after we dock but it will be a hell of a crush, so don't feel you have to come down. I will try to phone you anyway. I hope you have got some beer and horse's necks and have sharpened the spade!

It has been an interesting few months but not a time I particularly want to go through again (even if I did destroy more aircraft than anyone else!). I just want to get home to you 'orrible lot now. I am trying to get a bit of a tan now as it is getting quite sunny and I'm sure you must be brown by now.

Take care anyway, love, and I will see you on the 22nd if not the 21st. You will have to apologise to the Boggits because I haven't got them any presents. It's a bit tricky, not having been ashore properly for 97 days now!

I love you very much. See you soon.

D

As we left Ascension we gathered on the flight deck for a final farewell to those who would not be returning with us: those we knew well and those who were just names, some whose bodies would never be found, all who had paid the ultimate price. Well over a thousand men stood, heads bared, as the tropical sun sank gently into the western horizon. We sang the traditional hymns and recited the prayers for the dead before standing silently to remember, each with his own thoughts. A Royal Marine bugler played the Last Post and one hundred red roses were cast into the ship's wake. There was no sound for a full minute save the gentle throbbing of the engines through the steel deck. After the service, I made my way back to my cabin, not wanting to talk to anyone for a while. How I envied Neill Thomas.

COME SUMMER

When summer's calm
Does follow winter's raging seas
And cautious rays of warming sun
Replace cold morning's dread,

When enigmatic moors
No longer ring to clash of steel,
And snipe-rich bog and craggy mount
Forget the sound of pain

When peat-brown scars
That shroud the silent youth grow
Green and lush with living nature's
Warmth, against the rain,

Then think of these,
Who fought and drowned and flew
And prayed and cursed
And gave their all for you.

Some of the news we received at Ascension was not welcome. There were strong rumours that the RAF had decided to pillory Bertie Penfold. It seemed that someone had decided that he had disgraced the air force in front of the Royal Navy and had to be punished. Rumour had it that he was to be court-martialled for 'lack of moral fibre'. We were all incensed that such a crass decision could be made by senior officers who had never seen action in their lives and who had no idea of what it was like to be shot at or to take a human life. Bertie had done more in his first day at war than the whole of the Air Force Board had done in their entire collective careers. It was clear that the navy was doing all it could to have this outstanding instructor posted back to Yeovilton to finish his tour but the RAF was insisting that he was one of their officers and they would deal with him as they saw fit. It was desperately depressing to realise that the RAF was quite happy to accept the plaudits when you did well but instantly ready to shit on you if they perceived that you had provoked bad publicity. Who was it described the British army in the First World War as 'lions led by donkeys'? It seemed that little had changed.

The following day there was a rumour that most of the aircraft were to be flown off and returned home using in-flight refuelling from the Victor tankers based at Ascension. Andy Auld gathered us together to ascertain who would be qualified to fly the aircraft.

'OK, who is current on tanking?' was the first question. No one put up his hand. 'All right, who has ever tanked in a Sea Harrier?' he asked. Still no hands. 'OK then, has anyone done the tanking course at Brize Norton?' was the next question.

'I did it on the Buccaneer ten years ago, boss,' said Mike Blissett.

'I saw a Victor at Yeovilton Air Day last year,' called someone else and the discussion descended into farce. Two days later it was announced that the aircraft would be staying on board until we could fly directly to Yeovilton. Naturally, everyone hoped that he would be chosen to fly an aircraft home but we knew that some of us would have to stay on *Hermes* until she docked in Portsmouth a few days later.

On the 14th I flew a quick air intercept to combat sortie just to keep my hand in and was met by Mike Blissett on landing.

'I'm sorry, Mog,' he said. 'We have just received a signal from FONAC that there will be a large amount of press coverage when the aircraft arrive at Yeovilton and that all the pilots are to be dark blue; no crabs allowed.'

I was naturally disappointed that I would have to wait a further couple of days to see my family but as a new boy I had not really expected to be included on the list of those to fly ashore. I was however really pissed off that someone in Naval Air Command was being so short-sighted as to allow petty inter-service rivalry to ruin the terrific rapport that had grown up between the light- and dark-blue elements of the *Hermes* Air Group. As it turned out, a further signal, sent the following day, rescinded that order in no uncertain terms; common sense and decency finally won the day. Even so, the only light-blue representative on the final disembarkation was Ted Ball, who had not achieved any kills and therefore did not dilute the sense of RN victory. It all left a rather bad taste in the mouth.

Two days later we passed the Canaries. The weather was beautiful with light southerly winds and clear blue skies. The ship was making good speed to the north, which resulted in very light winds over the deck. A large number of the ship's company were on the flight deck, either running or just soaking up the warm sun, and a number of us were relaxing on the quarterdeck over a lunchtime drink. I was idly supping my pint of CSB and looking out over the stern rail when someone remarked that there was a helicopter astern. I thought this was a little unusual, as we were not closed up at flying stations, and a small knot of pilots gathered to look at the aircraft as it gradually got closer. At a range of about five miles I saw that it had a very unusual tandem-rotor configuration.

'Christ, it's a bloody Hormone! Where the hell has that come from?' I exclaimed, and a few minutes later the camouflaged shape of the Kamov KA-25 was hovering off the port quarter, with the Russian red star clearly visible on the rear of the ungainly fuselage. I had only seen this aircraft in recognition tests but it must mean that there was a Russian ship in the area and we had been caught with our pants down. So much for the Fishead's surface picture!

'Hands to flying stations! Hands to flying stations! Cease ditching gash. The flight deck is now closed for recreation,' came the pipe from Flyco, followed closely by, 'Launch the Alert 20 Sea King, launch the Alert 20 Sea Harrier!'

Dave Smith looked at me, then his half-empty pint. His jaw dropped and he spluttered, 'Shit, that's me!' before plonking his glass on the table and following the Sea King crew as they hurried off the quarter-deck, pursued by the catcalls of the assembled company. The Russian crew waved back at the serried rows of raised glasses and flew around us for a couple of minutes before heading off south again, hotly pursued by a gallant 826 Sea King. Before Dave could get airborne, a Soviet *Kresta 2* guided-missile cruiser appeared astern, making a good twenty-five knots as she carved through the calm blue water. She took up station off our port quarter, looking magnificent under the midday sun, her array of missiles and guns a grim reminder that there might be other battles in the world yet to fight. After a while she broke away to the west and we continued on our course for home.

We were by then getting more regular news from home and listened with some emotion to the commentary on the arrivals of the first task force ships to return. It seemed that masses of people were crowding the docksides and approaches as each ship arrived. John Locke wished to present *Hermes* in her best light and had started a programme of repainting the ship. The captain vetoed this; he thought she should return looking as if she had fought a war. For once I agreed with him; there would be time enough for painting once in harbour. Now was the time for the ship to revel in her battle scars, like a rugby player after a hard-fought game on a muddy field. She was rust-streaked and battered by the South Atlantic's furious seas, the Camrex paint was scabbing off her deck in any number of places and her funnel and masts were smudged by the oily smoke from her boilers. On the starboard side of the island, however, was a tally of her achievements. The black silhouettes of aircraft destroyed, ships sunk and special forces raids carried out stood out starkly against the grey of the ship's side, a proud reminder of her pivotal role in the operations of the last few months.

On the 19th those of us who were remaining lined the island as all but six of the SHARs disembarked. One by one they lined up on the centreline, gave a final salute to the FDO and accelerated off the ramp. One final fly-past and they were gone, small dots against the northern sky as they climbed to height for the transit back to Yeovilton and that other, normal world over the horizon. Everyone was now preoccupied with the impending arrival in Portsmouth. All personal gear and aircraft equipment was packed and readied for disembarkation and the following day we sighted the coast of Cornwall.

That morning some of the Sea Kings left us, chattering away towards the misty coastline of Lizard Point to meet their loved ones at Culdrose. I felt a melancholy as I watched them grow smaller against the skyline rather like the loneliness at the end of a boarding-school term when your parents are the last to arrive to take you home. We had enjoyed an excellent evening in the bar the previous night and no doubt I would see many of my comrades again but I still had that feeling of loss. Another of the pillars which had supported the tenuous fabric of life over the last few months had been removed. A carrier without its air group is a peculiar place. The Fisheads continue to polish and clean and carry out manoeuvres but the heart of the ship is gone; it is an empty shell waiting for its lifeblood to return.

There were arrivals as well as departures that day and we were delighted to see Brian Hanrahan and his team back on board to cover our return. They were greeted like long-lost brothers, and that evening as we steamed slowly up the Channel towards Portsmouth there were great celebrations in the wardroom. The rafters rang to the sounds of 'Don't cry for me Galtieri', 'The A25 Song', 'What shall we do with an Argie Mirage?' and a hundred other traditional and more topical refrains, as we all noisily celebrated our own survival and silently mourned our losses. Brian was as appalled as we were when he heard of the threat of court martial reputed to be hanging over Bertie's head and promised that evening to do all he could to help. We discovered later that, true to his word, he had asked some very pointed questions. These resulted in Bertie being given a medical discharge, regaining his flying category after a few months and joining Airwork as a Hunter pilot.

Our mood was tremendously lifted the following morning by a visit from the prime minister. We breakfasted well on bacon, eggs, sausages and champagne before lining up on the flight deck to meet the VIPs. Rarely do the services take a politician to their hearts but the cheers for 'Our Maggie' were loud and heartfelt. Her handshake was firm and her blue eyes piercing as she moved down the line, a formidable personality. Some years later I read an appreciation of the conflict by an eminent Russian general, who expressed amazement on several counts: first that a war could be won against such overwhelming odds, both on the ground and in the air; second that it could be fought at all with such an extended supply line; and third and most important, that there was the political will to even attempt such an endeavour. As the joke went, 'Why does Maggie Thatcher not wear miniskirts?'

'Because her balls would show!'

AS I UNCLIPPED the watertight door and stepped over the lip onto the grey flaking paint of the starboard Seacat missile sponson later that morning I was greeted by a glorious day. There was just a thin layer of high cirrus cloud partially obscuring the sun and a light westerly breeze caressing the grey waters of the Solent. The ship was hardly moving at all, sliding smoothly through the calm sea, leaving a mere ripple in her wake. Nabb Tower, its Napoleonic defences barnacle-encrusted and dripping with seaweed, slipped by to port as we formed up in Procedure Alfa for our return to Portsmouth.

The full pageantry of the Royal Navy was certainly a stirring sight: 1800 men lined up on every available foot of deck edge and catwalk, all straining for their first glimpse of home after fourteen long and arduous weeks away. On the flight deck was the ship's volunteer band, busying themselves with their instruments, preparing to play us in. Forward of them the six remaining Sea Harriers were lined up, with ZA177, the aircraft in which I had achieved my two Skyhawk kills, in the pole position high on the ski-jump. I now took my place alongside the rest of the ship's crew, a lone light-blue figure in a sea of dark blue. Brian Hanrahan had warned us that we might not get the rapturous welcome that had greeted *Canberra* a week or so earlier. He had explained that this was not because our deeds had been forgotten but just that the country had now become used to ships from the task force returning and it was no longer the novelty that it once had been. We were all therefore resigned to a quiet homecoming followed by family reunions.

As we closed to within a few miles of Southsea I noticed that there seemed to be a funfair or something similar on the beach. As we got closer I realised that it was a huge crowd of people, a massive throng of bodies all waving flags and banners and cheering so loudly that we could hear them across the intervening stretch of water. Brian, that bastion of truth and honesty whom we had trusted implicitly throughout the conflict, had deliberately and unashamedly lied! It was the biggest crowd I have ever seen and snaked along the coast for nearly five miles.

As if this were not enough, a small armada of boats now appeared – dinghies, fishing boats, cabin cruisers, yachts, anything that would carry people. They milled around the rust-streaked hull of *Hermes*, their occupants waving and shouting and holding up hand-printed messages. One banner read, 'HERMES STRIKES MORE OFTEN THAN ASLEF', a reference to the rail strike planned for that day. Unknown to me and lost in the fleet of small craft and the cheering crowds, my mother had secured a place on one of the fishing boats which circled the ship. While most in England were glued to their televisions, she had a front-row seat, although I never did actually spot her.

A very well-appointed ocean racer came close up the starboard side with a gentleman in blazer and cravat at the helm and two gorgeous young ladies on the foredeck. This was too much for our sailors who, with one voice, started the traditional naval chant inviting them to remove their T-shirts. After a glance at 'Daddy' and with broad grins, they duly obliged to a great roar of approval from the ship's company, a truly wonderful sight after nearly three months of enforced celibacy. How I would have liked to thank those two girls personally!

As we approached the entrance to the harbour, a fly-past of Harriers and Victor tankers roaring overhead, I suddenly realised that it was truly over. We had sailed over 12,000 miles, fought an intense, bloody war and survived. I also thought of those who were not coming home, those we had left behind beneath the grey rollers of the South Atlantic or the cold earth of those far-flung islands. I knew that the last few months had changed us all. No one could come through such a maelstrom of emotions without being affected; only time would tell how much. Some would recover quickly and get on with their lives, others would never come to terms with what they had seen and done. Most of us would survive well enough with only a few nightmares but all of us had changed.

As the bands on the jetty struck up 'Hearts of Oak' and hundreds of red, white and blue balloons were released I felt tears starting to trickle down my cheeks. After a furtive look round I realised I was not alone and everyone was suddenly blaming the funnel smoke for their smarting eyes.

We were home.

EPILOGUE

THE CONFLICT WAS over but not my association with those distant islands. The first couple of weeks at home were spent winding down and I soon grasped that it was going to take a while to return to normal. I was irritable and jumpy and very reluctant to make everyday decisions. I can remember being extremely annoyed when Carol asked me what I wanted for tea. This was a simple enough request and my sharp reply was unwarranted. It seemed as if I had become so used to making life-or-death decisions that I had lost the knack of dealing with the mundane.

I also began to realise that part of my mind was still in the South Atlantic. Whenever my brain was not fully occupied images of the conflict would surface and flit through my subconscious. After a while these images flowed together and it was like having a video playing on a continuous loop in my head. Another disturbing symptom was the twenty-third psalm.

I have never been at all devout, quite the opposite, but the verses kept running through my mind, sometimes on their own and at other times in the form of the popular hymn:

The Lord's my shepherd,

I shall not want.

He maketh me to lie down in green pastures.

He leadeth me beside the still waters.

He restores my soul.

He leadeth me in the paths of righteousness

For His name's sake.

These thoughts became ever more intrusive and I started to worry that something was seriously wrong with me. After three weeks however I was informed that I was to fly back down to the Falklands to reinforce 809 NAS on *Illustrious*. This did not impress me much but I found that when I was airborne the thoughts stopped. This was a great relief and helped to mitigate the disappointment of once more being separated from my family.

The three further months in the Falklands passed slowly but did give me the opportunity to get ashore and see something of the islands. Stanley was still a mess but the Upland Goose was open for business and Dave Smith and I spent a few nights staying there rather than in tents on the airfield with the No. 1 (F) detachment. The owner of the Goose had put up Argentine officers there during the conflict and was selling Argentine banknotes as souvenirs. He also had a reasonable stock of Argentine wine which the invaders had left behind. On the first evening we had a meal with some of the RAF pilots and he served us several bottles of this wine and then demanded payment! He received a very short and to-the-point answer.

The GR3 boys had set themselves up in a small city of tents among the sand dunes and were flying fairly normal training sorties, practising both ground attack and air defence missions. On our second day ashore we were invited to act as the enemy for a four-ship attack mission. We duly attended the mission briefing at which Bob Iveson went over the route and targets in a very professional manner and then proceeded to cover the rules of engagement. He briefed the GR3s not to fly below 250 feet and us to remain above 500. I pointed out that the SHARs were cleared to fly as low as fifty feet and that this would give us all much better training value.

Bob became quite agitated and told me in no uncertain terms that the islands were now governed by peacetime rules and if we didn't want to abide by them he would do without our participation. I thanked him politely and we left the briefing, having already made a note of their route and targets. It was no coincidence that we came across them four or five times and bounced the hell out of them. We were not invited to the debrief!

The following morning we arrived in our commandeered Mercedes jeep and were met by Flight Lieutenant Jim Ludford, who told us that the station commander wanted to see us in Stanley. I suspected we were about to get a bollocking for kicking arse on the RAF and I told Dave that I would take the rap as I was the formation leader. We were kept waiting for some time in the group captain's outer office. Yup, I thought. Standard bollocking procedure.

We were eventually ushered in and invited to sit down. *Not* standard bollocking procedure! Ian Dick leant across his desk and said, 'Congratulations, David, you have been awarded a Mention in Dispatches.' He then turned to me and said, 'And, Moggie, I am delighted to tell you that you have been awarded a Distinguished Service Cross.'

I was absolutely stunned. It was almost unheard of for the navy to award this medal to an RAF pilot; in fact it had only been done on eleven occasions before, the last time being in 1956 during the Suez crisis. That evening we flew back to *Illustrious* for a very good party.

On my return from this second stint in the South Atlantic I was able to settle back into a fairly normal routine as an instructor on 899 NAS, and after another eighteen months or so the flashbacks stopped and I felt that I had managed to cure myself of whatever it was I had been suffering from. The cottage was all I had hoped and the family were very happy there. However, Antje's marriage did not last and after eighteen months she separated and we began stealing time together when we could.

In 1984 I transferred to the navy and trained as an air warfare instructor before joining 801 NAS. The next few years saw me spending increasingly longer periods away at sea and this combined with infidelity on both sides finally resulted in Carol leaving home. There followed a bitter fight in the divorce courts which ended with me being granted care and control of Elizabeth and Charles. It was during this period that my previous problems came back to haunt me. I became very depressed and started to drink rather more than was advisable. I also forgot to eat on a regular basis and lost nearly thirty pounds in weight. I had already broken off contact with Antje in a vain attempt to save my marriage and sometimes it was only the children that kept me going.

In July 1987, I met Caro at the Yeovilton Cocktail Party. Despite me being as drunk as a lord she saw something in my eyes and we started going out together. She helped me pull myself back from the brink and we were married in 1990. I was still suffering from bouts of melancholy and eventually took the decision that I would have to leave the forces.

I had resigned my commission in 1990 and was looking forward to leaving to start a career in civil flying when the first Gulf War broke out. My squadron was put on notice to sail for the Middle East and the frantic preparations began. Out of nowhere my symptoms returned with a vengeance. They were as severe as they had been in the immediate aftermath of the Falklands conflict and I decided to seek professional help as soon as we returned from the Gulf. To this end I went to see Surgeon Commander Liz Hodges, our PMO at Yeovilton. Liz was an old friend and listened with great sympathy to my list of symptoms before announcing that I was describing a classic case of post-traumatic stress disorder.

I asked if I could be put on a PTSD course when the crisis was over and after some thought she gave me two options. I could stay behind when the rest of the squadron left for the Gulf and rejoin 899 NAS or, if I was not prepared to do this, she would ground me. I protested that the boys needed me but she wouldn't budge and the following morning I stood up in front of the squadron and told them that I would not be coming with them. It was one of the worst things I have ever had to do but I handed over to Brave, who did a grand job looking after them. In fact their ship never got further than Cyprus and just steamed around in circles for months before coming home. I am very glad that Liz insisted on me staying behind as the inaction would have crippled me.

The PTSD course helped me come to terms with my problems but I still suffered from periods of depression and anxiety until some years later when I was referred to a wonderfully caring and expert therapist near my home in Dorset. Sally led me along the convoluted path back to health and it was during this period that I decided I must relive my past and write my experiences down.

ALTHOUGH I HAVE made strenuous efforts to achieve historical accuracy in this account twenty-year-old memories are not completely reliable. In any case it is not meant to be a history; there are better general accounts of the conflict written by more eminent writers than myself. I am content if it sheds a little light on the extraordinary actions of a band of extraordinary men that I am proud to call friends.

INDEX